FREDERICK THE GREAT

LUDWIG REINERS

Frederick the Great

AN INFORMAL BIOGRAPHY

Translated and adapted
from the German by

LAWRENCE P. R. WILSON

NEW ENGLISH LIBRARY
TIMES MIRROR

First published in 1960 by Oswald Wolff (Publishers) Ltd.
© by C. H. Beck'sche, Verlagsbuchhandlung, Munich.

*

FIRST NEL MENTOR EDITION 1975

*

NEL Mentor Books are published by
New English Library Limited from Barnard's Inn, Holborn, London, E.C.1.
Made and printed in Great Britain by Hunt Barnard Printing Ltd., Aylesbury, Bucks.

45002240 4

Contents

CHAPTER ONE

*

The Enigma

FREDERICK II OF PRUSSIA became a legend even during his life-time. An English newspaper called him 'one of the greatest soldiers ever born.' In English inns his portrait was hung beside that of George II. In London his uniformed effigy was set on an ass and led in triumph through the City. In the peasant huts of Bavaria, pictures of the king who had twice delivered the country from the Austrians were placed beside those of the local saints. In Venice, in the monastery of San Paolo, the monks fought a pitched battle to decide whether they should pray for the Catholic Empress, Maria Theresa, or Frederick, the heretic King. The King of Sardinia called Frederick his 'hero', but when Frederick entered Moravia the King of Naples reinforced the city garrison – you never could tell with that extraordinary man, his cavalrymen might suddenly come storming across Alps and Apennines to water their horses in the Gulf of Sorrento. In Sicily, in 1786, Goethe was besieged for news of the King's health, but he was afraid to mention his death in case he made himself too unpopular. During the Seven Years War, Switzerland was said to be more Prussian than the Prussians, and in France, when Marshal Belle-Isle told Madame de Pompadour after the battle of Rossbach that Frederick would soon be in Paris, Louis XV's mistress made the surprising reply: 'Then at last I shall see a king.'

Nettelbeck, Mayor of Danzig, told of a youthful visit to a waxworks in Lisbon and how, confronted suddenly with an effigy of Frederick, he had been moved to declare: 'I, too, am a Prussian!' Whereupon the Portuguese had fallen at his feet and begged him to tell them of the Great King. From Constantinople the Austrian Ambassador reported that the Sultan had

7

asked 'about the strange country called Brandenburg that could hold its own against four powerful and warlike neighbours,' and Peter III declared it was a greater honour to be a Prussian general than the Czar of all the Russias. Of Frederick, William Pitt the Elder said he demonstrated the heights which human nature could attain. Goethe called him 'the Pole Star', while Thomas Mann, certainly no militarist or ardent friend of Prussia, confessed 'boundless sympathy' for Frederick and added, '– a sympathy of which I shall never be ashamed.'

Such was Frederick's fame. But it sprang from strange beginnings. As a young man he had been somewhat effeminate, given to versifying, flute playing and amorous delights. From his father, who chastised him in public and once all but sentenced him to death for desertion, he inherited a scattered kingdom of two million inhabitants. On his death forty years later, he left a country universally recognised as a Great Power.

But the achievement was hard-won. Frederick gave battle to countries totalling fifty times the population of his own, resisting their onslaughts long after his army had been reduced to a band of shabby mercenaries officered by smooth-cheeked, fifteen-year-old lieutenants, when enemy cavalry were clattering through the narrow streets of almost every town in Prussia and all but himself had abandoned hope. No detail was too small for the King's attention: he it was who prescribed the line of march and the point of attack for each of his battalions, who rode out on reconnaissance, arranged for food supplies and remounts, interrogated prisoners and briefed spies. He was used to sleeping by the campfire on a bundle of straw and used to enemy bullets: he was wounded several times and five horses were shot from under him. At the disaster of Kolin, Frederick himself seized the standard in an attempt to rally his men, and would have led them to the attack if his retinue had not stopped him with: 'Does Your Majesty intend to capture the enemy batteries single-handed?'

When Frederick finally returned to Berlin after an absence of six years the populace expected a triumphal procession. But spurning the gala coach which the city council had sent to meet him, Frederick chose to enter his capital by back streets in his old campaigning carriage and went to the garrison church, sitting alone with his head in his hands, weeping while Graun's *Te Deum* was played. But next morning at four o'clock, Frederick was at his desk, ready to tackle the reconstruction of his country, opening all the official post himself – first checking the seals, and then dictating his decisions.

Every decision affecting the welfare of the realm was made by the King in person: the leasing of Crown lands, the building of schools, the request of a village for the loan of army horses, an army officer's application for leave to marry, a private citizen's for permission to travel abroad, the appropriate season for planting mulberry trees, the maximum price of fine yarn . . . Frederick saw to it all, saw to it literally, with his own eyes. And woe to the mayor of that village where the houses were in bad repair or the fields looked poorly cultivated, or who was not ready with his answer when on one of his frequent tours of inspection the King gave proof of that terrible memory of his and demanded to know what had become of the shepherd who had told him about Spanish sheep-rearing methods five years before. Frederick was even more thorough when he inspected his army, which he did annually, regiment by regiment. If a squadron failed to measure up to his standards on parade, each trooper would be brought out and put through his paces separately, at the walk, the canter and the gallop. His seat in the saddle was scrutinised and the way he held the reins, and this would go on hour after hour, mercilessly, in all weathers, though the seventy-year-old King got soaked to the skin, though the gout in his right hand had forced him recently to learn to write with the left.

And Frederick was not only warlord and administrator, he was also a social reformer. Four days after his accession he abolished the use of torture. He expedited litigation, established a code of common law, built canals, fostered new industries and promoted settlement schemes. Moreover he established religious toleration throughout Prussia, the principle that everyone was free to choose his own path to heaven. And in all this Frederick proved indifferent to criticism or calumny. Coming upon a poster caricaturing him as a woman grinding coffee, after he had raised the import duty, he gave orders to hang it lower so that people could see it properly. A strange king indeed! And stranger still, in that age of absolutism, for calling himself the first servant of the State and his crown, a hat like any other, except that it let in the rain. It was the eminent German historian, Leopold von Ranke, who called Frederick the greatest man of his century.

Such is the picture drawn by Frederick's admirers. His critics see him differently. What, they ask, did Frederick's immense intellectual gifts, his extraordinary tenacity of purpose achieve? 'Frederick the Great made Germany small,' replies the poet, Ernst Arndt, referring to Frederick's seizure of Silesia, Austria's richest province, at a moment when the Empire itself was most

9

endangered. And indeed, by this and by refusing his support when Austria attempted to regain Alsace and Lorraine and her armies were investing Strasbourg, did not Frederick destroy the Habsburg claim to the leadership of Germany, wantonly, out of envy and malice, despite the fact that he had received the price of his support, the whole of Silesia? Again, it was Frederick, the ever-treacherous, who thwarted the reunion of Bavaria with Austria and who upset Austria's plans in the Balkans. Who, then, if not Frederick, was responsible for Germany's internal dissensions and the fact that she did not join the ranks of the Great Powers until eighty years after his death – and then for ever too late?

As Frederick destroyed Germany, so, it is said, he destroyed his own people. In the words of Ernst Arndt, 'his inordinate despotism crushed the tender growth of human feelings.' Frederick's Prussia, said Lessing, was the most slave-ridden State in Europe. Was Frederick himself the model for the typical Prussian, that stolid, hard-hearted, heel-clicking automaton? Was the massacre of Jena the fruit of his tyranny?

Yet other historians criticise Frederick's statesmanship, saying he incurred the enmity of half Europe by his tactless treatment of foreign rulers. Among his mistakes they point to the Treaty of Westminster, which alienated France, antagonised Russia and only partially gained him the friendship of Britain. Even among Frederick's admirers there are some who suggest that the Seven Years War was not a defensive war, but was deliberately engineered by Frederick for the purpose of conquest. And what of his military talents? Was he really a great commander? Napoleon detected grave strategic errors in all his campaigns, and whereas Frederick lost about half the battles he fought, the superior training and equipment of his army have led one modern critic to declare that, granted no more than competent generalship, the majority should have been outright victories.

Frederick has been acclaimed for his tolerance, particularly in the religious sphere. But what kind of tolerance was it which allowed the most scurrilous attacks to be printed against religion itself and which ordered foreign journalists who criticised Prussia to be flogged by army officers and then, as an added insult, be forced to sign a receipt that they had received their punishment?

And then: Frederick's intellectual and literary pretensions. . . . What miserable verses he wrote in his beloved French, what trite philosophical treatises, this German who, as he himself confessed, spoke his native language like a coachman! Bismarck laughed at the vanity of the man who could note beneath one of his own poems, 'not bad on the eve of a great battle,' and Macaulay mocked the hero-king who went about with a dram of poison in one pocket and a bunch of bad verses in the other.

Certainly, Frederick was an enigma, a wraith almost, flitting in the half-world between nightmare and reality, incapable of responding to Nature or women or of opening his heart to anyone. He himself said he lived 'divorced from the world,' and to the end he remained cynically detached, scorning men's spiritual aspirations, envying and hating their capacity for happiness, delighting in cruel jokes and in scandalising the pious with venomous blasphemies. Yet he left his stamp on the world and profoundly affected the fate of Europe – whether for better or for worse, scientific historians must decide. They will find no lack of evidence, either for the prosecution or the defence.

*

CHAPTER TWO

Ancestral Portraits

AT THE SECOND BLOW of the axe, the head that had worn the crowns of France and Scotland went rolling down the steps of the scaffold. As it struck the ground, wig, bands and false curls fell off and the horrified spectators saw the bald head of an ageing woman. Mary Stuart had atoned for conniving at murder by a brave death.

Sixteen years later, her son, James VI of Scotland, ascended the English throne and her granddaughter Elizabeth married a Wittelsbach, Frederick, Elector Palatine of the Rhine. Ambitious like all the Stuarts and thirsting for adventure, the beautiful, seventeen-year-old Elizabeth induced her weak-minded husband to accept the crown of Bohemia from the Protestants of Prague, and for the next thirty years Germany was the scene of blood, tears and devastation. For one winter Frederick kept his crown, then the troops of the Catholic Emperor drove him from Bohemia.

Thereafter the royal couple wandered friendless through Germany, barely able to feed the twelve children, which Elizabeth bore in fifteen years of impecunious marriage. When her husband died, the Rhinelanders pelted the coffin of their one-time Elector with horse dung. Elizabeth consoled herself with a series of lovers until her son Philip stabbed one of them to death. Six of her children ended their days in beggary, and at last, at the age of sixty, Elizabeth herself, the ex-Queen of Bohemia whose nephew now sat upon the throne of England, died as the wife of an English cloth-merchant. But amongst her surviving children there was one, Sophia, who was destined to be the ancestress of the Kings of England and of Prussia and the great-grandmother of Frederick the Great.

Frederick inherited much from the sharp-tongued Sophia.

She was as hard as granite and as unequivocal as cold steel. In her memoirs she proudly told how, when she was fourteen, she had slapped an importunate cousin of the House of Orange in the face with a handkerchief dipped in a chamber-pot. But like most of her forebears, Sophia had to pursue a tortuous path to reach her destiny. She was first betrothed to a Prince of the House of Guelph, George William von Celle, until in Venice – as Sophia cheerfully relates – her fiancé contracted venereal disease from a Greek woman. The bride-to-be was then relinquished to a younger brother, Ernest Augustus of Hanover, George William promising never to marry so that the Duchy of Celle could pass to Sophia's descendants.

Sophia was delighted with the arrangement. She and Ernest were duly married, then settled down to wait for the sizeable heritage. But they waited in vain, for suddenly, despite his solemn pledge, George fell in love and announced his intention of marrying, Eleonore d'Olbreuse, or 'that person', as Sophia called her, was a French lady of ancient lineage but inferior pedigree, and as Sophia could not hope to separate the lovers she did her utmost to bring home to her brother-in-law the political and social objections to the match. She persuaded him and, with more difficulty, Eleonore that their formal union was really not necessary and that morality and religion would be satisfied if, before suitable witnesses, they declared themselves bound by a 'marriage of conscience'. In a ceremony of her own devising, Sophia herself then joined the hands of George William and Eleonore, she and Ernest Augustus signing a certificate as witnesses. Neither the Church nor the public were informed of this arrangement, nor, of course, did Sophia feel it necessary to point out its consequences to the happy couple: their children, if any, would be illegitimate, hence the Duchy of Celle would in due course pass to Sophia's children, as previously agreed. But when Eleonore gave birth to a daughter, she realised this for herself and at once began a campaign for the child's legitimisation. Ten years later, she and George William were legally married in church and their daughter, Sophia Dorothea, the future grandmother of Frederick the Great, though born out of wedlock, became their legitimate heir.

Sophia was furious. Her first reaction was to try and prevent the girl from marrying, but as she was a wealthy heiress this was difficult and Sophia quickly realised that the stories she was putting out about Sophia Dorothea visiting servants in their bedrooms would be hopelessly inadequate to ward off eager suitors. That being so, there was only one alternative: Sophia Dorothea should marry Sophia's own eldest son, George. In due course, all barriers fell before Sophia's relentless assault and the betrothal took place when Sophia Dorothea was sixteen. She had matured early and was now a full-bosomed, sensual-mouthed young lady. Her cousin George was twenty-three. A profligate of coldly calculating temperament, for some time now he had been in the habit of sharing his father's concubines. By him Sophia Dorothea had two children in close succession, then there were scenes of domestic violence, the parents became estranged and George returned to his paramours while his wife acquired a lover.

This was the Swede, Count Königsmark. His sister, Aurora, was a mistress of Augustus the Strong, Elector of Saxony, and Königsmark had recently been made commander-in-chief of his army. For five years he and Sophia Dorothea kept their liaison a secret, then it gradually became common knowledge. When the news reached Ernest Augustus, who had meanwhile become Elector of Hanover, he acted promptly. Königsmark was kidnapped, or, as Ernest's wife, Sophia, put it in a letter to a relative: 'Königsmark must have been carried off by a witch – he left here a fortnight ago, since when we have heard no more.' But the witch was Sophia herself: Königsmark had been murdered on the Elector's instructions and his corpse walled up inside the castle. In vain Augustus the Strong demanded the return of his commander-in-chief; Ernest feigned ignorance of his whereabouts. The marriage of Sophia Dorothea to George was dissolved despite her mother Eleonore's plea that there was wrong on both sides and George had committed adultery not once, but dozens of times. On this argument Liselotte of the Palatinate commented in a letter to her aunt Sophia in Hanover: 'What husband is there in the world who loves only his wife and does not have something to do with mistresses or boys? If wives behaved as badly, no husband could be sure their children were his own. Does not this Duchess know that a wife's honour consists in having relations with no one but her husband and that a husband is put to shame, not by having a mistress, but by being made a cuckold? Misfortune will at any rate teach your daughter-in-law the truth of this.' Poor Sophia Dorothea! She had plenty of time to learn. Sophia had never ceased to hate Eleonore and at her instigation Sophia Dorothea was banished to the small country seat of Ahlden, where she lived completely alone until her death thirty years later. Despite her entreaties, she was never allowed to see her children again.

Meanwhile the widowed Electress Sophia was hatching new plans as she passed her days tending her aviary of forty canary-birds. Her son George's marriage had ended in disaster; all the greater her joy at contriving a good match for her daughter, Sophia Charlotte, who was studying philosophy under the great Leibniz and fast becoming a blue-stocking. For Sophia Charlotte her mother's eye rested on Frederick of Brandenburg-Prussia. Fop though he was with his pretty curls and a fool to try and outdo Louis XIV in extravagance, he had inherited from his father the most powerful State in North Germany and soon after his marriage to Sophia Charlotte he obtained the Emperor's permission to style himself King Frederick I of Prussia. In due course his wife bore him a son. They christened him Frederick William.

When Frederick William was twenty, the Electress Sophia set the seal on her dynastic ambitions by marrying him to his first cousin, her other grandchild, Sophia Dorothea, daughter of the prisoner in Ahlden. The bride's distaste for her podgy, stocky cousin and the Church's rigmarole about prohibited degrees of consanguinity were swept aside by the Electress and the King of Prussia in their combined enthusiasm for the marriage. For once, Frederick I could indulge his mania for extravagance with a good conscience by providing a gargantuan wedding feast: 640 calves, 100 fat oxen, 1,102 turkeys, 650 ducks, 1,000 doves, 7,200 eggs . . . . Thus the couple were joined who were to bring Frederick the Great into the world.

For the Electress Sophia this marriage was a personal triumph, but Fate was to confer a yet greater. When Queen Anne of England died without issue, the English Parliament resolved that the Electress's son George should succeed to the throne as the last surviving Protestant Stuart.

With her son King of England and her daughter Queen of Prussia, the aged Electress began to mellow and occasionally now the two great-grandmothers of Frederick the Great, herself and the Huguenot, Eleonore, both of them over eighty, would meet and exchange tired smiles at Herrenhausen. But to the last the Electress preferred Frederick William to her other grandson, George II of England, for in him, as she said, there were 'too many mouse-droppings mixed with the pepper,' and by that she meant too much Huguenot blood. Sophia never forgave 'that person', while Eleonore could never forget that, but for Sophia, her daughter would have been Queen of England instead of re-pining at Ahlden. So, beneath their cautious smiles and quavering conversation the two old women sensed a gulf that could never be bridged.

.   .   .   .   .   .

15

So much for Frederick the Great's maternal ancestors. On his father's side, the story is simpler and more quickly told. His great-grandfather, Frederick William, had acceded to the Electorate of Brandenburg in 1640, when Germany was still enveloped in the Thirty Years War. The Swedes were devastating the March, the French and Spaniards his Rhenish possessions. Once already, at the instigation of the feudal estates, the army had been reduced to 4,000 men, and the young Elector was soon compelled to reduce it still further. Brandenburg thus became the laughing-stock of Germany, a virtually defenceless State in times when only the language of the sword was spoken or understood throughout Europe. The Elector was the first to realise this, and before long he was building a fresh army with the aid of a French subsidy. By 1655, when Sweden and Poland went to war, he had a regularly paid and properly organised body of troops totalling 26,000 men and could play an effective part in the struggle. His aim was to obtain formal sovereignty over East Prussia, at that time a dependency of Poland. Fighting first with the Swedes, he obtained their recognition of his claim, then, as soon as the King of Poland offered to cede East Prussia in return for his help, the Elector changed sides and fought with Poland. Thus by ruthless opportunism he obtained a clear title to East Prussia.

For forty-eight years Frederick William, rightly called 'The Great Elector,' threw his restless energy into extending and consolidating the territory of Brandenburg and establishing an orderly system of government. In war an opportunist, in peace he was an enlightened reformer, fostering education and trade, revising the system of land tenure, introducing a postal service, building roads and canals. His achievements were great, but they remained far behind his hopes.

Frederick had chosen a wife from the House of Orange. A pious and homely individual Louise Henriette was a granddaughter of William the Silent, the man who had freed Holland from the Spanish yoke. They were the parents of the dandified Frederick (King Frederick I of Prussia) and it was he who, as we have seen, provided that outsize banquet at the wedding of his son Frederick William to Sophia Dorothea the granddaughter of Eleonore d'Olbreuse, the future parents of Frederick the Great.

A few weeks after their wedding the aged Electress Sophia wrote to King Frederick saying she hoped God would soon make him a grandfather and adding: '. . . to which end, as I hear, they are working night and day in Berlin.' Frederick read the letter aloud at the dinner table and the ensuing laughter so embarrassed the young bride that she had to leave the room. Within barely a year an heir to the throne was born, but the Prince died when only a few days old, apparently as a result of the protracted ceremonial at his christening. A year later, a second son was born; he, too, died in infancy. Then came a daughter, Wilhelmina, and on Sunday, 24th January, 1712, a third son came into the world and was christened Karl Friedrich. The child lived, and still lives as 'Frederick the Great'.

*

CHAPTER THREE

The Heritage

THE ELECTORATE OF BRANDENBURG – whose ruler had caused a snigger in the courts of Europe by assuming the odd title of 'King in Prussia' – was at that time thirteenth among the States of Europe in size of population, with 2,000,000 inhabitants coming between the Kingdom of the Two Sicilies and the Venetian Republic. Its population was about one-tenth that of France, Austria or Poland.

It was doubtful, even, whether Brandenburg could be called a State; the territory did not form one coherent whole like Bavaria or Hanover, but consisted of small parcels of land acquired by conquest or intermarriage in every part of Germany – the barren, sandy plain round Berlin, for instance, and, separated from it by a three days' journey, the former Polish fief of East Prussia. Of these two areas, and these only, the Elector of Brandenburg was entitled to call himself King, as they did not form part of the Holy Roman Empire. Apart from them, there were five or six small counties in the west – Minden, Cleves, Tecklenburg, Nester. They would be quickly lost in the event of war and Brandenburg as a whole positively invited attack: throughout the kingdom not one town was more than a day's march from the frontier.

If there was hardly a Prussian State, still less was there a Prussian people. No one in Cleves, Minden, Magdeburg or even in Berlin called himself a Prussian. Properly speaking, the only people who deserved the name were the inhabitants of Königsberg and neighbourhood.

Brandenburg was peculiar in a third respect. Looking back at the end of the eighteenth century Talleyrand said: 'Not to have been alive before 1789 is never to have lived at all.' In

France perhaps, not in Frederick William's Brandenburg! The autumnal Baroque, the age of gallantry when men lived for pleasure and the fate of nations depended on the whim of a handful of exquisitely dressed and perfumed ladies, seemed to have stopped at the borders of Brandenburg, shivered in the east wind blowing night and day from the steppes of Russia, and gone elsewhere. There seemed to be no colour, warmth or joy in this forbidding land, only its king, fuming, threatening and giving orders in fluent French, execrable German or a mixture of both. Whereas in other countries men only worked if they had the inconceivable misfortune not to belong to the upper classes, here everyone, including the aristocracy, was caught up in ceaseless, mole-like activity under the ubiquitous eye of an implacable sovereign. Frederick William had the power and he meant to use it. From the aristocracy he demanded blind obedience. 'They shall dance to my tune or may the Devil take me,' he wrote. 'If they don't I shall treat them as rebels, I shall hang them and roast them like the Tsar.' When the nobles of Pomerania complained at his reforms, saying the country would go bankrupt, the King mocked: '*Tout le pays sera ruiné! Nihil credo!* But this I *credo* – the Junkers' authority will have to be ruined, for I mean to establish my authority like *un rocher de bronze.*'

And the King did mean it! In East Prussia a steward of the royal demesne had been sentenced to several years' detention for embezzlement. For a nobleman who in other respects had done good service the punishment was unusually harsh. On visiting Gumbinnen, where the man was imprisoned, the King sent for him and told him bluntly the sentence had been too lenient, he deserved the gallows. The prisoner replied courteously it had never been the custom to hang noblemen, moreover, he intended to pay back the money. 'I don't want your thieves' money!' roared the King and dismissed the prisoner. This story caused uneasiness amongst the local nobility, but there were ways of softening the King's heart. On the following Sunday the parson preached on the text: 'Be ye merciful, even as your Father is merciful.' Frederick William was pious, and during the sermon tears streamed down his face. That same day he summoned the members of the domanial court to the fortress, made them stand by a window overlooking the courtyard, had the prisoner released before their eyes and then drove home.

But Frederick William did not usually act on the spur of the moment. He was systematic rather than arbitrary. One day, for instance, he sent for his private secretary, Thulemeier, telling him

19

to bring plenty of good, thick paper and some 'black stitching twine mingled with thread of silver,' and began to dictate a code of Regulations for State Officials. The work lasted several days. The result was a manual containing thirty-five chapters and 297 paragraphs in which every public servant in Prussia, from minister to night watchman, could find his duties precisely set out. Senior officials, for instance, discovered that their work would start at 7 a.m. in summer and 8 a.m. in winter. A minister or councillor failing to attend a committee meeting would lose six months' pay. If he absented himself a second time he would be discharged with ignominy from the royal service – 'for we pay them in order that they shall work.' How long would the meetings last? Until the work was finished. If a meeting were not over by 2 p.m., half those attending could go for their dinner. The remainder would eat when the others returned. The meal on such occasions would be served in an adjoining room. 'For serving there shall be only one lackey at a time,' ordered the King, 'so that the room does not get filled with lackeys, and four plates and one glass shall be laid for each man. A large basket must also be available for the dirty crockery.'

As the King's officials anxiously perused the Book of Fate they quickly realised that the era of sinecures, corruption and official travelling on private business had come to an end. Periodic tours of inspection were, of course, still necessary – and obligatory – but henceforth dog-carts or light hunting traps only were to be used so that farm horses borrowed for the journey should not be overworked. No inspections were to take place during the ploughing season or the harvest, when the farmers would have no time to spare. In Pomerania, Cleves and the March of Brandenburg all Government officials were to be recruited from outside the province. Each administrative department was to maintain private agents so that it would be kept well informed. All appointments had to be approved by the King or one of his ministers. Sponsors would be answerable for their nominees. Throughout the Regulations the word 'responsible' kept on recurring. So that no one should misunderstand its meaning the King drew a gallows in the margin.

The Regulations were supplemented by further instructions drawn up in person by the King, prescribing methods of ploughing and threshing grain, erecting earthworks as a protection against flooding, and hunting wolves. In great detail the King dealt with the recruitment and training of gardeners, millers, midwives, lamplighters and with the manufacture of woollen goods, including a clause that anyone who exported raw wool abroad would suffer death by hanging, for only the export of treated wool brought profit to the nation. The King then turned to minor matters: market women were in future not to sit idle at their stalls but were to busy themselves knitting stockings. Any parson preaching for over one hour would be fined two talers. Those under forty were forbidden to indulge in rhetoric. Older men were recognised as incorrigible.

Laws, edicts and decrees were one means of stamping the King's personality on the nation, the other was more direct. On one occasion, hearing noise coming from a house, Frederick William thrust his way in and ordered the quarrelling couple to kiss and make up. He chastised some idle building workers in person, tore what he considered extravagant finery off the backs of females in the street and broke up games of skittles – in short, no one, army officers excepted, was safe from the royal stick.

It is said the King once gave chase in the street to an escaping pickpocket. Having caught him, the King asked why he had tried to run away. 'Because I's afeard!' replied the man. 'Miserable wretch! You ought to love me!' roared the King, raining blows in proof of his words. True to type, Frederick William could be sentimental at times. Then he would forget his violent outbursts and complain: 'God knows I am much too tranquil; I think it would be better if I were more choleric.'

But Frederick William was no mere buffoon. He founded twenty or more towns in East Prussia, brought 20,000 settlers into the country, encouraged farming, reclaimed marshes, stored grain in good times and sold it in bad, and wherever there was a lack of skilled craftsmen he recruited them abroad. 'Men I consider the greatest of all riches,' he told his son.

For two reasons Frederick William worked with tireless perseverance for the welfare of his people: he wanted to make Prussia powerful and that meant he had to have a large army which could only be paid for by a prosperous country, and secondly he was pious and held it to be the duty of kings to care for their subjects. But the country he ruled was poor; Frederick often called himself 'the beggar king'; all the greater was his insistence in urging his officials to increase the State income, in particular from the royal domains. He told them they had to 'make a plus'; the people called him the 'Plus-maker', and he spared no efforts to set them a good example. No candles were left burning at the Prussian Court, and like everyone else the King paid the consumer tax which he himself had imposed. He used to call himself 'the

21

Field-Marshal and Finance Minister to the King of Prussia', showing that, autocratic though he was, he was no despot, but considered himself the first servant of the State. Throughout his life he could never understand why his people felt so little affection for him. While neighbouring monarchs reduced their countries to beggary with their idle extravagance, Frederick William worked hard and lived frugally, taught his people to do the same and so visibly enhanced the power and reputation of his country. But they saw no reason to be grateful; on the contrary there was much cause for complaint, above all, at the large and splendid army which the King had given them.

Frederick William had a passion for soldiers, despite the fact that four men had to lift him into the saddle before he could review them. He gave Prussia an army as big as Austria's, a country ten times the size. In Prussia, one in every nine men was a soldier; there were 40,000 under arms. Another 40,000 were foreign mercenaries, obtained by the King's recruiting officers, who were feared throughout the length and breadth of Europe, particularly by tall men, for the King, himself only five feet three, had a preference for giants. He would go to any lengths to obtain one for his own lifeguards. For an Irishman of six feet eleven inches he is said to have paid 9,000 talers, or three times the annual salary of a minister. 'The most beautiful girl that could be got for me would leave me cold. But soldiers – there is my weakness; they can do anything they like with me there.' The King's devotion to his giants was such that he painted their portraits, man for man, from memory and was so pleased with the result that he began to wonder whether he could abdicate and earn a living as an artist. In reporting to his Government, the French Minister was at a loss to explain this mania and suggested that the mystery would remain unsolved until a post-mortem could be performed on the King's brain.

But though the King was far too proud of his giant grenadiers to risk them in battle, if they ever had to fight it was obvious they would give a good account of themselves. By making the recruitment of each non-mercenary regiment the responsibility of a particular province, the King made local pride the basis of his troops' morale. Moreover his whole army was trained to a level of efficiency and discipline which removed the weakness inherent in a half-mercenary, half-volunteer force. By killing every human ability except that of obeying orders with speed and accuracy, Frederick William produced a new type of soldier and one admirably suited to the defence of a country too young to generate

22

patriotism or possess a military tradition.

Foreigners used to the unco-ordinated movements of their own troops gaped when they saw a Prussian regiment on the march. These men did not simply walk, they advanced like some irresistible machine, marching, first the right foot, then the left, in time. This measured tread, or *Gleichschritt* as it was called, had been invented by a Prussian field-marshal, and made an uncanny impression. And not only the step, but the bearing, the movements, the dress down to the smallest buttons – yes, even the appearance of each man was the same. The pigtails were all docked to precisely the same length and the beards, in those regiments which wore them, were identical in cut. If a man could not achieve the right shape, its outline was painted on his face. And the troops not only marched like a machine; as one man they knelt, aimed their muskets, fired, reloaded and fired again – six times a minute, thrice as fast as in any other army, thanks to another Prussian invention, the iron ramrod.

The discipline in Frederick William's army was due also to the quality of the officers. The King was the only monarch in Europe who did not sell commissions to the highest bidder, but gave them to members of the aristocracy strictly according to merit. The pay was miserable, but the status of officer was high. At Court the most junior ensign took precedence over the most senior civilian official and army officers were accorded a number of special privileges. In return they had to work hard to bring their recruits under the yoke of an iron discipline and keep them there until death gave them their release from the King's service. There were frequent attempts at suicide – one a fortnight in the Berlin garrison alone – and the King tried to reduce the rate by making a standing order that the corpse of a soldier who had taken his life should be tied by the feet to a horse and dragged through the streets to the knacker's yard.

But one order the King never gave: the order to shoot. Frederick William was the most unwarlike monarch in Europe. In London it was said that he only acted the wolf in his own fold, while Peter the Great remarked that he kept the peace not from a dislike of fishing, but for fear of getting his feet wet. These comments contained a grain of truth. Despite his devotion to duty, conscientiousness and administrative ability, Frederick William lacked the self-confidence, the subtlety and perhaps the taste for duplicity which make a successful opportunist in the international field.

Yet, with the unifying force of the Holy Roman Empire steadily declining, chances of aggrandisement had seldom been better.

Since the Treaty of Westphalia in 1648 German States had possessed the right to conclude treaties with countries outside the Empire, and although agreements directed against the Emperor were barred both Bavaria and Cologne had fought on the side of France in the recent wars against Louis XIV. Moreover, though German princes still owed nominal allegiance to the Emperor, some of them ruled territories outside the imperial jurisdiction – the Elector of Saxony, for instance, who was also King of Poland, the Elector of Hanover and Frederick William himself, King of Prussia. The fact was that, though still nominally intact, the Emperor's powers existed only on paper and in practice would not suffice to raise a single penny or set one soldier in motion. If it came to the point, therefore, men and money would have to be begged from the German States, with the certainty that by no means all would make their contribution to a cause which had ceased to exist. Every Sunday throughout Germany prayers were still offered for the Emperor, but for the rest of the week the German princes pursued their own policies and forgot him.

In this tempting situation, Frederick William raised longing eyes towards the Duchy of Jülich and Berg on the lower Rhine, hoping to acquire the territory with the Emperor's agreement when its ruler died. But he defeated his end by clumsy action and the naïve belief that his wishes would be deferred to because he had an army of 80,000 men and a war-chest of 25,000,000 talers. In fact, as far as his prestige in Germany was concerned, these assets were outweighed by his notorious political ineptitude. He played his cards badly and was considered too unreliable to be wooed, as he thought he should be, like a wealthy heiress. 'Thanks to his instability, the King of Prussia is neither useful to his friends nor dangerous to his enemies,' reported the French Minister from Berlin.

But Frederick William's inability to shine in the company of cut-throats was, after all, not entirely discreditable; in fact it sprang from positive virtues. First among these was an appreciation which no contemporary possessed of the living reality of German nationhood underlying the moribund Empire. Frederick William spoke of 'us Germans' and swore to put 'pistols and daggers in the cradles of my children to keep foreign nations out of Germany.' And to him, the Emperor still personified Germany. 'I'll not depart from the Emperor,' he said, 'unless he kicks me out.'

These sentiments were unusual for the times and the Emperor Charles VI ought to have appreciated the fact. But he showed singularly little gratitude. Having promised support for Frederick William's claim to Jülich and Berg, he then confined it to Berg, and a few years later to Berg minus its capital, Düsseldorf. Soon after, Charles VI withdrew his promise altogether by reserving to himself the right to decide on the succession to the Duchy. The King of Prussia complained he was being treated as though he were the 'Prince of Zipfel-Zerbst.' That he was deeply hurt is revealed in a letter which he wrote to Dessauer. 'This world is past my comprehension. God grant me a speedy and peaceful end so that I shall have done with all this knavery. It can be endured no longer.' With mournful irony he painted a fanciful portrait of himself as the comic Lord of Misrule and wrote beneath: '*In tormentis pinxit.*' With advancing age, his depression deepened (and his German spelling became more and more arbitrary): 'I wish now for nutten more in the vorld than to find in forein land far from mine own lands a bretty lonely blace where I can live in peace, for I am no use for nutten in this vorld and everyting is burden to me, wherefor I wish to lead a filosophish life.'

Frederick William could beat, hang, admonish and chastise his own subjects, but in his dealings with foreign rulers who were his equals all the weakness and confusion in his irascible, authoritarian nature were revealed. 'Beware of imitating me in all that touches diplomacy,' he told his son, 'for I have never understood anything of that.' Sometimes the inferiority complex that lurked behind the bluster would rise and all but smother him. When an entire squadron of his hussars, complete with arms and equipment, deserted abroad, Frederick William could only say: 'Now the whole world will think I treat my people badly.' Finally, towards the end of his life, he sadly confessed: 'God knows what a small opinion I have always had of myself.'

*

CHAPTER FOUR

Fritz

A SUMMER'S EVENING in 1721. The King of Prussia was sitting alone, brooding over his son. In front of him was a plain deal table that served as a desk. He was wearing a colonel's dark blue uniform, and, as the material was expensive and worth keeping clean, a grey apron and green armlets over it. Judging by his expression, the King was not pleased with the nine-year-old Fritz. His mouth, always small, had almost disappeared between his compressed lips and the large pink face like a Rubens cherub was rigid and purple with anger.

For all his sickliness and his slight frame, Fritz was proving an awkward young cub to train. Why was it that the time-honoured precepts drawn up by the King's grandfather, the Great Elector, applied with success in the education of his father, and with minor changes in his own, seemed to be producing the exact opposite to the desired result in the case of this boy? Admittedly, the King had altered them somewhat, but with the object of making them more specific, more watertight, not less. First and foremost the tutors of the Crown Prince had been instructed to instil into him a love of soldiering. The moral of all their teaching was to be this: only the sword could bring honour and glory to a prince – only by the sword could he win fame and respect. If he was not a soldier, he was nothing. To drive home the point and accustom him to the din of battle, the King had arranged for a daily discharge of cannon beneath his son's window. At the age of five he had been given a miniature company to drill, drawn from the children of the aristocracy. At six he had been introduced to horse management and equitation. At seven he had exchanged a nursery governess for two tutors, and for the last three years these men had been dinning into him another crucial precept: the greatest of all sins is sloth. For the rest, the boy's education was founded on good sense. German and French were to be taught him, but no Latin. No Latin – on this the King was adamant. Why, he never explained, but no doubt as a practical man he scorned Latin as the language of pedants. Finally, as the model he wished his son to imitate, the King realised the importance of not losing his affection, and whenever the boy was naughty the tutors could threaten to tell his mother, but never his father.

All this Frederick William had done for Fritz. And what was the result? A slovenly, blubbering, womanish coward who went about on tiptoe like a dancing master, covered his hair and face with powder, seldom went near cold water, looked like a sack of potatoes in the saddle, was already speaking French better than German and spent all his spare time playing the flute. And how he loved to show off, be different to everyone else! That time, for instance, when he had gone out hunting with his father and worn gloves because he said his fingers were cold; when he said he could not manage the normal two-pronged fork and refused to eat until he was given a fork with three; when on the trip to Magdeburg he had refused to accept the loyal citizens' gift of money, and why? To make himself popular, because his father had a proper respect for money and was not in the habit of refusing! The spiteful, treacherous young – !

But, after all, Fritz was only nine. All this must be the fault of his tutors. They were not obeying the King's orders. Well, he would have them thrashed – thrashed and clapped into jail. But were the tutors to blame? Or was it the Queen, the plump and ever plumper Sophia Dorothea, 'Olympia', or Fifi as her husband called her in roguish moments? No wonder Fritz gave himself airs with his mother spoiling him as she did and telling him he was one day to marry Amalia, daughter of the Prince of Wales and granddaughter of King George I of England, and that his sister Wilhelmina was to be the wife of the Duke of Gloucester! It was Sophia, with her extravagance, her foolish ambitions and her attempts to monopolise her children's affection who was to blame. Her influence must be diminished. The children must be forbidden to see her. And her allowance must be cut. Now for the tutors: the King might have known they would find loopholes in their instructions. They were not interested in carrying out the spirit; they were not loyal enough for that. What they needed was something so precise, so detailed that the spirit and the letter became one and betrayal of either would cost them their heads.

Frederick William gave a hitch to his armlets and took up his pen:

> On Sundays he [the Crown Prince] is to rise at seven. As soon
> as he has his slippers on he shall kneel at the bed and say a short prayer
> to God loud enough for all present to hear, as follows: 'Lord God,
> Holy Father, I thank thee from my heart that thou has been pleased
> to preserve me through this night. Make me obedient to thy holy Will
> and grant that neither this day nor all the days of my life I may do
> aught to separate myself from thee, for the Lord Jesus, my Redeemer's
> sake, Amen.' After which, the Lord's Prayer. Then speedily and with
> all despatch he shall dress and wash himself, be queued and powdered;
> and getting dressed as well as breakfast – tea, which is to be taken
> while the valet is making his queue and powdering him – shall be
> finished and done in a quarter of an hour, that is, by a quarter past
> seven.

Then followed general prayers and hymn-singing with the servants and with Duhan, the tutor, who was also to read a chapter
from the Bible.

On each week-day the Prince was to have seven hours of study,
four in the morning and three in the afternoon. Then, on Saturday
morning:

> . . . until half-past ten, everything that he has learnt during the week
> in History, Writing and Reckoning shall be repeated, and in Morality
> as well, to see whether he has profited. If Fritz has profited then the
> afternoon shall be his own. If he has not profited, then from two until
> six he shall repeat all that he has forgotten in the preceding days.

All this the King wrote out in his own hand and signed it, confident that Fritz would now be moulded to his will.

Meanwhile, the nine-year-old Prince was sitting by the hearth
in his living-room, reading a book. Without waking his tutor
who slept beside him, he had crept out of bed to this corner where
no one would see the light. The book was in French, the language
he had learnt from his Huguenot governess, Madame de Rocoules,
who had brought up his father before him. In the forty years she
spent in Prussia she had never learnt a word of German, and
throughout his life her pupil was to have difficulty even in understanding his people's tongue.

Duhan was also French. He was teaching the boy many things
which the King had forbidden, including a little Latin, well aware
that if he was found out his only reward would be to feel the royal
boot come into painful contact with his person. The Queen also
braved the King's displeasure by having her children with her in
her apartments during his absence. Whenever they heard the clink
of his spurs in the corridor they had to hide. Once, after the King

had returned home earlier than expected from a hunting trip, he went to sleep in the Queen's armchair, and for some hours Wilhelmina in hooped skirt lay squashed under the low bed, while Fritz had to remain in the only place he had been able to find – the toilet.

The marriage of Fritz's parents had been a disaster from the start. The Queen was herself the daughter of an unhappy marriage and she began her own with a prejudice against the male sex caused by her mother's suffering. While Frederick William was tortured by self-mistrust, his wife had the arrogance of the Guelphs allied to the enterprising rashness of the Stuarts. Each aggravated the other. Frederick William's timidity exasperated the Queen, while the mere fact that she was George II's sister sufficed to make him hate her. Within a few months of their wedding Frederick William was already threatening her with divorce, to which she replied: 'Believe me, I set no store by my own life. You embitter it too much for me to mourn for it.' Of what did the King accuse her? 'You persist in saying that I dislike living with you, but what have I done to cause such a belief? In fact I love you and am trying my hardest to demonstrate a love which will live longer than the malignant phantoms of your imagination. I thank God that I have no cause to reproach myself with anything, unless with loving you too much.'

Such letters left the King unmoved. Sophia Dorothea was a thorn in his flesh and in the body politic. While he was hard working and parsimonious and taught his subjects to be the same, she spent her life in frivolity and extravagance, spending money like water, running up huge debts, gambling for high stakes, and in ducats, too, though at the first sign of the King's approach she might sweep them off the table and substitute coffee beans. He was not fooled. And he got his own back. If the Queen thought him uncouth, he would be uncouth, mock her intellectual pretensions by ridiculing her former tutor, Leibniz, load distinguished men of letters with foul-mouthed abuse – and force her to eat his favourite dish of pickled scrag end and pease pudding, helping her to choke by jumping up and proposing a toast to the downfall of England, in other words, of her own family. At times, admittedly, Frederick William felt an upsurge of tenderness towards his wife; for instance when she inherited 3,000,000 talers from her mother. 'To obtain control of this sum,' reported the Austrian Minister in Berlin, 'the King lavishes endearments on the Queen and nothing is too much to put up with. The moment the money has been transferred to his treasury no doubt this will become less apparent.'

29

But the King sent to Hanover in vain. When his privy counsellor arrived with a number of stout iron boxes, the King's brother-in-law surrendered not a single coin. At once the endearments were abandoned and in his wife's presence the King gave the toast: 'To hell with all Hanoverians!' This sentiment, however, did not deter him from begetting fourteen children by his Hanoverian wife. Later he began to sense that at least one of them despised him.

At dinner one day with the War Minister, Grumbkov, Frederick William started lecturing his son Fritz. The boy was then twelve. There was nothing in his attitude to provoke his father – Fritz listened and answered dutifully – but for the very reason, perhaps, that he lacked all pretext, Frederick William grew more and more angry. He had started by tapping and pinching his son's cheek; soon he was boxing his ears, hitting him, pulling his hair until suddenly the King was seized with a kind of fit and he jumped up and started hurling plates at the wall. Feigning drunk, Grumbkov tactfully did the same, while the Crown Prince stood by, trembling, and pale with contempt.

The fact was Fritz was very different from his father's conception. He was not in the least a mother's darling, was not lazy, unpractical or a day-dreamer. But he was unloved, and so completely rootless, unattached to either parent. He spoke French better than German, but neither perfectly. Despite the two hours' daily religious instruction decreed by his father he was irreligious. As for childlike spontaneity, enthusiasm or trust, all that had been destroyed by the need for calculating duplicity in the remorseless struggle with his father. Fritz could not afford to be sentimental – he cultivated the flute, a clear, rational instrument, rather than the violin. At the age of fourteen he approached the envoys of France and England to ask what would happen if the King died, or if . . . In reporting to their governments, the ambassadors stated they dared not commit to paper everything the Crown Prince had said. Was he expecting that his father would lose his reason, or was he planning a *coup d'état*?

Meanwhile, knowing nothing of this, the King was arranging for his son's scriptural knowledge to be tested by a clerical friend. The pastor questioned and Fritz answered, skilfully evading fundamentals, but showing he understood the letter if not the spirit of the Gospels. Frederick William nodded. That would have to do. So much for book learning. He discharged Duhan and the other tutors, put the Prince in the Guards and appointed four officers to watch over him, making them answerable with their heads for any irregularities of behaviour which they failed either to correct or report to the King. Fritz had now reached the age of puberty, and suspecting that it might lead a boy of his repressed character to seek new outlets, the King ordered that one at least of his escorts was never to leave his side.

Satisfied that he had made all necessary arrangements for his son's moral welfare, the King then made ready to leave for Dresden, where his friend Augustus the Strong, King of Poland and Elector of Saxony, was waiting to be his host. Frederick William had not intended to take Fritz with him, but at the last moment was prevailed upon by his host to do so. Reluctantly, then, the King set off with his son for the most pleasure-loving Court in Germany.

In Dresden Fritz entered a new and glittering world: vast state apartments where at night a thousand candles shone amidst a sea of mirrors and subtle perfumes rose from agate incensories in which Arabian spices glowed. Wandering in the gardens between trim hedges and past splashing fountains, the boy caught a glimpse of marble statues gleaming palely under the moon, while Moors dressed all in silver held huge torches aloft to light the guests. Everywhere there was music: fifes and fiddles played from the galleries, and outdoors invisible choirs sustained a murmurous hum. Fritz was enchanted. Here were no threats and thrashings. Seductive women sought his company. He was treated with respect. He played the flute? Excellent! And the company listened with discernment while he played with the orchestra and afterwards gave their sincere applause. When Fritz talked, people listened. He waxed eloquent, quoted philosophy and found he could turn epigrams and paradoxes with the best. He was admired, flattered and lionised. Best of all, his wishes were consulted. Would the Crown Prince care to dance or would he prefer to watch the players? See a ballet or a masquerade? Fritz had only to speak and his will was performed. It was intoxicating.

And what a contrast between the intelligent young Prince and his oafish father, who had split his dancing breeches and, having brought no second pair, had been obliged to retire from the ball! While the King strode, fat and fretful, beside his host, trying to remember how to be pleasant, his son was contemplating the beauty of the young Countess Orczelska, daughter of Augustus, now his concubine and also the mistress of one out of some dozens of sons he was said to have fathered by members of his harem.

As a good host shares all with his guests, so one evening, while Augustus was showing Fritz and his father round the palace, a

31

wall-tapestry in one of the rooms was suddenly raised, revealing the fairest of Augustus's ladies, the Countess Formera, reclining nonchalantly on a couch in the splendour of complete nudity. With one swift movement Frederick William doffed his hat and covered his son's eyes – too late! Fritz had seen, and according to Wilhelmina, before he left Dresden the Countess Formera had become his first mistress. His sister also stated that he returned to Potsdam with venereal disease, but that seems improbable, particularly as Wilhelmina's memoirs are among the most mendacious ever written.

In September 1728, encouraged perhaps by his success in Dresden, Fritz tried to come to terms with his father. The letter has been preserved.

My dear Papa. For a long time I have not ventured to come to my dear Papa, partly because I was advised against it, but also since I was to be anticipated an even worse reception than usual; and from fear of vexing my dear Papa with my present request I have preferred to make it in writing.

So I ask my dear Papa to show mercy to me and I can herein assure that after long reflection my conscience does not accuse me of the smallest thing wherein I have to reproach myself; have I however done anything against my knowledge and intention that may have distressed my dear Papa, I beg herewith most humbly for forgiveness and hope that my dear Papa will lay aside the cruel hatred which I have clearly been able to discern in all his actions. I hope that my dear Papa will reflect all this and will once more be well disposed towards me, meanwhile I repeat my assurance that as long as I live nothing shall wittingly be lacking on my part. . . .*

That same day Frederick William replied, addressing his son in the third person:

He has a wicked stubborn mind which does not love his father; for if he loved his father he would do his will, not only in his presence, but even when he can not watch everything. He well knows withal that I can not stand an effeminate fellow whose inclinations are not human, who can not ride or shoot and is also *malpropre* in his person, curls his hair like a fop and will not have it cut, and I have reproved this a thousand times, but all in vain and no improvement is in nothing. Moreover he is arrogant, full of conceit and does not speak with the people, does not ingratiate himself and is not affable, but pulls faces as though he were a jester and does my will in nothing unless

* In this as in all letters and documents quoted in the text an attempt has been made to reproduce in translation the peculiarities of spelling, style and syntax contained in the originals. – *Translator.*

compelled, never from filial love, and he never wants anything but to do as it pleases him and nothing else. This is my reply.

Frederick William.

Six weeks later Fritz made another and more desperate attempt to conciliate his father, this time in company. The scene was reported by Suhm, the Elector of Saxony's Minister in Berlin. Sitting next to the Minister and opposite his parents at a big dinner party, Fritz took Dutch courage and then turned to Suhm and made some remark about his father, adding pointedly: 'All the same, I love him.' Frederick William wanted to know what the Prince had said. Suhm replied that the Crown Prince was tipsy and did not know what he was saying. 'He's only pretending,' retorted the King. 'I want to hear it.' Suhm then told him the Crown Prince had said that although the King made him drink too much, he was very fond of him. Again the King said: 'So he pretends.' Then Fritz got up and leaning over the table insisted in kissing the King's hands. Then he tried to embrace him. 'Bravo!' cried the guests. 'Long live the Crown Prince!' At this the Queen left the room in disgust and Fritz went staggering round the table to kneel before his father, clasp his knees and swear that he loved him and his only wish was to serve him. 'All right then,' said Frederick William. 'From now on, see you act like an honest fellow.' Then the Prince was assisted to bed and for the rest of the evening the King was reported to be 'very merry.'

But the honest soldier-king was surrounded with intrigue and the very next day was persuaded that Fritz had only been play-acting: Prussian interests might be served by a reconciliation, but the relationship between father and son was connected with a project which affected all Europe and on which opinion was divided. This was the double marriage between Fritz and Wilhelmina and the children of George II of England. The project was anathema to the Emperor Charles VI, and in order to prevent its realisation he had appointed Count Seckendorff as Austrian Ambassador in Berlin. Seckendorff had a good reputation as a general and was also well liked by Frederick William, whom he had met long ago in the Low Countries during the wars with France. Seckendorff wasted no time in coming to an arrangement with the King's War Minister, Grumbkov, whereby Grumbkov received 1,000 ducats yearly in return for allowing Seckendorff access to the King's secret files. A further 40,000 guilders would be forthcoming if Grumbkov persuaded the king to drop the double-marriage project.

Meanwhile Seckendorff cemented his friendship with Frederick

William by admiring the Prussian army, riding, smoking and drinking litre for litre with the King. He also bribed the groom of the chamber, who in turn bribed one of the Queen's maids to pass on the gist of conversations between the Queen and the Crown Prince, so ensuring that the latter's plans would be known in Vienna almost as soon as he conceived them. Finally, von Reichenbach, the Prussian Ambassador in London, received substantial sums from Seckendorff, and in due course Frederick William learnt from him that his son's intended bride, the Princess Amalia, was becoming uglier every day, while Wilhemina's intended husband, the Duke of Gloucester – now Prince of Wales – was ruining his health in profligacy. News also came from London that as a result of the double marriage the English were keenly looking forward to giving orders to the King of Prussia, and, as an alternative means of persuading him to drop the project, a hint that the House of Hanover was becoming increasingly unpopular with the islanders and might soon have to re-embark, bag and baggage, for the Continent. In London, meanwhile, the Prussian Ambassador felt it only right to warn the Prince of Wales that Wilhelmina was stupid, frigid and of hideous appearance. So that von Reichenbach would appear to be almost uncannily well informed, Seckendorff supplied him regularly with items of Potsdam Court gossip so that he could weave them into his reports to Frederick William.

Von Reichenbach played his part with great skill, not forgetting to obtain from Seckendorff a guarantee of a post in Vienna in case his perfidy came to light. In Berlin Grumbkow also took precautions, carrying with him at all times a document appointing him field-marshal in the Austrian Army – even Frederick William would think twice before hanging a field-marshal. But though in Wilhelmina's opinion Grumbkov's whole character was a tissue of vice, he was not the only corrupt minister at the Prussian Court. Everyone had his price, and the conflicting currents of intrigue were such that even the arch-corrupter, the fifty-two-year-old Seckendorff, confessed that he preferred the outright slaughter of the battlefield to the furtive throat-cutting practised in Frederick William's entourage.

Meanwhile, the rift between father and son was deepening. To Frederick William the mere thought of that seventeen-year-old unsoldierly, emasculated aesthete sitting on his throne was galling and made him fear for his life's work, let alone the thought of Fritz with an English wife. King George no doubt expected greater advantages from an English princess in Potsdam than from the marriage of his son to Wilhelmina, but that could not be helped. In no circumstances, decided Frederick William, should his son marry the Princess Amalia. In that case, came the reply from London, there would be little point in Wilhelmina marrying the Prince of Wales. Frederick William felt hurt. His pride was wounded. He complained that his daughter was being bargained for as though she was a common prostitute. He could not look at her now without tears springing to his eyes. Then rage took hold of him. The English – 'that rabble', as he called them – could keep their princess. He wanted no English madam at his court, giving herself airs and beating even Sophia Dorothea at the game of intrigue. As for Fritz, 'that snot-nose, he shall have the whip before he has a wife. He's an abomination. But I'll make him see reason yet. The Devil take me if I don't change him for his own good. I'll give him some medicine of a kind he's not expecting.'

But this was mostly bluster. Frederick William knew well enough that Fritz would not listen to his father, so once again he delegated the task of disciplining his son, this time to Colonel von Rochov, now the Prince's equerry. His son, the King told Rochov, was an idle wretch. He was to rid him of his 'lascivious preoccupations,' teach him to look people straight in the eye, to stop walking on tiptoe and to stop making silly faces. He was to 'drive the sleep from his head and persuade him to an open, honest manner so that he can freely question great and small, for that is the way to learn everything that is going on.' As proof of his serious intentions, the King then reduced Fritz from the rank of colonel to ensign and made him sit at the bottom of the table at mealtimes where he was often forced to rise before he had had a bite to eat.

Now aged forty, Frederick William was becoming daily more irascible. Whether the reason was physical, emotional, or both, he would get into blind rages and rain blows on all within reach. The effects of provoking him were out of all proportion to their cause. Haunted by insomnia, he would spend whole nights wandering aimlessly, while by day, when some explosion had drained his vitality, he would sit silently weeping for hours on end. He asked the French Minister if he would report it to Paris if he started chastising his ministers. 'I trust Your Majesty will not put my discretion to that test,' replied the diplomat. The most frequent object of the royal outbursts was Fritz. Wherever he happened to be, in private or in public, Frederick William would suddenly seize him by the throat and throw him to the ground, force him to kiss his boots and beg forgiveness, and then accuse his

35

son of cowardice. 'If my father had treated me like this I would have put an end to my life long ago. But you have no courage.' Small wonder that Fritz complained to his sister: 'Every day here we go through the most unutterable scenes. I am so tired of it all. I would rather beg my bread than go on living like this.'

As Frederick William would not accept an English princess for Fritz and, unless he did, Wilhelmina could not marry the Prince of Wales, the King now found an alternative husband for her in the shape of the fat, loose-living Prince von Weissenfels. Anyway, the King was tired of bargaining with George II, that all too closely related monarch whom Frederick William called 'the red cabbage' because of his red uniform. Not only were they first cousins – George II's father and Frederick William's mother having been brother and sister – but Frederick William had married George II's sister and so became his brother-in-law. Yet each hated the other, partly because as a boy Frederick William had been stronger than George and had once given him a bloody nose, whereas now he had to look up to him as the ruler of a larger and more powerful State. There was also a bone of contention between them. As long as he lived Frederick William treasured the memory of the beautiful arched eyebrows of his first love, Caroline of Ansbach, whom George had stolen from him and made his bride. Periodically the King of Prussia still expressed the wish to challenge 'the red cabbage' to a duel.

Meanwhile, Wilhelmina had been saved from her impending fate by an event which occurred fifteen hundred miles away in Seville, where England and France had made peace with Spain. England had obtained fulfilment of all her overseas demands in return for the recognition of Spanish claims to Tuscany, Parma and Piacenza. Not that these territories were English – they belonged to the Habsburg Empire. Hence England was now trying to out-trump the Emperor. The highest card of all was undoubtedly Prussia's 80,000 grenadiers, and so it was that an envoy extraordinary now appeared in Berlin to resume discussion of the double-marriage project on behalf of George II.

Sir Charles Hotham was a general in the English Horse Guards and Frederick William took to him at once. But that did not mean he was prepared to discuss the double marriage. He would gladly send von Weissenfels packing and reserve Wilhelmina for the English heir apparent, but as for Fritz . . . The English general, thought Frederick William, had better be told straight away; soldiers don't like beating about the bush. So, hardly was Sir Charles seated, pipe in mouth, at Frederick William's *Tabak-*

kollegium, or Smoking Session, than the King gave a toast to the betrothal of Wilhelmina to the Prince of Wales. Immediately, as though it had been prearranged, all present leapt to their feet in a chorus of congratulation – all, that is, except Sir Charles, who had instructions to negotiate the double marriage or nothing. He now asked the King for a private audience.

In their bluff soldierly way, Sir Charles and the King reached a compromise. The double marriage should take place on the understanding that upon his marriage the Crown Prince should be made Governor of Hanover. Thus Frederick William would be rid of the son he hated, extend his influence over Hanover and be saved, as well, the entire upkeep of the Prince's household. Referred to London, the plan met with George II's entire approval (with the mental reservation that Hanover would not be Prussianised, but the Prince anglicised). It only remained to make a secret agreement with the Crown Prince that he would refund his uncle the cost of his governorship upon his accession to the Prussian throne and then George II said yes.

But now that his plan had been accepted, Frederick William began to doubt whether it was a good one. He changed his mind about it three times in forty-eight hours, and was no doubt on the point of changing it a fourth time when his thoughts were interrupted by an invitation. Augustus the Strong was holding an immense military review in Mühldorf, Saxony, and asked the King and the Crown Prince to be his guests. So to Mühldorf the Prussian Court transferred to watch mock battles, the illumination of the Elbe flotilla and a meal being served at one sitting to 30,000 troops. While the monarchs rode on horseback between the tables and toasted each other to the thunder of cannon, the second course was served, consisting of a cake measuring forty feet by sixteen and containing 5,000 eggs, 6,000 pounds of flour and 2,000 pounds of butter. . . . All very impressive, but anxious thoughts were still revolving in Frederick William's mind. Once in Hanover, how would Fritz behave? Would he side with England against Prussia? Did he deserve his independence? Might not this double marriage one day involve Frederick William in war with the Emperor, or as the Emperor's liegeman, with his own son? How many giant grenadiers would that cost him? Perhaps Grumbkov and Seckendorff were right, perhaps this double marriage could spell the doom of Prussia. It all depended on Fritz, and Fritz was not yet eighteen.

On returning home, Frederick William sent for Sir Charles Hotham and told him about his son. He was very young for his age. The King had found it necessary to reduce his army rank from colonel to ensign. The boy was not ready for responsibility yet, either as an officer, or as Governor of Hanover, or as a husband. In ten years' time no doubt he would be. Meanwhile, the plan for his marriage had better be postponed – until he was twenty-eight. Then, of course, it could go forward, and the governorship of Hanover would best be forgotten. . . . Sir Charles took note of these words and then went to see the Crown Prince. Fritz seemed only too glad to wait and volunteered a promise never to marry anyone except the Princess Amalia. Sir Charles then reported to London, where Frederick William's proposals were interpreted as a polite refusal of the double marriage project and with equal politeness declined.

There remained one last hope of persuading Frederick William to accept the double marriage and that was to give him proof that his own minister, Grumbkov, had been working against it in connivance with the Emperor's Ambassador Seckendorff and the Prussian Ambassador in London. Letters from Grumbkov to von Reichenbach had already been intercepted by the British secret service and copies had been sent to Sir Charles, who had shown them to the King. When questioned, Grumbkov had denied their authenticity. Now, on 10th July, 1730, Sir Charles was due to take his leave of the King before he returned to London. In his pocket was an original letter of Grumbkov's which had been brought out to Berlin by the British Minister, who had been in London on holiday. After a few pleasantries, Sir Charles reverted to Grumb-kov's denials and said that in view of them, 'I have been ordered by the King my master to transmit to Your Majesty one of his original letters.' Hotham then produced it and gave it to the King. Surely that would convince Frederick William of his minister's treason? No doubt it did. But the British envoy could not know that the King had always mistrusted his servants because he mistrusted himself. He had never believed he was the kind of man to whom people could be loyal. Proof of Grumbkov's treason now showed that belief to be justified – or so it seemed. The King glanced at the letter, then threw it down. A prop to his self-esteem had been shattered, leaving him angry and confused. 'I've had enough of this affair!' he said, and left the room, slamming the door.

Sir Charles was outraged. He had been acting on his master's instructions. An insult to him was an insult to George II. A few hours later the King made a half-hearted apology, saying he regretted his action, but coming from Grumbkov the letter had

38

deserved no better treatment. Hotham then made a reasonable suggestion: let the King grant him another audience, accept the letter and consider it on its merits. Frederick William declined, whereupon Hotham left Berlin.

So ended the double marriage project between England and Prussia. For another twenty years Wilhelmina still lived in hopes. Then, in his father's lifetime, the Prince of Wales died and she saw that, even if she had been married to him, she would never have been Queen of England.

CHAPTER FIVE

*

The Conscience of the King

AMID THE JOUSTING and jocularity at Mühldorf, Frederick
William had found time to humiliate his son. Eighteen now and
restored to the rank of colonel in the army, the Crown Prince
had been seized on in public, kicked, beaten, dragged along the
ground by his hair and sent off, bleeding and dishevelled, to make
his official appearance at the pageantry. While the marriage
project was still under discussion, he had waited. Now that it had
been finally abandoned, and with it his hopes of an independent life,
he prepared for the only possible alternative – flight.

Fritz told two friends of his plans, a high-spirited young page
named Keith, to whom he was passionately attached, and a
twenty-five-year-old lieutenant, Johann Hermann von Katte. As
a schoolboy Katte had been lampooned for his swarthy, pock-
marked complexion:

> He who Katte's look displays
> On the wheel will end his days,
> Else can be his only hope
> To die a-dangling from a rope.

But Katte was intelligent, could play the flute, was refined, witty,
a man of the world and a free-thinker. His father was a general
and his grandfather a field-marshal. At this moment he seemed
to be on the threshold of a brilliant career. He and Fritz made
ideal companions and were devoted to each other. Together they
sold the jewels from the Prince's insignia to provide money for
their flight. Fritz had already approached his uncle George
through the British Ambassador with a request for asylum in
England. But for fear of driving his brother-in-law into the

40

Imperial camp, the King had firmly declined. Instead, not wanting to quarrel with his nephew, he had made a suggestion: in return for a promise to abandon all idea of flight, he would pay the young man's debts.

Fritz had received this news one evening in July 1730. While Katte kept watch, the English envoy met the Crown Prince under a gateway and handed him his uncle's written reply. The Prince's debts amounted to 7,000 talers. He gave them as 15,000. No doubt the envoy raised his eyebrows, but he paid. Fritz now approached the French Government and received a favourable reply: he could count on finding refuge in France. So far, so good. But Fritz was a newcomer to the art of conspiracy and so failed to observe the very first rule, concealment. From now on, his every action invited disaster. He talked and boasted and trailed his secret until finally his father got wind of it. Grimly incredulous, Frederick William then took precautions: Keith was transferred to Cleves and the Prince's bodyguard was strengthened. The Danish and French envoys now warned Fritz that he was being watched, but he ignored them. His father was about to set off for Ansbach in southern Germany, and in order to keep his eye on him proposed to take Fritz. This, thought Fritz, would be a splendid opportunity to make good his escape. Katte was entrusted with the surplus money that Uncle George had unwittingly provided and also with a box of compromising letters which the Queen and Wilhelmina had written to Fritz. As Katte had not been detailed to accompany the royal party, it was agreed he should apply for leave of absence from his military duties and follow as soon as possible. Meanwhile, he and the Prince would keep in touch through the ordinary post.

Well content with these arrangements, before the royal cortége left Berlin Fritz bought a bright red cloak. Then, early on 15th July, 1730, the heavy coaches rolled out of Frederick William's capital. By the end of the day it had become obvious to Fritz that Colonel von Rochov and the two other officers travelling with him had been ordered not to let him out of their sight.

For five days Fritz waited for news; then he got a letter from Katte saying he had been unable to obtain leave. Without money, friends or freedom of movement, Fritz might have realised that his plan could not succeed. But he persevered. Among the royal pages, as it happened, was a younger brother of his friend Keith. Fritz took Keith junior into his confidence and as the party was approaching Mannheim, not far from the French border, told him to procure two horses for three o'clock on the following morning –

41

two hours before the King was due to move on.

Next day – it was 5th August – Fritz dressed at 2.30 a.m., donned his scarlet cloak and went to wait for Keith by the barn which the King had assigned to his retinue for the night. Three o'clock came, three-fifteen, and still there was no sign of Keith and the horses. Meanwhile, the Prince's valet had become suspicious of his intentions and woken Colonel von Rochov, who had been sleeping fully dressed. Now, as Fritz stood shivering in the morning mist, a voice beside him suddenly said 'Good morning'! At this precise moment the horses appeared, led by Keith. 'Who are those horses for?' asked the colonel. 'For the pages, sir,' replied the boy. 'The devil they are! Take them away!' So in despair Fritz withdrew to his quarters, wondering whether the colonel had guessed his intentions and would tell the King. There was no doubt he would, if he obeyed his orders.

Later that day the Prince had a chance to contact Keith junior again. He told him to procure the horses for the same time on the following morning. But Keith had been caught once: a second time and he might lose his life. Next morning, as Frederick William was coming away from divine service, the terrified Keith threw himself at his feet and told him all. If ever the King felt mad with rage it must have been at that moment. But he had to restrain himself. He was the official guest of the Elector Palatine and the strictest etiquette controlled his every movement. For the time being he could do no more than seize a fleeting opportunity to tell Colonel von Rochov the news and make him answerable with his life for the safe arrival of the Crown Prince at Wesel.

Wesel was in Prussian territory, but before they reached it the King and his Court were due to visit three foreign States: Hesse-Darmstadt, Frankfurt and Cologne. Here again no jot of the official ceremonial could be curtailed for fear of causing offence. Outwardly, the King remained calm; the only hint of the turmoil in his mind was an incident in Darmstadt when, turning to his son, he remarked with studied irony: 'I am surprised to see you still here. I thought you would be in Paris by now.' Not yet aware that Keith had confessed, Fritz replied casually: 'I would have been, if I had wanted.' But his suspicions were now aroused and that evening Keith received the note: 'Things look bad. Arrange for us to get away.'

That was on 6th August. On the 8th the party reached Frankfurt and a letter was handed to the King written by his son and addressed to Lieutenant von Katte – inadequately addressed, hence the letter had been opened and in view of the contents returned not to the writer but to his father. Though Frederick William was already convinced that Fritz planned flight, final proof had hitherto been lacking. This letter supplied it. Now the King knew everything. His fury deepened. And still the smiling procession continued, by ship down the Rhine to Cologne, where the Prince-Bishop was waiting to welcome Frederick William and his heir apparent. Before the Crown Prince was allowed to disembark the King summoned Colonel von Rochov and in a loud voice so that Fritz could hear told him that immediately the ceremony was over he was to be brought back on board, alive or dead.

Two days later the King was on Prussian soil again at Wesel. The Crown Prince was brought before him under armed escort. Convinced that his son was guilty not only of attempted desertion but of conspiring with England and France against the throne and his own life, the King now ordered him in the presence of the garrison commander, General von der Mosel, to confess everything. If he did, he would receive justice tempered with mercy. Fritz responded with the plot for a novel. Yes, he said, he had planned to escape, with the intention of going to Italy and taking up military service there so that he could earn his father's favour by distinguishing himself in battle. For days, the King had forced himself to smile, and even act the affectionate father. Now, at this glib and foolish tale his pent-up fury overwhelmed him and he seized his dagger. But before he could strike, General von der Mosel sprang forward. 'Sire! If it's blood you want, take mine, but spare your son's!'

There was a pause. Then, in a thick voice, the King commanded that the Crown Prince be taken forthwith and by the shortest route to the fortress of Küstrin in East Prussia and there detained until he made known his pleasure. From now on, Fritz was a prisoner. Keith junior had already made good his escape. The King ordered that the journey to Küstrin was to be made without stages. The prisoner was to eat and sleep in the carriage. 'If he has a need to satisfy, it is to be done in open fields where there is a wide uninterrupted view and no hedges or bushes.' Care was to be taken to avoid entering the territory of Hanover or Hesse as attempts to rescue the prisoner might be made from either. In the event of an armed attack in overwhelming force, General Buddenbrock, the commander of the escort, was to ensure that the prisoner did not fall into enemy hands alive. So Fritz set off, dreading that the stab which General von der Mosel had averted might be given him by another hand at his journey's end.

When the Queen heard of her son's arrest she had no less cause

43

to fear for her own life, for she knew that among his papers must be letters from herself and Wilhelmina ridiculing the King and condoning Fritz's plans for escape. But to her great relief the box of letters which Fritz had left with Katte was restored to her with seal unbroken, and then her only concern was that Frederick William might come to hear of its existence and demand to see the contents. What should she do? At all costs he must be prevented from reading the letters; yet it would be useless merely to destroy them. His imagination would then supply contents even worse than the reality. . . . It was Wilhelmina who found a solution. Day and night before the King returned to Potsdam, she and her mother wrote new letters, dating them appropriately and filling them with edited versions of the old with additions to make up length. The fakes were then put in the box and the originals destroyed. It was hectic work, but Sophia Dorothea and her daughter would have belied their Stuart blood if, with their necks almost in the noose, they had not felt a fearful joy in hoodwinking the tyrant, as well as pleasure in savouring anew the malicious phrases they had once applied to him.

Meanwhile, Frederick William spent some days hunting before he could bring himself to return to Berlin and face the problems that awaited him there. Should he have the prisoner in Küstrin executed as a deserter, or should he compel him to renounce the succession in favour of his younger brother, Augustus William, who had always taken after his father? This seemed the better solution, but how to bring it about? Having renounced the throne under duress would the prisoner keep his word, or, the moment the King was gone, would he start plotting to oust his brother? If he did, what would become of the royal authority, that *rocher de bronze* that Frederick William was working himself to death to establish, and what would become of Prussia? In any case, the act of abdication would not be valid without the approval of the Imperial Diet, the assembled Princes of Germany to whom Frederick William's army of 80,000 men gave him the right to condescend, but who instead condescended to him. It was they who would be judging between father and son, weighing them up and finally siding, perhaps, with the prisoner against Frederick William. . . .

A week later, when the King reached Berlin, he was still un-decided. He greeted his Queen with the words: 'Your unworthy son is dead.' For a moment she believed him. 'But that's inhuman! You mean you have put him to death?' 'Yes . . .' But the Queen saw that her husband was lying. He had turned now to the box of letters and had begun to read them, scowling as he realised they gave him no pretext to insult his son's mother. Then Wilhelmina spoke up, pleading for her brother's life, while the younger children joined her and threw themselves at their father's feet. The King exploded with rage, gave his daughter a stinging slap on the ear and made to strike at the others with his stick. They fled under the table, pursued by the King until suddenly their nurse barred the way. 'Out of my sight, baggage!' But the woman bravely stood her ground and risked her life by scolding Frederick William: 'The devil take you if you don't leave the children alone!' And she hustled them out of the room. Next day the King thanked her.

Meanwhile, Katte had been arrested in Berlin. He was interrogated by the King and with dignity and composure told frankly all he knew. He solemnly assured Frederick William that he had not expected the Prince to attempt flight during the tour of southern Germany, as he, Katte, had retained all their money. But the King was in no mood to show clemency to his own son let alone to Katte, and when the latter's father appealed to him to show mercy Frederick William replied: 'Your son is a knave, mine too; but what can we fathers do about it?' If the confessions of Fritz and Katte failed to reveal the international conspiracy to dethrone him which he felt sure existed, the King was prepared – until dissuaded by Grumbkov and Seckendorff – to extract the 'truth' from them by torture. In prescribing every detail of the daily routine at Küstrin, he had already done all he could to put Fritz in a malleable state of mind. He was, of course, in solitary confinement and his jailers were strictly enjoined not to speak to him. If he asked questions, they were not to reply. The only books allowed him were the Bible and Psalter. When the prisoner asked if he might receive Holy Communion, the King's reply sounded ominous: 'It is not time yet; first the court martial must be held, then it will be time.'

But Fritz showed no signs of hesitation or weakness when he appeared before the commission his father had appointed to conduct the preliminary inquiry. The Prince looked cheerful, asked several times during the hearing whether there was anything further the commissioners (among them Grumbkov) wished to know and stated bravely that his father's maltreatment had forced him to attempt flight, and that if it continued he would be obliged to try a second time. He also attempted to shield Katte by stating that his friend had been acting on his orders.

Some days later at a second hearing the prisoner was confronted with no less than 178 written questions drawn up with his father's approval. He answered them all with precision, including the last question, which read, 'Has he anything further to say in his defence?' to which Fritz replied, no, he had already admitted his guilt. Then, at the end of this ordeal, the prisoner was required to answer eight more questions devised by Frederick William himself and so clearly inadmissible that the assessor had only agreed to include them on a direct order from the King. The last four of these questions read:

(1) What does a man deserve who forfeits his honour and conspires to desert?
(2) Does he think he deserves to become King?
(3) Does he or does he not desire to be made a present of his life?
(4) As he has rendered himself unfit to succeed to the throne by forfeiting his honour, does he wish to save his life by renouncing the succession and does he wish such renunciation to be confirmed by the entire Roman Empire?

Though the traps in the questions were obvious enough, the Prince was obliged to give his answers. They showed that the long and nerve-racking ordeal had left him with mind still lucid and will unbroken:

(1) I do not think to have acted against my honour.
(2) I cannot be my own judge.
(3) I submit to the King's mercy and pleasure.
(4) I do not set such store by my life, but His Majesty will not show such great severity towards me.

Having refused to be browbeaten into renouncing the throne, the Prince now sugared the pill of his defiance with a final plea:

He realises that all in all and on every point he has been at fault; what distresses him most is the concern he has caused His Majesty; he begs His Majesty to believe that his intentions have never been criminal; that he has not sought to cause the least harm to His Royal Majesty; that he submits in all things to the will and mercy of the King. His Majesty can deal with him according to his pleasure, and he begs His Majesty's pardon.

On receiving the protocol Frederick William immediately tore up this final appeal. His anger at the prisoner's evasion of his questions was reflected in an immediate order tightening up the conditions of his imprisonment and adding 'If that *coquin* asks after my health, or my wife's and children's he is to be told that no one remembers him, that my wife refuses to hear his name mentioned and that his sister Wilhelmina is under lock and key in Berlin.'

It seemed the King's rage could mount no higher, but soon

events were to give it further impetus. Katte had stated under oath that the Crown Prince had told him it had been his father's intention to make him enter the Church of Rome so that he could marry the Archduchess Maria Theresa. This, according to Fritz, had been one reason for his attempted flight. Somehow this story had leaked out to appear in foreign newspapers and arouse considerable sympathy with the Prince throughout Protestant Germany. But the King, a staunch Lutheran, had clearly been maligned. 'God knows,' he stormed, 'I could never be such a rascal! It is a wicked invention.' Now, truly, his fury was at its peak and to the Dutch Ambassador, Ginkel, he revealed in confidence his plans for revenge. They were so terrible that the envoy dared not commit them to paper; he merely reported his protest that the Crown Prince was, after all, the King's own flesh and blood. 'Blood!' Frederick William had roared. 'As for that . . .' – and speechless with rage had pointed to the veins on his wrists, meaning that blood would surely flow. Later, the King threatened that any of his subjects caught repeating the story should have their tongues cut out.

In this mood of ungovernable frenzy the King thirsted for an immediate victim. Inquiries had revealed that the Crown Prince had been conducting a harmless flirtation with a Berlin precentor's daughter named Dorothea Ritter. He had visited her once or twice when her father was out and they had played music together. Was that all? The King sent a surgeon and a midwife to examine the girl, but their report was disappointing – her virginity was intact. Nevertheless she was clapped into jail. Then the monarch wrote out this order:

> His Majesty commands *Hofrat* Klinte to arrange that the precentor's daughter at present here in arrest shall be publicly whipped tomorrow. . . . First she shall be whipped in front of the Town Hall, then before her father's house, then at all corners of the town. . . .

Then she was to be imprisoned in the house of correction at Spandau. For how long? The King wrote *'ewig'* – 'for ever.' She was sixteen and a half.

Ranging farther afield, the King then found Fritz's secret library containing books which his father had forbidden him to read. The King asked the custodian how much the Crown Prince had paid him. 'Twenty hellers a week,' replied the wretched man (about two shillings). The King was mollified. 'That's really not very much, is it?' he said, and banished the man no farther than Memel.

Meanwhile, solitary confinement and uncertainty were gnawing at Fritz's morale. In an attempt to end both he asked to be allowed to make a statement. Before Grumbkov and the other members of the commission he then declared his readiness to renounce the throne in return for the King's pardon. But if he was to lose his life, he asked that he should be informed of the decision as soon as it was made. With an eye on the royal favour he also asked permission to be allowed to wear uniform again, but of course it was refused: 'I would not have such a bad officer in my army, let alone in my own regiment.' Finally, Fritz had the temerity to suggest that the King should put in a good word for him with his mother! One cannot but admire his defiance.

But soon the Prince had solid grounds for hope. He noticed that Grumbkov was treating him with more respect. There could be only one reason: Grumbkov was looking to the future. That, at any rate, ruled out the possibility of the death sentence or of an enforced abdication. At once Fritz regained his high spirits. When he was told that the King had reduced his maintenance allowance to a derisory eight groschen a day, he retorted: 'It's all the same to me whether I starve in Küstrin or in Potsdam.' Anyway, he was not starving. Many of his jailers were seizing the chance to be of service to their future sovereign, and Fritz had all the food, books, paper and candles he wanted. At this time he wrote to Wilhelmina:

> Dearest sister, at the court martial which it has now been decided to hold I shall be branded a heretic, for not to agree with the lord and master on every point is enough to earn one the title of arch-heretic. You can imagine therefore how neatly they will docket me. For my part, I shall not be in the least distressed by anathemas hurled against me. . . . From the bottom of my heart I could wish there were no need of interpreter between us, and that those blissful days might again be ours when your *principe* and my *principessa* embraced,* or in plain language, when I can say to you in person that nothing in the world can have the power to diminish my love. Adieu! – The prisoner.

When Fritz wrote this mannered epistle the court martial on himself, Katte and Keith was already sitting in Köpenick. All three were accused of desertion, the term which Frederick William had applied from the start to his son's attempted flight. The court comprised fifteen members, all of them army officers, under the presidency of Lieutenant-General Count von Schulenburg. His instructions were to take no further oral evidence, but to base his findings on the existing written material. The court

* His flute and Wilhelmina's lute.

48

had been sworn on 25th October, nearly three months after the Prince's attempted escape.

Keith was unanimously sentenced to death *in absentia*. The members of the court also agreed that they were not competent to try the Crown Prince. As regards Katte, opinion was divided. Nine members voted for the death sentence, but with a plea in mitigation. Six voted for life imprisonment on the grounds that Katte had sought to dissuade the Prince from flight. It was also considered that the Prince would never regain his peace of mind, but would hold himself responsible if his friend were executed. Count von Schulenburg had therefore to use his casting vote. He recorded it in words which plainly reveal the delicacy of his position:

> . . . but in all good sense and as I cannot conceive that even in the greatest crimes a distinct difference must not exist between the actual performance of the intended pernicious deed and between [*sic*] the measures at first taken thereto . . . so, according to my best will and conscience and also in accordance with the judicial oath sworn with such heavy penalties for infringement, I cannot agree to the death sentence for Katte, but impose the sentence of life imprisonment.

This was soundly reasoned. But unless the court martial recommended the death sentence Frederick William could not shield himself behind their prior advice if he chose to impose it. It was not justice he wanted, but a scapegoat. No wonder he was furious or that he accused the court of 'trying to make the plans of the Crown Prince and his supporters appear to the whole world as no more than a childish game, undeserving of serious punishment.' Moreover, by refusing to pronounce the guilt of the Crown Prince and handing him back to his father, the court had made the whole affair seem like a family quarrel with rights and wrongs on both sides. Bitterly the King complained: 'For every ten who side with the King, ten and more will now say that the Crown Prince was justified.' He called the findings of the court 'an act of perfidy.' He thought he had appointed 'honourable men who would consider only their conscience and the King's honour.' Instead of which, the officers had acted with an eye to the future. But the King would find an opportunity 'of destroying those people who have tried to side with my children against me.' He ordered the members of the court to dispense justice 'and not pass over it with a feather duster. As Katte did act indeed, the court martial is to reassemble and pronounce a different verdict.'

But the members stood by their recommendations, the seventy-one-year-old president of the court adding with trembling hand three quotations from the Bible, one of them from the Gospel: 'Take heed how ye judge, that your judgments be not unto men but unto God.'

Katte's life now lay in the King's hands. As the supreme authority in the State he was entitled to overrule the findings of the court martial, and the law allowed the death sentence for attempted desertion. If he accepted anything less it would be ascribed to a guilty conscience. As for the Crown Prince losing his 'peace of mind', in Frederick William's view that was no argument against Katte's execution; on the contrary it would do the Crown Prince nothing but good to lose his complacency. The shock of Katte's execution might bring him to his senses, awake him to the realities of life and to a sense of duty. So the King decreed:

> Concerning Lieutenant Katte and his crime and the sentence passed on him by the court martial, though it is not His Majesty's custom to increase sentences of military courts, but rather, wherever possible, to reduce them, nevertheless this Katte is not only an officer serving in my army, but is also a soldier of the Guards, and if loyalty and devotion to me are required of all officers in my army, then doubly so of those officers serving in regiments attached to my person.
>
> As, therefore, this Katte has been plotting desertion with to-morrow's Sun and weaving conspiracies with foreign ministers and envoys . . . His Majesty does not know what empty reasons have induced the court not to declare his life forfeit, for in future His Majesty would not be able to trust any of those officers or servants by oath and in duty bound to him, for such crimes once committed can occur again, the offenders believing that, as Katte had been dealt with leniently, so leniency would be shown to them. But His Majesty went to school in his youth and learnt the Latin adage: *fiat justitia et pereat mundus.*
>
> Therefore it is our will that justice be done and that Katte, though lawfully he should be torn with red-hot pincers and hanged, shall, solely out of regard for his family, instead be brought from life to death by the sword. When the military court informs Katte of the sentence, it shall be told him that His Majesty is sorry, but it is better he should die than that Justice should vanish from the world.

Katte heard the sentence with composure, saying: 'I surrender myself completely to the decree of Providence and to the will of the King. I have committed no base action, and if I die it is in a good cause.' But the attitude of stoic resignation proved impossible to sustain. Katte was young, and soon after his despair found expression in this appeal which his grandfather, Field-Marshal Wartensleben, transmitted to the King:

The fallibility, weakness, rashness of my youth, a mind which meant no evil, a heart swayed by sympathy and affection, a youthful illusion devoid of hidden treachery – it is they, my King, which most humbly beg and beseech your hearing – your grace, mercy, pity and compassion. . . .

To this the field-marshal added his own appeal, hoping 'Your Majesty will be most graciously pleased to give ear to the supplication of a very old man.'

In his reply the King expressed regret, but the Field-Marshal knew well enough what punishment the crime deserved. The King had already shown consideration for the Field-Marshal and the prisoner's father by commuting the sentence to death by beheading. The King now ordered that Katte be taken to Küstrin and executed in the presence of his son, the Crown Prince. Katte had regained his composure and wrote a farewell letter to his father, Lieutenant-General von Katte, asking him to seek consolation for his death in the fact that God had given him other sons whose lives would perhaps be happier than their brother's.

The execution was fixed for 6th November, 1730. Katte was not informed until the preceding day, when he arrived in Küstrin. Still he remained calm, deriving comfort from the ministrations of Pastor Müller, who had come with him from Berlin, and the garrison chaplain. That evening, after the major in charge of the execution and other officers had prayed with him, Katte wrote a short letter to the Crown Prince saying that he did not reproach him and advising him to look into his heart and submit to God and the King. Then, with the officers and clergy, Katte prayed again, asking for courage to die well.

Next morning at five o'clock – two hours before the execution was due to take place – the Crown Prince was informed that Katte would be beheaded immediately below the window of his cell. It was the King's order that he should be a witness. Until this moment, Fritz had heard nothing of the findings of the court martial, nothing of the sentence and nothing of the time or place of the execution of his beloved friend. He gave one terrible cry, then sobbing called: 'Jesus! Take my life for his!'

In the time that remained, Fritz pleaded to be allowed to send a messenger to the King, pleaded for postponement of the execution, swore he would renounce the succession in return for Katte's reprieve, would gladly spend the rest of his life in prison, offered his life for his friend's: for two hours he talked, wept and paced his cell like a trapped animal, delirious with remorse and despair. In vain.

At seven o'clock the Prince was led to the window of his cell. Below him the troops were already in position. It was a cold, grey morning. In a moment, Katte came into view, walking steadily between the two chaplains from a corner of the fortress. As he passed below the window he looked up and Fritz cried: 'My dear Katte . . . I beg your forgiveness . . . a thousand times . . .' and sent him a kiss. In a voice loud enough to be audible Katte replied:

'No need of forgiveness, sir. I die for you with the greatest joy.'

Katte said goodbye to the officers of his regiment; handed his wig to a bystander; 'quite ordinarily and cheerfully' took off his coat; knelt down and, restraining the hand that came to blindfold him, began to pray. The sword severed his head at the first stroke. At the window, the Crown Prince collapsed unconscious into the arms of his jailers.

. . . . . .

Every detail of the execution had been meticulously arranged by the King and, even more precisely, the sequel. The corpse was to lie exposed until 2 p.m. Meanwhile, the moment the execution was over, or 'before the executioner has finished wiping the sword', as the King put it, Pastor Müller was to enter the Prince's cell and attempt to stir 'his softened heart' to contrition.

'If you find the Crown Prince in a state of contrition,' wrote the King, 'you are to encourage him to fall upon his knees with you, and also the officers who are with him, and beseech God with tearful heart for forgiveness. But in all you must act prudently, in the proper manner, for he has a crafty wit and you must take good care that he does all with true repentance and a broken heart.' The pastor was also to rid the Prince of his belief in the dangerous Calvinist heresy of predestination, so that in future he could not quote in defence of his bad behaviour the inefficacy of good works as a means to salvation.

But when Müller first entered the cell, he found the Prince prostrated and unable to converse. Throughout that night the delirium continued. Next morning the Prince was, if anything, worse: he was suffering from delusions. 'The King imagines he has taken Katte from me, but he is here still, before my very eyes!' Müller tried to calm him, to exhort him to examine his conscience more systematically. At once the Prince felt a fearful dread. Was the pastor trying to prepare him for his own death? Had the heap of blood-soaked sand beneath the window been left there for a second victim? When Müller offered the Prince a sedative powder, he suspected poison and made him swallow some first. Then Müller started to speak of God's mercy, but the Prince kept changing the subject to the one nearest his heart – the mercy of the King. Finally he asked Müller outright whether he had come to prepare him for death, and the pastor had the utmost difficulty in convincing him that his instructions left no room for doubt that the King intended to restore his son to favour so long as he showed true repentance and submission and abandoned his Calvinist beliefs.

Fritz felt a surge of relief. Was that all his father asked? Well, he should have it. Fritz knew how to act submission. As for his 'beliefs', the word was altogether too flattering. But of course he could not surrender them without a semblance of a struggle. And so for hours he schooled himself to discuss religion, generating a zeal which filled Pastor Müller with profound satisfaction. Even then the Prince was not content, and to probe matters more deeply he asked Müller to send him a short concordance so that he could look up all the passages in the Bible that referred to his problems. When he returned the book, the pastor found inside the cover a drawing of a man kneeling with crossed swords over his head and beneath: 'Psalm LXXIII, 25.' The passage reads, 'Whom have I in heaven but thee? . . . For lo, they that are far from thee shall perish.'

There remained the question of predestination. Was the Prince ready to renounce his heresy? After a further show of argument, he was, and Pastor Müller reported the glad news to the King. Frederick William was now content. He had wrested his son, as he said, 'from the clutches of Satan' and was ready to restore him to limited freedom in return for a solemn oath to obey the King's orders and 'act in all things as befits a loyal subject and son.'

On 17th November, 1730, a commission headed by Grumbkov reached Küstrin to witness and record the Crown Prince's act of submission. Next day, Grumbkov had a long private talk with the Prince, of which nothing is known except that, as a gesture of reconciliation and also, perhaps, because it was becoming a burden to him, Fritz presented Grumbkov with Katte's last will and testament. But the desire to bury the past must have been mutual. To Fritz, Grumbkov was a valuable ally against his father; to Grumbkov, Fritz was 'tomorrow's Sun' and in view of the King's poor state of health he had no time to lose if he was to be sure of basking in its rays. They emerged from their conversation formally reconciled.

Next morning, in the presence of Grumbkov and five generals, the Prince took the oath of submission in words which his father had prescribed. He was then informed of the King's plans for his future. He was now free to leave his cell, but instead of returning to Potsdam he was to be confined to the boundaries of Küstrin, where he was to start work immediately as the most junior member of the provincial administration board, so learning, wrote the King, 'that the welfare of a country without doubt depends on the ruler understanding everything himself and being a good husband-man and administrator. Otherwise, if this does not happen, the country will be at the disposal of the favourites and chief ministers, who will use it for their own profit and set all things in confusion.'

Now Fritz was given back his sword, but not his status as an officer. He appealed to the King to reverse this decision, but his father was adamant. That vexed him, but not for long, for life and freedom were never so sweet as in the days that followed, nor, as the Crown Prince started work as office-boy in the Küstrin *Kriegs- und Domänenkammer*, the sense so strong of being one with the people he was destined to govern. At the end of his first fortnight, the chairman of the board, *Kammer-direktor* Hille, was able to report to Frederick William: '*Seine Königliche Hoheit sind lustig wie ein Buchfink*' – 'His Royal Highness is as merry as a chaffinch.'

CHAPTER SIX

*

The Student Prince

ON MONDAY, 20TH NOVEMBER, 1730, the Crown Prince started work as junior referendary on the Board of War and Domain Lands, taking his seat at the bottom of the council table as his father had expressly ordered. Once again Frederick William had drawn up a list of Do's and Don't's. Fritz was to learn how, on the land, every taler had to be earned by toil and sweat, how ploughing, sowing and manuring were done, how beer was brewed, husbandry organised, taxes collected and on what terms domain lands should be leased if they were to 'produce a plus.' On the other hand, Fritz was not on any account to dance or listen to music, dine out or entertain. He was not to order oysters from Hamburg, not to buy light summer suits, not to burn candles after nine at night and not to speak to strangers except in the presence of the Master of the Household or of the two young noblemen who were attached to his person. Even with these he was only allowed to discuss administrative questions, agriculture and the Word of God; politics were banned and, above all, 'plans for the future.' Reading of any kind, except, of course, devotional books, was not allowed, and when Fritz's mentors relaxed the restrictions to exclude textbooks on administration and fiscal systems the King asked indignantly 'if they would not like to give him back his flute and contrabass as well.' Even geometry and military engineering were banned as frivolous subjects, and if the Crown Prince allowed his tongue to stray to such invigorating topics he was to be told to keep silent. This time there were to be no airy fancies or whimsical conceits: the young man's nose was to be kept firmly to the grindstone.

But though every member of the Board understood that Fritz

was expected to work hard in atonement for the past, they could not forget that, one day, he would be their King. How unwise, therefore, to interpret his father's orders too literally, and how foolish to let slip this unique opportunity of earning the Crown Prince's gratitude!

So it was that, one day at a meeting of the Board when Fritz asked leave to speak, he was met with encouraging smiles. He had been thinking, he said, addressing the president, the Brandenburg nobleman von Münchow, in sweetly reasonable tones, that as he had been behaving so well he might soon perhaps be given some small Government department of his own to administer – the Navy Department, for instance, as there seemed to be no vacancy on land. . . . At this the president, who had been listening with his usual benevolent detachment, looked mildly surprised, but the Prince continued: As it flowed into the Baltic the River Oder would, of course, come under the Navy Department and with it the village of Kiez-in-the-Marsh, whose mayor, as the gentlemen knew, had recently come to him with a complaint. Now this complaint . . .

It was the complaint, it seemed, that the young man really wanted to talk about; the rest was merely a flourish, a sample of his royal wit. Once again all present smiled, or tried to. But, Lord, how far-fetched! If only the Prince would stop trying to be waggish and apply his brains, for he was clever, there was no doubt of that. But how vain! And how excessively ignorant! In one of his periodic reports to Frederick William, the chairman of the Board, *Direktor* Hille, wrote: 'The Prince has Aristotle's Rules of Poetry at his finger-tips, but whether his ancestors won Magdeburg at a game of cards, or otherwise, he cannot say.'

Meanwhile, the Prince had aired the problems of Kiez-in-the-Marsh, von Münchow had smiled at the ceiling and Hille had taken charge of the case. Then the Board returned to the agenda. The chief function of the *Kriegs- und Domänenkammer* was to let and supervise the management of the royal domain lands which comprised one-quarter of the area of the province. It was also responsible for local government, but this was not a very onerous task as in practice it was carried out by the land-owning aristocracy. So, with well-feigned interest, the Crown Prince would hear that a marsh was to be drained in Wolfsberg and that after the brewery had been built in Karzig the rental of the estate could be raised by 640 talers. Before long he himself would be visiting these places and making long and detailed reports to the King on the fertility of the soil, the state of repair of farm buildings

56

and the annual profits that might be expected to accrue to the royal revenue. Was he really interested?

In those first few weeks Fritz must have found it hard to decide which was the more boring: the long daily sessions with the Board or his off-duty life of monastic seclusion with the Master of the Household. In the afternoons, at any rate, Fritz the Poet, Musician, Moralist and Natural Philosopher (as he called himself) would have time for higher pursuits, versifying, for instance; he could compose one hundred verses now in just over two hours. Later, after his father had allowed him more freedom and he had been able to make new friends, he would be sending some of these compositions to a young colonel's wife, Frau von Wreech, with a letter which began:

> Madam, The host of grasshoppers which has been devastating this region has so far been considerate enough to spare your estates. Instead, some insects yet more uncouth and dangerous are on their way to you. They are called 'verses', possess four feet, sharp teeth and an elongated body. Their basic principle is a certain rhythm, and it is this which gives them life.

And then come the 'verses'. The first one reads:

> *Permettez-moi, madame, en vous offrant ces lignes,*
> *Que je fasse part de cette vérité;*
> *Depuis que je vous vis, j'ai été agité,*
> *Vous êtes un objet qui en êtes bien digne.*

But these diversions could not make up for one fact: so far, Fritz had failed to come to terms with his father. It was not for lack of effort on his part. In order to cement his alliance with Grumbkov, he had compelled himself to address the arch-knave as 'dear friend' and accept from him pages of advice on how to approach the King. To Frederick William himself he had written reports strewn with information selected to delight the royal heart: for instance how the glassworks at Marienwalde ought to show a better 'plus' this year – at least 857 talers, 21 groschen and 3 pfennig. Then Fritz had written about his hunting and how he had killed eight wild boar and two sows at Neumühle; about a wonderful tall fellow he had seen at Major Röder's who would have been just the thing for dear Papa's regiment, and how his heart had bled at being unable to obtain him; about a piece of specially fat pork he was sending dear Papa from Wollup; how it would give him infinite pleasure if the King would send him a copy of the new Infantry Regulations – how he longed to be a soldier again, and how the King could dispose of him as he chose – he was entirely at his service – he owed all to his father, who was the only source of true happiness and honour. . . . And what had this abject self-abasement achieved? Nothing. For Wolden, the Master of the Household, had been foolish enough to tell the King that the Crown Prince still believed in predestination.

The King wrote back to Wolden that the Crown Prince should cleanse his heart of falsehood and diligently seek God's mercy, and when Wolden reassured him of his son's good behaviour, he received the reply: 'In time you will get to know your Saint better and realise there is nothing good in him – except his tongue, there is nothing the matter with that.' Soon after, the King was told that the Prince was ill. He replied sarcastically: 'As it is predestined, all will be for the best. If there were any good in him he would die, but I am sure he will not die, for weeds always prosper.' When the heard of this letter, Fritz hastened to inform Wolden that he no longer believed in predestination and Election by Grace.*

At last, a year after Fritz's attempted flight, the King came to Küstrin in person. Fritz flung himself at his feet and his father proceeded to sermonise him on his faults. When Fritz admitted he had intended to escape to England, Frederick William said: 'Now hear what the consequences would have been! Your mother would have fallen into the greatest misfortune, because I would naturally have thought she was privy to the plan. Your sister I would have put where neither sun nor moon would have shone on her for the rest of her days. I would have entered Hanover with my army, burnt and laid waste the country even at the sacrifice of my life, my country and my people. . . .'

Then the King asked if Fritz still called military uniform a shroud, whether he liked it in Küstrin and if he had given up trying to make witty remarks. Twice the Crown Prince fell at his feet and again, in full view of the public, as the King was about to leave. Deeply moved – it was his birthday – Frederick William clasped his son in solemn forgiveness and was heard to say: 'Behave well, as I see you mean to do, and I will take care of you.' Then he climbed into his coach and was driven away. Eyes filled with tears, Fritz watched him go, then turning to Hille, said: 'I would not have believed until now that the King felt the least affection for me. At this moment I am convinced that he does.'

Restored to the royal favour, Fritz felt he could afford a dig at Grumbkov, Wolden and others. Showing them first to Hille,

---

* Calvin's predestination did not refer to the events of this life, but to the world to come, where human beings were predestined for salvation or otherwise irrespective of their actions on earth. – *Translator.*

who remarked, 'Quite good for a Prince, nothing much for an ordinary person,' he sent Grumbkov some verses:

Advice to myself

Though your life is full of care
You must all with patience bear,
Whatsoever may befall,
Think your thoughts, but that is all.

When your household overseers
Behave themselves like buccaneers,
Simply do as you are bidden –
Think your thoughts, but keep them hidden.

Lasting gratitude express
For a minister's friendliness,
Thank him for it most sincerely,
Show you love him very dearly.

Next, Fritz again asked his father to be allowed to rejoin the army. He received the withering reply:

What's the use? If I really tickled your heart, if I sent you a *maître de flûte* from Paris with a dozen or so instruments and books of music together with a whole troupe of actors and a large orchestra, if I ordered you Frenchmen and French women, also a couple of dozen dancing masters and a dozen coxcombs, this would be sure to please you much more than a company of grenadiers; for in your opinion the grenadiers are just *Canailles*; but a fop, a *petit-maître*, a Frenchy, a *bon mot*, a hack comedian, a scratch quartet, there's something much more noble, that's fit for a king, that's *digne d'un Prince*!

All the same, the restrictions on the Prince's movements were relaxed slightly after the King's visit to Küstrin, and for the first time since his trial he was allowed to see Berlin. The occasion was Wilhelmina's wedding to the Hereditary Prince of Bayreuth.

It was no cheerful family occasion that Fritz found on his arrival. After his attempted flight the King had invoked the tortures of hell to plague his English relatives and finally abandoned the marriage project. Instead, he informed Wilhelmina that she was to marry the Prince of Bayreuth. She could raise no objections, said her father, because she did not even know the man. If she agreed, he would restore the Queen to favour and pardon her brother Fritz. If she refused, he would have her imprisoned in the fortress of Memel and order her governess and confidante, a certain Fräulein von Sonsfeld, to be publicly whipped. The gentleman of the household entrusted with this message for

Wilhelmina added his own assurance that it would give him the greatest pleasure to see the blood running down von Sonsfeld's pretty back. So Wilhelmina said yes, the King embraced her and gave her his blessing, then sent her to the Queen, who, still toying with hopes of the English marriage, swore at her roundly. The Queen also gave the bridegroom a difficult passage. Did he know history, geography, Italian, English and music? 'Yes,' replied the young man, refusing to be intimidated, 'and I know my Catechism, too.' Then he was handed over to the King, who made him drunk every day, 'to deepen his character and educate him.'

On the day before the wedding, Sophia Dorothea implored Wilhelmina to live as brother and sister with her husband so that the door could be left open for the Prince of Wales and the marriage annulled as not consummated.

On 20th November, 1731, amid tears and artillery salutes, Wilhelmina was wedded to the Prince of Bayreuth. Then came the festivities. They lasted for three days and ended in a ball for 700 couples. Wilhelmina was leading them in a quadrille when she noticed a man dressed in grey civilian clothes standing in a corner of the ballroom. Grumbkov had to tell her it was her brother. Still not recognising him, she ran towards him – yes, it was Fritz, but fatter and not so handsome – and flung her arms round his neck. Then she rushed to the King to thank him and ask for her brother's complete forgiveness; it was for his sake, after all, that she had agreed to the marriage. She took her brother by the hand, gave him 'a thousand caresses' – but Fritz was as cold as ice and spoke only in monosyllables. She presented the Prince, her husband: Fritz looked at him and said nothing. Wilhelmina was aghast. Was her brother angry with her for marrying this man, for not waiting till he could arrange a good political match? Had Fritz turned politician? Or was he merely embarrassed at being allowed by his father to make only this strange, belated appearance at her wedding and constrained by the knowledge that the King was watching him? Later in the evening, she asked him outright. 'I have my reasons,' he said.

With Wilhelmina's marriage, the Crown Prince's apprenticeship at Küstrin was nearing its end, and with it the first and last flirtation of his life. Frau von Wreech, twenty-four to his nineteen, had charmed away some of the tedium of his stilted routine and answered him verse for verse, keeping his ardour within bounds by telling him that her husband, who was considerably older, had helped her with the rhymes. She allowed Fritz to call her 'cousin'. She must have thought him a strange young man.

Before he went to Berlin he wrote her a letter, picturing his entry into the capital of Prussia:

> Before me will proceed a herd of swine with orders to grunt for all they are worth. Following them will be a flock of sheep, then some cows and immediately behind them, I myself seated on a donkey. . . . Instead of pistols, I shall carry two bags of assorted seeds. In place of a saddle there will be a sack of flour on which my noble form will be enthroned. I shall carry a stick instead of a whip and on my head will be a straw hat. . . .

In such hectic wit Fritz squandered his energy, little knowing what further trials awaited him.

CHAPTER SEVEN

*

Marriage

WITH WILHELMINA MARRIED and Fritz subdued and pardoned, Frederick William felt it was time to find a wife for him. The search was simplified by the fact that England was now finally ruled out. The King hated the country more than ever, for meanwhile the only person in London for whom he had any regard had died – Caroline of Ansbach, the girl with the beautiful eyebrows, whom long ago his cousin George II had carried off to make his Queen. On her death-bed Caroline had advised her husband to marry again, to be met with the tearful but indignant retort: 'No, no! I shall have mistresses.'

Frederick William wanted nothing more to do with England. Instead, he had a plan by which he hoped to change the face of Europe: Fritz should marry the Princess Elizabeth of Mecklenburg, niece of the Czarina Anna and heir presumptive to the Russian throne. The Russian Court was enthusiastic and Fritz was not averse to the plan: 'She is getting a dowry of two to three million roubles; just think of the life I could have with her!' But then Frederick William made it a condition of the marriage that his son should renounce the succession, and Fritz indignantly refused.

Even more indignant at the project was the famous general and statesman, Prince Eugene of Savoy. As commander of the Imperial armies he foresaw and feared the military alliance of Russia and Prussia, whether or not the Crown Prince renounced the succession. But he need not have worried. As so often in foreign negotiations, Frederick William overbid his hand by insisting not only that the Crown Prince should remain a Protestant – which the Russians agreed – but that the children of the marriage should be baptised in the Reformed Church. This the Russians could never accept, and so the strange chimera of a second dual monarchy faded. But Prince Eugene was still not content, for, unlike other Austrian statesmen, he realised one fact: of all the nations of Europe, Prussia with her large standing army presented the greatest potential threat to Austria. So he decided to arrange the Crown Prince's marriage himself.

The position of Austria was at that time a difficult one. Though the Habsburg eagles held sway from Brussels to Breslau and from Palermo to Belgrade and the Austrian territories included, apart from hereditary lands, Silesia, Bohemia, Hungary, the south part of modern Baden, Lombardy, Naples, Sicily, North Serbia and Wallachia, in many cases Austrian suzerainty was contested by at least one neighbouring State. Moreover, the Emperor Charles VI had no male heir. Instead, he possessed a document – the Pragmatic Sanction – by which, with great difficulty and at the price of considerable political concessions, he had persuaded almost all the States of Europe to agree to recognise the Archduchess Maria Theresa as his heir. The Emperor was proud of this document, but Prince Eugene valued the Prussian army more highly and had already tried to secure Maria Theresa's bethrothal to the Crown Prince. Had he succeeded, German history would have taken a different course and Europe might have been spared a sea of blood and tears. But Maria Theresa was a Catholic and the plan proved impossible.

Later, the Crown Prince himself had revived it. Some months before Wilhelmina's marriage, he had woken Hille in the night and dictated to him a peculiar 'statement'. In it, Fritz offered to marry Maria Theresa and renounce the succession to the Prussian throne on two conditions: he should not be called upon to change his religion and, until the death of her father, Frederick William should pay for the upkeep of his household. Telling Hille he hoped by this plan to be restored to his father's favour, Fritz asked him to send it at once to Grumbkov. As soon as he received it, Grumbkov despatched a copy to Prince Eugene and then hurriedly burnt the original. To Hille he wrote that the King would certainly hang anyone who dared mention such a project. Eugene found it a 'strange document', but suggested that the Crown Prince's intention had merely been to discover whether the King had any other marriage plans in mind.

Prince Eugene now decided to act. Whom should the Crown Prince marry? The answer was simple – a Protestant relative of the Imperial house. Only one person answered this description, the Princess Elizabeth Christina of Brunswick-Bevern, a niece of the Emperor's wife who had been a Protestant before her marriage. Prince Eugene initiated Seckendorff into his plan and together they began to prepare the ground. First of all, Seckendorff reported that the Crown Prince was deeply in debt. Eugene suggested paying off his debts at the rate of 2,500 ducats a year, in small sums so as not to attract attention. The Prince's lackeys, for instance, would certainly be the King's spies, bound on pain of death to report all that passed in the Prince's household. Seckendorff thought the rate too low and suggested 6,000 a year, on the understanding, of course, which should be made clear to the Crown Prince, that once his debts were paid he could expect no further sums from his Imperial Majesty. This was agreed.

Prince Eugene then told Seckendorff how he was to broach the marriage to the King. The Princess of Brunswick-Bevern should be mentioned casually. There must be no funny jokes against the English royal family and the King must on no account be allowed to see that Seckendorff was in his son's confidence or that he himself had any particular interest in the plan.

Before long, encouraged by the tactful present of some fine *lange Kerle* (tall fellows) for the grenadiers, the King had swallowed the bait and was even beginning to look on the Brunswick-Bevern plan as his own. Meanwhile Fritz was enjoying his salary without asking questions and it was not until the King's letters to him in Küstrin suddenly became strongly affectionate in tone that he realised that Nemesis was approaching. All remaining doubts were dispelled when presents from the King began to arrive, first a horse and then a silver dinner service of such weight that the donkey carrying it could barely totter. Fritz was now 'feverishly alarmed.'

Then, before dawn on 4th February, 1732 he was woken by an estafette from the King. The letter was confused and arbitrary in tone:

My dear Son Fritz, – You know that I am very fond of my children when they are obedient and so, when you were in Berlin, I heartily forgave you all and from that time since I have not seen you, have thought of nothing but your well-being and establishing you in the army and also with a suitable daughter-in-law and seeking to have you married during my lifetime. You may well be persuaded that so far as possible I have had the Princesses of the continent surveyed by other persons for their *conduite* and upbringing; I then found the eldest von Bevern Princess, who is well brought up, *modeste* and retiring: so women ought to be. You should write me your *sentiment*

How to turn a shelf of paperbacks into a shelf of books for only £2.

You simply open a leather-textured Chancery Library hard cover, insert a paperback, and shut it.

Self-adhesive strips inside hold the cover firmly, permanently in place.

In minutes and for pennies, Chancery Library hard covers transform your new paperbacks and old favourites into your own private library. And apart from preserving them from damage, they will add a distinctive feature to your home.

CHOICE OF COLOURS Chancery Library hard covers are finished in a material that looks, feels, and practically smells like leather.

The difference is, it just wipes clean with a damp cloth.

Choose from red, bottle green or blue, all with stencilled gold lettering.

CHOICE OF SIZES All Chancery Library hard covers are the same height and width as the average paperback — $7\frac{1}{4}'' \times 4\frac{1}{2}''$

They're available in 3 depths: $1''$, $1\frac{1}{2}''$ and $2''$. The narrowest takes one paperback up to 350 pages; the deepest takes one paperback up to 900 pages.

Or, if you prefer, you can bind two paperbacks in one cover.

A reference list inside Volume 1 gives you a catalogue of your library and makes sure you know exactly where each title is.

CHOICE OF PRICES Chancery Library hard covers come in any number of volumes, in sets of three. Volumes 1 to 3 for example are £1 for the set. Volumes 1 to 6 are £2 for the set. Volumes 1 to 30, £10, etc.

And we're not talking about deposits, we're talking about total costs. Postage and packing 25p U.K. and 50p abroad.

If you're not satisfied, you can return the covers and have your money refunded within 7 days.

START YOUR LIBRARY NOW.
POST THIS COUPON TODAY.

at once. . . . The Princess is not ugly; not beautiful, either. You must tell nothing of this to anyone, but you may write to Mama that I have written to you, and when you have a Son, then I will let you travel, but the wedding cannot be before the coming winter, meanwhile shall see about opportunities for you to meet together several times in all *honneur*. She is a God-fearing creature and that is everything. God give his blessing on it and bless you both and your Posterity and preserve Thee as a good Christian, and have God always before your eyes and do not hold to that damnable faith of Election, and be dutiful and obedient and so wilt Thou prosper, here temporarily and yonder eternally, and may he who heartily desires the same reply Amen.

Your faithful father unto Death,

Fr. William.

Fritz saw that the inquiry for his 'sentiment' was merely a formality. What could he do? For over a year he had been acting the dutiful son, the zealous administrator, the pious Christian simply in order to get Küstrin and its slavery behind him as quickly as possible. Certainly, it would be no pleasure to marry this girl who, reading between the lines he gathered was prim, dim-witted and ugly, but if he did so he would at least have some kind of freedom. So, having no alternative, Fritz replied saying he would fall in with his father's wishes. But privately he seethed with rage. In a letter to Grumbkov two days later he said he would prefer the greatest whore in Berlin to a bigot, that he would rather marry 'Fräulein Jette without money or possessions' than this stupid princess – and Fräulein Jette being Grumbkov's own daughter, he would no doubt appreciate the force of the argument. 'For the sake of Christ's wounds,' implored the Prince, let him at least be allowed some alternative choice, and he signed: 'I am yours as the Pope is the Devil's.'

Forty-eight hours later Grumbkov received another letter. This time the Crown Prince said he would not be forced into a marriage of any kind. As a good Christian, his father ought not to commit the sin of inviting subsequent infidelity or divorce. 'I have been unhappy throughout my whole life and I believe I am fated to remain so. But come what may, I have no cause for self-reproach and I have endured enough for a crime that was no more than an aberration. I will not put myself under an obligation to prolong my sufferings to all eternity. . . . A pistol can release me from them and I believe God in His mercy would not damn me, but give me eternal salvation instead of this miserable life.'

Grumbkov was scandalised. How could the Crown Prince ask

him to dissuade the King when he had already submitted to his father's pleasure? If Grumbkov spoke against the marriage it might cost him his head. He replied indignantly: 'I am not obliged to cast myself and my poor family to destruction merely for love of your Royal Highness who is not my master and whom I see running headlong to destruction. I fear God too greatly to attach my heart to a Prince who intends to take his own life without cause. . . . Monseigneur, however much intelligence you may have, your thoughts are not those of a Christian. . . .' Then the godly Grumbkov added this threat: 'I will always remember what the King said to me at Wusterhausen when your Royal Highness was in Küstrin and I attempted to take your part. "No, Grumbkov! Remember this! God grant I may be wrong, but I do not think my son will die a natural death. God forbid he should come into the hands of the executioner!" '

The King ordered the Crown Prince to Berlin for the betrothal. Grumbkov thought of the Prince's letters and trembled, but Fritz behaved impeccably until the ceremony was over. Then, after he had exchanged rings with Elizabeth Christina and stood beside her while they received the customary congratulations, he turned to his friends and never gave her another glance. Three weeks later, on 4th April, 1732, he left Berlin for Nauen to take command of his regiment. Suspecting that Grumbkov would pass on his letters to Vienna, he continued to vociferate, hoping perhaps that the Emperor would change his mind about allowing Elizabeth Christina to marry him. Seckendorff, too, was left in no doubt of the Crown Prince's feelings: 'Marriage confers majority and as soon as I come of age I shall be the master in my house and my wife will have no right to give orders there. At all costs, no petticoat rule! A man who lets himself be ruled by women is in my opinion the biggest fool in the world. So when I marry . . . I shall let Madame go her ways and as far as I am concerned I shall do as I please. And long live freedom!'

And in another letter Fritz wrote: 'I wish her the best of luck and pray from the bottom of my heart that the Emperor of Morocco will fall in love with the report of her charms, abduct and marry her. Empress of Morocco is worth twice as much as Crown Princess of Prussia. Judge by this if I am not a good Christian and am not well disposed to the source of all my woe. . . . I can't conceive how anyone could be so kind!'

These and similar letters found their way to Prince Eugene and left him greatly perturbed. 'Would to God the wedding day were here!' he wrote to Seckendorff, and asked how the bride's feminine contours were developing. Then, holding that money, like muck, is no good unless spread, he systematically bribed the whole of Fritz's entourage. Wilhelmina received the price of her support for the Bevern marriage, and the ex-tutor Duhan. Even the future Mistress of the Princely Household was given, on Seckendorff's suggestion, an annual allowance, the figure to be fixed by Prince Eugene, 'at your Serene Highness's enlightened discretion.' In this ducat-saturated atmosphere the Crown Prince rapidly improved his borrowing technique, working alternately with whines and threats, with 'I'm completely dry' today, and tomorrow: 'I would prefer to put myself in your hands than anyone else's.'

So the Habsburgs bled to maintain the Prince whose letters revealed such boundless contempt for his betrothed, the Habsburg Emperor's niece. This was galling enough, but what would they have thought if they had heard how she was spoken of in Berlin? One day at table, in the presence of the servants, the Queen said to Wilhelmina: 'Your brother is in despair at having to marry her, and he has some reason. She is a proper goose. Whatever you ask her, she just says "yes" or "no", with a stupid laugh that makes you feel quite ill.'

Then Wilhelmina's younger sister, Charlotte, spoke up. 'Oh, Your Majesty does not know all her good points! The other day I was present at her toilette. She stinks like the plague. I think she has at least ten or twelve fistulas. . . . I also noticed that she is misshapen. Her bodice is padded out on one side and one hip is higher than the other.'

But Frederick William was well content. He had been told that Frau von Wreech, Fritz's partner in literary flirtation, was expecting a baby and that he was thought to be the father. 'Bravo!' cried the King. 'Then he will do the same to the Bevern girl!'

Meanwhile, Prince Eugene and Seckendorff were coming to the conclusion that a premature wedding might be worse than none, for as long as the Crown Prince detested Elizabeth Christina there would be little chance of her influencing him in Austria's favour. So months passed while attempts were made to polish her manners and enliven her wit, the Crown Prince was anxiously watched for a change of attitude and Frederick William allowed to relapse into his customary mood of indecision. So it was that the date of the wedding was postponed until 12th June, 1733. But in February of that year, Augustus the Strong, King of Poland, had died and of the three candidates for election to the throne

one was Louis XV's father-in-law, Stanislaus Leczynski. While France threatened to treat opposition to his election as a breach of the peace, the Emperor was equally determined to prevent it. On the brink of war he began looking for allies, and found England, at a price: the marriage of the Crown Prince of Prussia to Princess Amalia, daughter of George II.

On 11th June, the day before Fritz was due to marry Elizabeth Christina, 'the abominable object of my desire,' as he called her, and Hohenzollerns and Brunswick-Beverns were already exchanging uneasy courtesies at the bride's home at Salzdahlum while the champagne was being cooled for the morrow's wedding, Seckendorff received a letter from Prince Eugene: the marriage must not take place – the Emperor desired the Crown Prince to marry the Princess Amalia. At first, Seckendorff doubted whether diplomatic immunity would suffice to protect him if he dared make this suggestion to the irascible Frederick William. Grumbkov, his old accomplice, would have nothing to do with it, mumbling something about 'a dishonourable plan.' So if Seckendorff went to the King, he would have to go alone. He went – and found Frederick William in bed.

After obtaining the King's promise to listen calmly, Seckendorff conveyed the Emperor's proposal, in the same breath meeting the first and most obvious objection to it: it was too late to cancel the Crown Prince's wedding to Elizabeth – the guests were already assembled. Not at all, said Seckendorff. Let there be a wedding, but the wedding of the Crown Prince's sister Charlotte to Elizabeth's brother Charles. After all, it had long been under consideration. . . .

Frederick William listened calmly. Three things were clear to him at once. First, the Queen and the Crown Prince were behind this plan – whereas, in fact, they knew nothing about it. Second, his cousin George was trying to make a fool of him by reviving a plan he had already emphatically abandoned – here he underestimated the English desire to restrain French ambitions in Europe. Third, he must somehow contrive to make a plus out of the new situation – and here he overestimated his own skill in diplomacy. The King answered that he could not possibly break his word to the House of Brunswick at this stage. But he was prepared to marry his second son to the Princess Amalia if George II would give the boy the Duchy of Courland as a means of supporting her. Seckendorff sighed with relief and withdrew. He passed on the counter-proposal, but it was, of course, never answered. Next day, the Crown Prince was married to Elizabeth. As soon as the ceremony was over, he wrote to his sister: 'Thank God it is finished! I hope I shall see you again soon. . . . I am wholly yours. . . . Adieu, Frederick.'

Frederick was married, but what did that mean? Seckendorff wrote to Prince Eugene: 'There are rumours that the King had to use much persuasion and threats to get the Crown Prince into the bridal bed, where he stayed no longer than an hour, afterwards showing himself publicly in the garden at Salzthal.' As soon as he could after the wedding, Frederick returned to Rüppin, to the north-west of Berlin, where his regiment was stationed. He contrived to arrange that his wife stayed behind alone in the capital.

There is only one sympathetic character in this sordid affair: the eighteen-year-old bride. She had curly, ash-blonde hair, pale blue eyes, a dazzling white complexion and a pretty mouth, but her childlike face was disfigured by crooked black teeth, she was plump, held herself awkwardly, was gauche in her manners and embarrassingly slow of speech. Of the shifts and stratagems surrounding her she can have understood little or nothing, while the reasons for her husband's ill will must always have remained a mystery. Fortunately, she had no suspicion of what was to come. The first five years of her married life she spent mostly with the Crown Prince in Rheinsberg, doing her best to gain his affection. Her choleric father-in-law gave her fine clothes and a dancing master. He even inquired occasionally after the progress of her laborious studies in ancient philosophy. But all to no avail. Hardly had Frederick become King than he banished her from his Court. Potsdam and Sanssouci were closed to her; instead, she was allotted apartments in the Schloss in Berlin and given the smaller residence of Schönhausen. She only saw her husband on State occasions or when the Queen Mother, who felt sorry for her, invited them both to dine. Officially she was treated as Queen, foreign envoys paid their respects to her and she was given enough money to live on, but privately she was an outcast. Her sister and sisters-in-law were invited to Potsdam, she herself never. So that no one should be in any doubt as to the character of this marriage, her husband gave his brother the title traditionally borne by the heir to the throne and made him Prince of Prussia.

For another sixty years almost, Elizabeth Christina lived in peace and charity with her neighbours. Of the 40,000 talers allotted for her expenses she gave 24,000 to the poor. She never lost her love for Frederick, but though he respected her qualities it was never returned. Shortly before she died at the age of eighty-one she said of herself: 'It has so pleased God to watch over me that I have never knowingly committed an action whereby any human being has been diminished in his happiness.' Let this be her epitaph.

CHAPTER EIGHT

*

A Philosopher Looks at War

SOME MONTHS AFTER FREDERICK'S ENGAGEMENT the King had
made him Colonel Commandant of the Goltz Regiment of Foot –
after all, if he was not fit to fight he was hardly suitable for marriage.
The King warned him that the Goltz were not to become a *Salat-
Regiment*, a sloppy regiment.

'I have drilled, I am drilling and I shall drill – that is all I
have to report,' wrote Frederick to Grumbkov. But in fact only
a small part of his day at Rüppin, where his regiment was stationed,
was taken up with military duties; most of it was devoted to
reading, for which, at the age of twenty-one, he now had leisure
for the first time in his life. And he was not at all averse to playing
the regimental commander. A good observer reported to Vienna
that the Crown Prince seemed even fonder of soldiers and soldiering than his father was. At any rate, when the horses were saddled
for a war with France Frederick was delighted: he was still
young enough, he said, to master the art of war. And no doubt
violent action would release some of the tension that had built up
in this much-tried individual over the years.

France and Austria were at war over the Polish succession; the
German Reich took part; Prussia provided a contingent according to treaty and Crown Prince Frederick accompanied the
Prussian forces to the Rhine. Naturally, precise instructions from
his father went with him. No detail was to be too small for his
attention. He was to learn, for instance, how the men's boots were
made and how much wear they were good for, how the hundred-
pound cannon was discharged and how Cousin Eugene, the
Generalissimo, worked out his dispositions. Frederick was to be
economical: no more than eight dishes for luncheon, with an

71

extra six if Eugene was his guest. Gaming, drinking and women were strictly forbidden. On the battlefield Frederick was to spend the forenoon with Eugene to learn the technique of military command and the rest of the day with the Prussian infantry.

These instructions were admirable but, as it turned out, largely superfluous, as there was no battle. The ageing Generalissimo decided not to attack the French in strength and the fighting was confined to skirmishes. None the less Frederick was delighted with all he saw and Frederick William, too, with the copious notes and diagrams his son sent home. The Crown Prince found that his bridle-hand remained steady under enemy fire and he emerged from the campaign with a profound contempt for the Austrian army. He proved himself far from being the milksop his father imagined, and from this time on he never tired of deriding the literary stay-at-homes who had never heard the hum of bullets. He now felt he had a foot in both camps, the literary and the military, and as a philosopher-soldier and warrior-poet felt himself superior to both soldiers and poets.

In another sense the campaign proved fateful. Frederick William had visited his men in the field and taken pride in living with them as an ordinary officer, sleeping in a tent and rising at dawn. Over-exertion and emotional stress – the chaos prevailing in the Austrian army made him nearly sick with rage – combined to lay him low with heart trouble and acute attacks of dropsy and gout. The doctors despaired, and as a precaution he prepared Frederick to take over the reins of government, telling him precisely whom to hang and whom to banish as soon as he was dead and assuring him that if he bungled he, Frederick William, would laugh at him from the grave. Meanwhile he prescribed his own medicine: 200 grenadiers were marched into his sick-room and their martial aspect helped to revive him.

And what were Frederick's feelings as he stood on the threshold of kingship? Seckendorff reported that the Prince's eyes had been full of tears and that he had said to him: 'I would give an arm to prolong the King's life by twenty years.' But to Wilhelmina Frederick wrote in a different vein. The sympathy she had expressed for her father's suffering was due, he told her, to the fact that she had not seen him for some time. 'If you could see him again you would let him rest in peace without distressing yourself or him.' Or, as La Rochefoucauld might have said: 'Many parents, knowing their children's tender hearts, drive them to despair during their lifetime in order to mitigate their sorrow when they die.' And in another letter to Wilhelmina concerning his father-in-law, who died about this time: 'The Duke of Brunswick's behaviour delights me. Being a well-mannered gentleman, he has died to please his son.'

But to Frederick's horrified amazement, his own father did not die. Within the space of a few weeks he recovered sufficiently to be able to ride a horse, beat his servants again and fulminate against his son. 'I presume God must have had very good reasons for giving him back his life,' wrote the Crown Prince to Wilhelmina. 'The King's illness has been political; he gets worse when it suits him.' And the letter ends on a note of despair: 'Sickened by all I see of the world, I shall devote myself entirely to quiet contemplation. More and more I learn that there is no lasting happiness on earth.'

But Frederick was young and resilient, and it soon transpired that the King had been permanently weakened by his illness and perhaps as a result had become more indulgent towards his son. He now gave him 300,000 talers for the purchase and conversion of an old manor house at Rheinsberg, fifteen miles north of Rüppin. To help efface his memories of parental brutality and hatred, Frederick gave the interior an elegant simplicity and made it as cheerful as he could. The walls were decorated with classical motifs of vases and intertwining garlands against a background of pastel blue and pink. The furniture was upholstered in pale green silk outlined in silver. Mirrors and busts were placed in the corners of the rooms and on the library ceiling Minerva was depicted holding a book and surrounded by cherubs. Here Frederick cloistered himself, striving as a true son of the Enlightenment to master systematically the rudiments of all human knowledge. He made excerpts from the more important passages in his books and had them printed separately. His day began at 6 a.m. and ended after midnight. He even tried to do without sleep altogether, but after staying awake for four successive nights he developed cramp and colic and abandoned the attempt. An inscription was set up over the main portico: *Frederico tranquillitatem colenti* – 'To Frederick the cultivator of tranquillity.'

But study was not his sole occupation at Rheinsberg. One night, after a parson had censured him in a sermon, Frederick and some officers from his regiment broke in the man's windows and drove him and his wife (who was expecting a child) out of bed and into a nearby dungheap. Frederick thought it a good joke, and later when he was King never tired of telling the story at table. Even the lackeys were expected to laugh. But such pranks were not typical of life at Rheinsberg. There the young

Frederick surrounded himself with witty and cynical friends who could hold forth – in French, of course – on any subject under the sun: the art of living, the dramas of Racine, the immortality of the soul. Life and learning, in Frederick's opinion, should go together and 'the man who cultivates the sciences and lives without friends is an academic werewolf.' There might be anything from twenty to thirty guests at the dinner table, men and women, for in those days women still had a place in Frederick's life. They were 'indispensable', he considered, 'to society, quite apart from their services to the tender passion. Without women every conversation falls flat.'

But even then, and young as he was, Frederick began to reveal a strange erotic cynicism. To a young countess who regularly visited Rheinsberg he wrote anonymously:

> Still art thou full of pride and prim defiance,
> But heed the call of love, show time compliance,
> Or else the passion that from thee took fire
> Despised may in a bawdy-house expire.

'Nothing can surpass the pleasure of observing the different effects this epigram has had,' wrote Frederick to his sister. 'I feel as malicious as an old monkey at having wrought confusion in the realm of love.' The same coarseness is revealed in a letter to Grumbkov. 'I am much obliged to you for your good wishes regarding my propagation, and if I have anything in common with the stags which are now in the rutting season, in nine months' time it may happen as you desire.' And to a friend while on a visit to East Prussia: 'If you were here I could offer you a choice between the prettiest Lithuanian girls and the finest mares from the royal stud . . . for between a daughter of these parts and a mare there is no more difference than between cattle and cattle.'

About half the guests at Rheinsberg were French. Precedence depended on skill in conversation. 'He's a rogue, but amusing at table,' said Frederick of one of them. 'We play Reason here as elsewhere people make up a game of Ombre.'* And then there were theatricals, masked balls, musical parties and, for Frederick, who ranked it as an amusement, correspondence. In those days when letter writing was an art he was a notable exponent, and in that year of 1736 he wrote his first letter to the person he considered to be the greatest of all living men and among the very greatest of all ages – to Voltaire.

Then aged forty-two, Voltaire was already looked on as the

* A card game popular in the seventeenth and eighteenth centuries.

embodiment of the French nation and of the century in which he lived. As a dramatist, historian, philosopher and poet he was famous throughout Europe. From England pilgrims trudged their way to his home in Cirey and paid £6 for a chance to gaze at him. After the first performance of his tragedy, *Zaire*, the Paris mob had embraced his carriage horses. Never, before or since, have such extravagant flatteries been bandied between two people. Frederick:

> You, dear friend, are to me an incomprehensible being. I doubt whether a Voltaire lives; I have invented a system to deny his existence. No, for sure, the gigantic output ascribed to him cannot be the work of one man. In Cirey there is surely an academy comprising the élite of the entire world. Philosophers are there to translate Newton, epic poets, Corneilles, Catulluses, Thucydides, and the works of this academy appear under the name of Voltaire as the deeds of a whole army are ascribed to its commander.

In short, as Frederick wrote on another occasion: 'You had to come into this world so that I could know happiness.' Nothing loth, when Frederick compared Voltaire to Plato, Aristotle, Anacreon and Jupiter and less frequently to Apollo, Voltaire swore he saw Julius Caesar, Marcus Aurelius and Solomon combined in the person of the Crown Prince. Neither stinted his praise, for the fact was each was greatly flattered by the other's admiration and expected positive gain from the friendship, Voltaire financially and Frederick artistically. Moreover, Voltaire had been imprisoned in the Bastille and his *Lettres Philosophiques* had been burnt by the public executioner. What revenge could be sweeter than the friendship of a prince who one day would have the power to put those same ideas into practice that Voltaire's fellow countrymen had rejected? Frederick, too, triumphed over his detractors through this friendship, and, before all others, over his father, who had never ceased to sneer at his intellectual and artistic pursuits. Now he was lauded by the great Voltaire himself as a combination of Virgil and Augustus; small wonder that he let the whole of Berlin know of his private corrrespondence with him, in the same way, in fact, as Voltaire was circulating Frederick's first letter to him through the *salons* of Paris. Finally, for Frederick there was the joy, deeper than perhaps he realised, of receiving for the first time in his life complete, unmitigated approval from another human being. Perhaps the cynical Frederick was not just turning an elegant compliment but speaking the literal truth when he described, as a young lover might, how he waited for his friend's letters:

Soon I am seized with impatience and rush to the window. A sound in the ante-chamber and I am there: 'Well? What is it? Give me my letters! No news yet?' My imagination rides faster than the galloping estafette. . . . At last, at last my post arrives. Quickly I break the seal, look for your writing, and the moment I see it – I cannot open the letter for sheer excitement. Now I am reading it, but so hastily I often have to read three times before my mind has quietened enough for me to understand the words, sometimes it is the following day . . .

But, like all men, Frederick wanted to be praised for virtues he did not possess, and, seeking approbation as a poet, he sent Voltaire his verses for criticism and improvement. Voltaire performed the task with grace and tact, suggesting to his Royal Highness that the word *opinion* was not spelt *opiniong* and possessed four full syllables. Moreover – 'for I owe you the whole truth' – *tête* did not rhyme with *trompette*. In case these harsh facts proved indigestible, Voltaire sent Frederick some of his own work for criticism and unblushingly maintained he had altered the fourth and fifth acts of his tragedy, *Mérope*, to accord with Frederick's suggestions. Occasionally in the correspondence we find Frederick writing: 'we poets . . .'

But not even Voltaire could turn Frederick's verse into poetry. Admittedly it was copious, contained many fine thoughts and was steeped in mythology, but one thing it lacked entirely, poetic imagination. This extraordinary man was all intelligence and will-power; how could he be expected to write poetry, and in a foreign language at that? His prose was a different matter. Here Frederick's penetrating mind succeeded in producing a series of light, elegant and lively essays which, according to competent French critics, might have been written by one of their own countrymen.

But this achievement was bought at a high price. In Rheinsberg and later in Sanssouci French was the only language spoken; German was reserved for the servants. Frederick read German books and classical authors in French translation. Gradually he came to see the whole world through French eyes: clearly and sharply defined, without the smallest trace of sentimentality. It was indeed a tragedy that, in addition to depriving him of all other emotional ties, Fate should have robbed Frederick of all contact with his native language.

It was in these circumstances that he threw himself into philosophy, finding himself attracted at an early stage to the system for which temperament and experience best suited him: Scepticism. But it was more curiosity and love of argument that drew

Frederick to philosophy than spontaneous enthusiasm for the subject. Hence he never delved deeply into theoretical problems. 'I maintain a proposition as long as I can in order to see how far the conclusions of logic will take me and on which side lie the most contradictions.'

His personal philosophy, his outlook on life and the motives of his actions derived from other than theoretical sources. He had been humiliated as a child, so he had to fight for admiration as a man. His insatiable desire to compel respect gradually diverted his energies from the enjoyment of the good things of life towards superhuman effort and self-denial. The need to be unshakable, to be proof against all the shocks of life, is the motif of all his verse, and to serve that need he tried to justify his belief in fatalism. In a letter to Voltaire he argued: In creating the world God must have had an object; consequently, as God is omnipotent, everything that happens in the world must serve the attainment of that object. Therefore all human actions must, whether we realise it or not, be in accordance with the plans of the Creator. Moreover as God is omniscient our future actions must be known to him, therefore we have no alternative but to perform them. Voltaire replied that if God is omniscient he must also know what he himself will do, therefore he has no free will either. But Voltaire himself could not see how divine prescience and free will could be reconciled. He then made a rather feeble attempt to undermine the concept of omniscience by pointing out that human beings, if they were sufficiently well informed, could also predict certain events correctly. Frederick replied, he had to laugh at a God who had to collect coffee-house news in order to prophesy the outcome of the campaign in Hungary.

When he was twenty-six Frederick became a Freemason and for a time practised freemasonry at Rheinsberg. But then the Freemasons aroused his derision and he never set foot in the lodge which was founded under his patronage in Berlin.

He still had to be cautious in what he said on religious questions, for his father still insisted on rigorous Lutheran orthodoxy. Outwardly, relations between the two had become peaceful, but inwardly they had not improved. Very occasionally Frederick forced himself to laugh at his father's enmity: 'No artist has ever had such a poor opinion of his own work as the King. If modesty is the reason, one must confess, it is carried a trifle far.' But the bitterness remained: 'I am obliged to consider him as my worst enemy. He spies on me continually, awaiting the right moment to deal the death-blow.' And in another letter: 'I would prefer a thousand times to beg my bread elsewhere than sustain myself on the vexations which I am forced to swallow here. . . . What crime I have committed I do not know, apart from being the heir to the throne.' Meanwhile, he had learnt how to confront his father's bitterest sarcasms with an expressionless face and then speak when he had a chance as though they had never been uttered. Yet he still had to act the dutiful son. To the King, who had sent him some game to Rheinsberg, he wrote: 'I have received in all submission my most gracious father's gracious letter and cannot thank my most gracious father enough for the grace he has shown in sending us some pheasants. I can assure my most gracious father that we are not consuming them otherwise than mindful of the most submissive gratitude which we owe him.'

How he hated the need for this hypocrisy, and doubly so now that he realised he was his father's superior in range and depth of intellect! As for literature and art, the King scorned and begrudged others the enjoyment of what he himself could not understand. And how ridiculous to imagine that, because his son liked playing the flute and was interested in poetry, philosophy and the theatre, that was all he was good for! Yet how else could Frederick employ his mind as long as his father was on the throne? Well, posterity would see whether a flute-player could rule, whether the son could not outdo the father in every sphere; in concern for the welfare of the people, above all in the extension of Prussian power. The youth whom the King had once threatened with the scaffold would perform such deeds as would stir and amaze the hearts of men for centuries to come. Only by the sword could he prove how greatly his father had underestimated him.

But was this thirst for glory worthy of a philosopher? Was it not a philosopher's task to put theory into practice, abjure the baser human instincts he was so skilful in analysing and be true to his chosen gods of Reason and Altruism? Perhaps, but where was glory to be found if not on the battlefield?

Thus in the young Frederick a struggle developed between the philosopher and the politician, a struggle which he crystallised in writing and published in the form of a critique of Machiavelli's political theories.

Frederick's contemporaries viewed Machiavelli in a simple light: the great Florentine had taught that States were so far from being bound by moral principles that a prince could only retain power if he shrank from no form of crime. To what extent Machiavelli's doctrine sprang from the political circumstances of his time and from his object in writing *The Prince* was a matter

78

of indifference to Frederick. He was not concerned to see the book in historical perspective, but, taking its arguments at their face value, to use them as a starting point for his own.

Frederick's criticisms expressed boundless moral indignation in a facile, rhetorical form.

'Machiavelli's atrocious perfidy fills his whole work as the stink of a knacker's yard poisons the surrounding atmosphere.' His arguments never get much stronger than that, or go farther than the thought that immorality is immoral: 'Of all the impulses which beset us with overwhelming power, none is so baneful or so opposed to humanity as boundless ambition, an excessive craving for false glory.' Sometimes Frederick seems to be trying to persuade himself more than the reader: 'Bravery and presence of mind are found in the highway robber as much as in heroes; the only difference is that the conqueror is an illustrious robber who impresses by the scale of his actions and compels respect by the force at his command, whereas the average thief is a nameless ruffian, the more disreputable, the more despised. The former reaps laurels as the reward for his violence, the other ends on the gallows. . . . New conquests do not make the territories a ruler already possesses more prosperous or wealthy; his subjects get nothing out of it, and if he imagines he will thereby become happier, he is mistaken.'

But the true Frederick was anything but sententious, and elsewhere in his *Antimachiavel* the philosopher with his trite generalisations discreetly withdraws and a different Frederick appears, the young man destined at any moment to exercise absolute power in a world where no two political situations are ever exactly the same. So we find the statement, 'to deceive is a definite political error,' qualified by: 'if the deceit is carried too far.' And in the last chapter, dealing with the causes of wars, after declaring a defensive war to be just, he asserts: 'No less justified are those wars by which a ruler maintains rights which others seek to contest. Kings are subject to no court of law and so their rights must be decided by the sword. . . . There are also some aggressive wars which, like the ones just discussed, carry their justification in themselves; these are the preventive wars which princes have good reason to undertake when the giant power of the biggest European States threatens to engulf the world.'

The *Antimachiavel* proves as self-contradictory as its author. But it does him a useful service, for in writing it he rids himself once for all of his scruples regarding war and conquest. Soon, too soon, as Grumbkov predicted: 'Junior will give the world a surprise.'

Meanwhile, life at Rheinsberg was costing more than Frederick William was prepared to pay, and the Crown Prince had to turn elsewhere for money. This time, the Empress of Russia's lover, the former stable-boy Duke Biron of Courland, was the source. To the envoy of Saxony at St Petersburg, who was acting as go-between, Frederick wrote coolly: 'The King is ill. You can use that as justification for a good advance to me next summer, for seriously: if I am to be put under an obligation, it must be done with all speed.' Was this not carrying deceit too far? The fact was that never at any time did Frederick perform the least service for anyone who lent him money, not even for the Habsburgs, who were still secretly transferring annual sums.

But before that could be realised in Vienna, Frederick William would have to die, and this he now did – appropriately enough, some months before the world situation faced Prussia with decisions which he himself would never have had the skill to handle.

At the very end of his life the King seemed to glimpse qualities in his son which he had never before suspected. 'There's a Frederick William in you,' he said after a successful parade of his regiment, and when he was angered by the Emperor he took comfort in the thought that Fritz would avenge him. But in the background, jealousy still simmered, breaking out occasionally in an ironic 'Your Majesty,' followed by: 'You must be patient for a while longer.' When, during his last illness, the Crown Prince suggested summoning an eminent doctor from Halle, the King retorted that his own physician, Eller, could kill him without assistance, and, turning to Eller: 'The rogue knows that once I am gone, no one will call him to account for the way he has treated me.' But three days before his death he said tearfully: 'I die content with so worthy a son to succeed me.'

As he drew towards his end in May 1740, Frederick William had the oak coffin placed beside his bed. During the last weeks of his life he was in constant pain from dropsy and gout. He had long since made his will and now he gave precise instructions for his funeral. After his death he was to be shaved and four hours later an autopsy was to be performed to establish the cause of death. The King was to be buried in his uniform and the Potsdam Grenadiers were to escort the coffin and provide pall-bearers. The royal servants were not to be dressed in full mourning – as it was, the funeral would cost a terrible sum – but were to wear a crape band round the hat. There was to be no funeral oration. Twelve salutes, each of twenty-four pieces of field artillery, were to be fired.

On 28th May the King spent two hours with the Crown Prince

explaining matters of State and giving him some last advice. At one o'clock on the morning of the 31st, feeling that the end was approaching, he had himself wheeled into the Queen's apartments and said to her: 'Get up! I am going to die.' Then he was wheeled back to his own room, which overlooked the royal stables. He ordered the horses to be brought out, and calling his oldest friend, the Prince of Anhalt-Dessau, and Colonel Hacke, the Adjutant-General, he told them to take one each as a parting gift. Dessau was too distressed to do more than gesture vaguely through the window, but the King saw he had pointed to a bad horse and made him select another. Then, as tears began to roll down Dessau's face, the King said: 'Nay, nay, my old friend. This is a debt we all have to pay.'

Seeing a stable-boy about to put a saddle covered with yellow velvet on a blue horse-cloth, the King told Hacke to 'go down and give the fellow a drubbing.' Then all present – the Queen, the Crown Prince, generals, ministers, clergy and the captains of the Potsdam Grenadiers – sang his favourite hymn. When they came to the verse, 'Naked I came into the world and naked shall I go,' – 'No!' broke in the King vehemently. 'That is not true. I shall be wearing my regimentals.' Soon afterwards he had a relapse. When he came to, the chaplain was beside him. They prayed together, the King complaining that he could not remember the words.

Hours passed and Frederick William gradually sank into a coma. In the early afternoon he revived a little, and, asking for a mirror, examined his face attentively. Shortly before three o'clock he spoke for the last time: 'Lord Jesus, in Thee I live, in Thee I die.' His breathing continued for a few moments longer. Then he expired.

*

CHAPTER NINE

Frederick Is King

THROUGHOUT EUROPE hopeful eyes were raised to the youthful, cultivated, high-spirited King. That he would maintain a gigantic court and fill it with poets, ballet dancers and men of learning was generally expected. In France it was believed he would apply the ideas of the Enlightenment and possibly make Voltaire his first minister. By the English he was confidently expected to reduce the Prussian army from 80,000 to 45,000 men. His own officials and the European Powers hoped that he would leave his ministers to do the ruling while he devoted himself to the arts. As for his friends at Rheinsberg, none doubted that an era of wealth had dawned, and when one of them received the news of Frederick William's death and dropped his purse in his haste to reach the young King's side, the architect Knobelsdorf was heard to exclaim: 'What! Stop to pick up groschen when it will be raining ducats!' But these hopes were soon disappointed.

An hour after Frederick William's death, the Prince of Anhalt-Dessau, organiser of the Prussian army and his most trusted counsellor, threw himself at the young King's feet to assure him of his personal devotion and incidentally express the hope that he would confirm him in his offices and authority. Wiping the tears from his eyes, Frederick assured the aged vassal that he wished him to retain all his functions. 'But as for authority,' he said, 'I don't know what you mean. I am the only one to exercise authority in this country.'

Some days later, Frederick entrusted Baron Pöllnitz with the funeral arrangements, telling him that no expense was to be spared to make it an occasion of fitting pomp and solemnity and ordering him to buy the necessary quantities of black cloth. 'And mind!' said the King as Pöllnitz was leaving, 'no cheating! No private arrangements with the purveyors, or I warn you I shan't pass the accounts!'

Pöllnitz told a friend he would give a hundred gold pistoles to have the old King back, and others must have thought the same. The Department of War and Domain Lands for the March had sought to ingratiate the King by asking leave to spend 195 talers on improving the road between Rüppin and Rheinsberg. 'I know the road,' came the reply, 'and the *Kammer* must think me a great fool.' The former friends of the Crown Prince had to content themselves with insignificant posts. To the closest of them, Groom of the Chamber Fredersdorf, Frederick confided: 'The pranks are over.' Lieutenant Keith was called home from London, made a Lieutenant-Colonel and Groom of the Stables, but was not admitted to the King's presence or allowed to serve in the army. Katte's father was made a Graf and promoted to Field-Marshal. For Dorothea Ritter, who had already been released from prison by Frederick William, the King did nothing. 'If this sort of thing continues,' complained the Saxon envoy, 'the father will seem a spendthrift and popular favourite compared with his son.' And the expected reduction of the army? Seventeen battalions of infantry, a regiment of hussars, a squadron of dragoons and a squadron of horse guards were – not disbanded, but added to the establishment. The King wore 'the shroud' every day. But if the financial economy and military character of the old régime survived, the King left no one in doubt that a new era had begun. On the first day of his rule he told his generals that the army should not oppress the people with its rapacity and arrogance. On the second day, the ministers were informed that they were never to set the King's interests before those of his people, and that same afternoon Frederick founded a periodical for literature and politics, announcing that he himself would be a contributor. Further changes followed in quick succession. The ragging of newly joined army cadets and the 'customary brutalities' of the press-gang were forbidden. Torture, except in cases of high treason, was abolished. The barbarous penalty for women convicted of infanticide was changed to death by beheading. The censorship of newspapers was in future to be confined to the political columns, 'for if gazettes are to be interesting they must not be under constraint.' The regiment of giants was disbanded as being too costly to maintain, public granaries were founded to reduce the price of bread, marriage between distant relatives was made easier, the State brewing monopoly was relaxed to allow country people to brew their own beer, a department for trade and industry was set up within the Civil Service, the building of an opera house was planned and the Academy of Science reorganised. It had pleased Frederick William's sense of humour to decree that the Academy's finances should depend on the sale of calendars showing on what days of the year oats should be sown and cows blanketed and that the 'court jesters' should be paid out of the receipts. Frederick appointed the French geographer Maupertuis as President of the Academy and learned men from all over Europe as members. Finally, he declared complete religious toleration throughout Prussia, on the principle that every man was entitled to choose his own path to heaven – all this during the first few weeks of his reign.

Those who had reason to fear Frederick's vengeance were pleasantly surprised. Apparently he had forgotten all the insults and indignities he had suffered as Crown Prince. He even promoted one of his most vicious persecutors, Colonel von Derschau, to Major-General.

Slowly a portrait of the new monarch came into focus. Here was no poetaster-king, no fond and foolish prince, but a ruler who was seriously concerned, as he himself wrote in a circular to his officials, to make his people 'happy and contented.' Throughout these early months of his reign Frederick was in an ecstasy of joy. Free at last! Free from tyranny, free to act. 'Adieu!' he wrote with innocent vanity to a friend. 'I still have to write to the King of France, compose a solo and a poem to Voltaire, alter the constitution of the army, and a thousand things beside.' And the poem reads:

> My heart on my People dotes,
> This God only will I serve.
> Fare ye well then joyous notes,
> Verses, flute no time deserve.
> Pleasures all, even Voltaire
> I abjure; duty alone
> I as my sole God enthrone.
> Heavy is the crown I wear!

In the accompanying letter Frederick wrote that, as the principle which had torn him from his literary work he had considered composing a poem against primogeniture, but on second thoughts he had decided that satire was not appropriate to princes. But at that moment Frederick was also considering a very different project.

For the last eight years Prussia had been arguing with the Prince-Bishop of Liège over the ownership of Herstal, a small village with a castle once famous as the seat of the Emperor

Charlemagne's father. Frederick William had offered to commute his claim for 100,000 talers. The Bishop had declined. Now Frederick consulted his ministers. They warned him that both France and the Emperor supported the Bishop; to use force would be out of the question – to which the King gave the written reply: 'When my ministers discuss politics, they are skilful people, but when they talk of war, it is like an Iroquois speaking of astronomy.' Frederick issued a two-day ultimatum to the Bishop demanding that he cease supporting the Herstal 'rebels.' The ultimatum began: 'Knowing all the assaults made by you upon my indisputable rights . . .' and continued in an abrupt and offensive tone calculated to provoke a negative answer. In fact, the Bishop ignored it. In that case, he had been warned, 'you will render yourself alone responsible before the world for the consequences which will infallibly follow' – and follow they did. Waiting at Wesel, Frederick had 2,000 men comprising three battalions of infantry and a squadron of dragoons together with ready-printed copies of a manifesto drawn up by himself and setting forth the reasons 'which have induced the King of Prussia to take just reprisals against the Prince-Bishop of Liège.' This manifesto was dated 11th September, 1740, that is, two days after the ultimatum, which had reached the Bishop on the 7th, was due to expire. Promptly on the 11th – no reply from the Bishop having meanwhile been received – Frederick set his troops in motion. Their commander, a well-seasoned officer, had been thoroughly briefed and knew exactly what he had to do: first, march fifty miles south-west to reach the River Maas at a point opposite the town of Maaseyk which lay in the Bishop's territory; second, cross the Maas by pontoons which his engineers would bring with them; third, occupy Maaseyk, levy a contribution of 20,000 talers on the burghers, placard the town with the King's manifesto and then await further orders. By the evening of 14th September this whole task had been completed without a hitch. As a result, as Frederick anticipated, the Prince-Bishop paid 200,000 talers to rid his soil of Prussian troops and enjoy the undisputed title to the village of Herstal. Included in that sum were the expenses of the campaign which amounted to 80,000 talers. Frederick at this time was aged twenty-eight; the Prince-Bishop was eighty-two.

The rest of Europe watched these events with impotent alarm. The French Minister, Cardinal Fleury, said that Frederick was consumed with vanity and thought himself 'the equal of the greatest princes.' But France did nothing. The Emperor spoke condescendingly, and in Latin, of 'hot-headed advisers who have misled the King of Prussia into performing unheard of acts.' But the Emperor did nothing, and no one dared even report his words to Berlin. To modern readers some of the phrases in Frederick's manifesto will have a familiar ring: 'His Majesty the King of Prussia . . . has with regret seen himself obliged to resort to arms in order to suppress the affront which the Bishop has attempted to put upon him . . . he has had no other course but to maintain the justice of his rights . . . this resolution has cost His Majesty much pain . . . unsuccessful attempts have been made to come to a friendly agreement, but the King's moderation only increased the Bishop's arrogance. . . .'

Europe was now very much concerned with the personality of this new King. The French Ambassador reported that his voice was soft, his manners so accommodating that they might be thought to spring from timidity. But on closer examination a mocking, contemptuous trait became apparent which the veil of courtesy only partially obscured. The King was good-looking, though a trifle fat. He held his head tilted slightly towards his left shoulder. The face was sunburnt, the very short-sighted, grey-blue eyes were lively. He spoke a great deal without listening to others, gesturing forcefully with white hands overloaded with rings. When provoked he could flare into uncontrollable rage. It was clear now that Frederick was not going to be a comfortable man to live with.

CHAPTER TEN

*

A Thirst for Glory

A SHIP LAY IN THE ROADSTEAD of Rio de Janeiro flying the con-
joined Crosses of St George and St Andrew. For the last three
months a boat had crossed daily from ship to shore and unloaded
textiles, hardware and negro slaves – a magic ship from *A Thou-
sand-and-one Nights*, or so it seemed, for already ten times as
much merchandise had been put ashore than there was room for
in the hold.

There was a story attached to this ship. When Louis XIV of
France had closed his eyes for the last time, a life of achievement
lay behind him. The House of Bourbon occupied the thrones of
Spain and France. The whole of South America and a third of
North America belonged to the Spaniards, and a further one-
third of North America to the French. When French enterprise
had opened up this gigantic territory the King believed that the
British monopoly of world trade would be doomed.

But Louis XIV had underestimated his opponents. At the
Treaty of Utrecht in 1713 Britain had been granted the right to
send one ship yearly to trade with South America. For long months
the ship lay unloading off Rio, and as fast as the holds were
emptied they were filled again from other ships. The traffic in
contraband also thrived and thousands of slaves were landed in
the Spanish colonies in defiance of the agreement made at Utrecht.
Administrative efficiency had never been one of the Spanish
virtues, and twenty-five years elapsed before, stung by this
procedure, the Government concluded a mutual assistance pact
with France and set about the British smugglers. Soon after, the
House of Commons was stirred to patriotic fervour by the sight

of one Captain Jenkins, who produced one of his ears in a bottle, claiming it had been struck off by Spanish coastguards when boarding his vessel on the high seas. So began the War of Jenkins's Ear between Britain and Spain, with France obliged by treaty to come to Spain's assistance. As so often in the past, the English-French rivalry threatened to engulf Europe in war.

This was the situation when, on 20th October, 1740, the German Emperor, Charles VI, died at the age of fifty-six, having first instructed his physicians that, in the event of an autopsy revealing the cause of death, one of them was to do away with himself and bring the news to him in heaven.

This ponderous and peevish person – 'he looked earnest even when he smiled' – had succeeded in the last five years of his reign in destroying all that Prince Eugene had built up in a quarter of a century and in leading Austria to the brink of ruin. In two foolish wars against France and Turkey he had lost Naples, Sicily, Serbia and Wallachia. In exchange for valuable portions of the Empire he had acquired a collection of signatures from the European States to a document – he called it the Pragmatic Sanction – recognising, as he left no son, his daughter Maria Theresa's accession in Austria, Hungary, Bohemia and the southern Netherlands. In vain Eugene had pointed out that only a strong army and powerful allies could keep Maria Theresa on the throne and to this end had suggested the Crown Prince Frederick of Prussia as a suitable husband for her. But the Emperor put his trust in his autograph book and married his daughter instead to Duke Francis of Lorraine, whom both he and the fair-haired Maria thought a splendid fellow. In fact, the emperor could have found no more unsuitable a son-in-law in Europe. Too lazy and frivolous to make a good ruler, too stupid for military command and too promiscuous for a husband, Francis had a yet more serious fault: he hailed from Lorraine. Neither Charles nor his advisers realised the significance of this fact. Just the reverse: the Emperor's minister, Professor Bartenstein of Strasbourg, conceived the idea of persuading Francis to renounce the succession to Lorraine in favour of France and become instead Grand Duke of Tuscany, thereby obtaining, as he believed, not only France's signature to the Pragmatic Sanction but the friendship of Austria's hereditary enemy. But only the signature was forthcoming, and that cost the silver-haired Cardinal Fleury precisely one minute of his time. As for friendship, Fleury was convinced that if Francis became German Emperor he would attempt to recover his hereditary dukedom of Lorraine and might even revive the claims of his

House to the throne of France. But these fears were groundless. Francis's warlike ambitions were confined to the battlefield of the boudoir and profitable trade in military equipment: in the Seven Years War his business enterprise secured him for a time the patronage of the Prussian army.

Apart from his pedestrian son-in-law and the egregious Professor Bartenstein, Charles VI bequeathed a dislocated army, a bankrupt treasury, the notoriously corrupt Chancellor, Count Sinzendorff, and three field-marshals, among them Frederick's old friend Seckendorff, all of whom were expiating defeat on the battlefield with imprisonment. This was the reverse of the coin. It was balanced by the head, that of Maria Theresa.

Charles had done nothing to prepare his daughter for the throne, and when she became Empress at the age of twenty-four she was totally ignorant of State affairs; it was no merit of his, therefore, that she became one of the great rulers of history, and almost the only one who could truly be called a benevolent despot. In Maria Theresa were combined strength of character and constitution with womanly sensibility, realism with an unquenchable faith in human virtue, respect for tradition and reforming zeal, courage and humility. To the sixteen children of her own she added a seventeenth, her people. She was born to rule and she was a born ruler, firm yet generous in the exercise of an authority which her own clear mind and pious heart gave her over her fellow men. There was not a trace of arrogance, ambition, rancour or vanity in her nature. Such was Maria Theresa, such the opponent against whom Frederick was about to pit himself.

For hardly had the courier who had brought the news of the Emperor's death to Rheinsberg finished rubbing down his horse than Frederick had made up his mind: this news was the cue for his great scene, now was the moment for him to burst upon the stage of history and avenge the humiliations he had suffered as Crown Prince. A long-cherished scheme stirred in his mind. The most urgent matter was seen to at once: he wrote to Voltaire, adding, despite his hurry, one or two verses of his own and a biblical analogy:

Dear Voltaire, for once the most unexpected occurrence in the world prevents me from opening my heart to you as usual and chatting as I should like. The Emperor has died. This death destroys all my peaceable thoughts and I think for the next month it will be more a matter of powder, soldiers and trenches than of actresses, ballets and drama. . . . The moment has now come when the old political system must undergo a complete change; for the stone has torn loose that struck Nebuchadnezzar's image of four metals and crushed them all.* . . . I shall get rid of my fever for I need my whole self and must extract the utmost from it.

Then Frederick called his chief minister Podewils and Field-Marshal Count Schwerin and informed them that he proposed to exploit the confusion in Austrian affairs brought about by the Emperor's death and seize the rich province of Silesia. His army would simply march in without warning; the negotiations could come afterwards. But both men thought it would be better to do the talking first. Maria Theresa might be willing to cede Silesia voluntarily in return for three things: a promise of Prussian support if Austria were attacked by another power, Prussia's vote for the Grand Duke Francis at the Imperial Elections and a contribution of 2,000,000 talers to Austria's empty treasury. If this offer were refused, Prussia could always agree with France, Bavaria and Saxony to partition Austria.

Podewils and Schwerin submitted this plan in writing. Frederick swept it aside: 'I give you a problem to resolve. When one has the advantage, should one make use of it or not? I am ready with my troops and everything. If I do not exploit my preparedness, I am holding something of value that I do not know how to use. But if I do exploit it, it will be said that I am not lacking in skill to take advantage of the superiority I possess over my neighbours.' In vain Podewils pointed out that Prussia's strength lay not only in troops but in alliances: 'the heat,' as he weakly complained to the Field-Marshal, 'seems rather to be increasing than otherwise.' Frederick replied with a brief note to the effect that as Britain and France were at loggerheads he would be bound to have one or the other as an ally, and 'a donkey-load of gold' would secure Russian neutrality. On the following day he gave orders for his army to march on 8th December. Now the aged Dessau added his warning to the others. Frederick replied that he would conduct the war alone and made no attempt to conceal the reason: the world should not think he was entering the field under tutelage.

Frederick's motives have often been argued, but the discussion is pointless as they are perfectly clear. If he had believed there was any moral or legal justification for the assault on Silesia he would not have instructed Podewils, as he did, to discover a pretext, nor when Podewils had done so and prepared a written declaration for the use of the King would Frederick have congratulated him with the words: 'Well done! That's the work of a good charlatan!' In any case, Frederick himself stated his

* See Daniel II, 31–45.

motive in a letter to his friend Jordan: 'My youth, the fire of passion, the thirst for glory, yes – to conceal nothing from you – even the taste for novelty, in short a secret instinct has torn me from the joys of quietude. The satisfaction of seeing my name in the newspapers and later in history has seduced me.' That this was no cynical pose, but the plain and all too terrible truth, is confirmed by a passage which Frederick wrote later in his *Memorabilia*: 'The possession of troops trained and ready for war, a well-filled treasury and a lively temperament: these were the factors which decided me for war.' It was not until Voltaire had pointed out the harm which these remarks might do him that Frederick revised them, adding that his House had an incontestable claim to Silesia and substituting for 'a lively temperament' the phrase 'an urge to make a name for myself'.

Meanwhile, as the Prussian regiments were making ready for war, Frederick understood the need for deception, and he covered his plans with a richly embroidered mantle of falsehood. In case his military preparations leaked out, he let it be known that as the Elector Palatine was dying he was making ready to press for territorial claims. At the same time he intensified the social life in Rheinsberg and wrote to a friend whom he could rely on to spread the news: 'Our pastimes could not be more frivolous. We are refining quintessential odes, torturing verses out of the language, studying the anatomy of thought and withal keeping a close eye on altruism. What else are we doing? We are dancing ourselves breathless, carousing till we burst, losing our money at gaming and titillating our ears with soft, voluptuous harmonies.' France sent no less a person than Voltaire to sound Frederick's intentions, but he could only report that the King seemed to be spending his whole time chatting, dancing and playing the flute. These negative results did not prevent Voltaire presenting his Government with a gigantic expenses account of 3,000 talers, which was duly paid: 'never', wrote Frederick to Jordan, 'was jester so highly rewarded by a great patron.' But when the British Ambassador, Guy Dickens, warned him against military adventures, Frederick became rude: 'I know that England, like France, is disposed to place other princes under her tutelage, but I have no desire to be guided by the one or the other. . . . I hope England will behave wisely, otherwise I foresee a new Thirty Years War.'

Rumours multiplied, but no one in Europe could believe that the 'Marquis of Brandenburg,' as some called Frederick, would dare to attack great Austria. The French Ambassador suggested there was probably some Masonic understanding between the King and the Grand Duke Francis.

But meanwhile Frederick's envoy in Vienna was talking darkly of Austria's need for allies and of how they would be cheap at the price of a gangrenous limb. Thoroughly alarmed, Maria Theresa sent a new and experienced ambassador to Berlin, a Genoese, the Marchesi di Botta. Crossing the Silesian frontier into Brandenburg, he had ample opportunity to note Frederick's preparations, and at an audience, three days before the invasion was due to start, he told the King pointedly that all roads in Silesia were flooded – to which Frederick merely replied he was not afraid of mud. On the following day, 6th December, he sent a note to the European Powers stating that he had resolved to send a body of troops into Silesia in order to protect his rights against claims on the territory that might arise from other quarters – but he remained, he said, a firm supporter of the House of Austria. At the same time he had a proclamation issued in Silesia announcing that his troops were entering the province with the agreement of the Austrian Government.

But it was not till ten days later, on 16th December, that the King himself entered Silesia with his troops. On the 18th his special envoy, Count Gotter, arrived in Vienna to offer the Grand Duke Francis Prussia's military support in return for the cession of Silesia. Gotter's manner suggested that 'his army was already on the march to Constantinople.' Francis was outraged and said he would rather perish than buy Prussian support at such a price. Sinzendorff thought some sacrifice was inevitable, and suggested it would be better to give Frederick half Silesia if he would guarantee to help Austria keep the rest of her territories intact. Britain, too, advised Francis to accept the offer.

But Maria Theresa and Bartenstein were against any concession, she because she believed in the justice of her cause, and the professor because he still hoped to win the friendship and military backing of France, and though Francis conducted the negotiations, twice when he was on the point of coming to an agreement with Gotter his spouse found an excuse to enter the room. Even Francis had the wit to realise that she had been listening at the keyhole. In the result, the Austrian refusal to discuss terms was so emphatic that Gotter wrote to Berlin suggesting the withdrawal of Prussian troops from Silesia.

In the light of subsequent events it may be asked whether Maria Theresa would not have done better to accept Sinzendorff's advice, corrupt though he was. Through a voluntary surrender of the whole or a part of Silesia, Austria would have been spared three wars with Prussia and also war with France and Spain. But who can say whether, as soon as he had Silesia, a man of Frederick's character would not have asked for Bohemia as well?

Now that Austria had declined to exchange Silesia for Prussian military assistance, Frederick informed the world of his 'legitimate' claims to the province. Hitherto there had been no mention of them either in Berlin or in Vienna. In November he had merely written to Podewils: 'The question of title is a matter for the ministers, a matter for you; it is time to start work on it in secret, for the orders have been issued to the troops.'

But strangely enough, despite Frederick's compliment to Podewils on the result of his labours, Prussia's legal claims to at any rate parts of Silesia were not so empty as might be imagined. Two hundred years previously, the Hohenzollerns had concluded a reciprocal treaty of inheritance with the Dukes of Brieg, Liegnitz and Wohlau, districts comprising a quarter of all Silesia, whereby each should succeed to the others' territories in the event of either line becoming extinct. But when, 150 years later, the Duchies died out, the Habsburgs had appropriated Silesia, leaving the Great Elector only one small area as compensation. This was the district of Schwiebus. If the Hohenzollerns had in fact received Schwiebus, they would have lost all claim to the province, but three weeks before the compensation was arranged the Habsburgs had persuaded the Great Elector's son, the Electoral Prince Frederick, to promise to hand over Schwiebus after his father's death in return for certain private advantages. This in due course he did, though only reluctantly and without committing himself to agree – as the Habsburgs required – that the surrender of Schwiebus did not entitle the Hohenzollerns to revive their claim to the Duchies. Thus the question was left open and in 1740 Frederick had in fact a certain legal title to Brieg, Liegnitz and Wohlau. Not that it interested him particularly, or his contemporaries, for as his friend Count Algarotti ironically wrote: ' . . . everyone is certain without having examined the question that Your Majesty's rights are incontestable.'

As the small bodies of Austrian troops for the most part withdrew without fighting, the occupation of Silesia was a military walk-over. In many places the population received the Prussians with rejoicing; the province had become Protestant during the Reformation, and then in the Counter-Reformation, thanks to the Liechtenstein Dragoons, known as the 'Soul-Savers', had returned in part to the Catholic faith; the jails were still full of Protestants who had been imprisoned because they had 'relapsed from the Faith,' in other words, because their great-grandparents had been Catholics. Frederick did what he could to win over the people. He danced with the burghers' daughters in Breslau, promised the Catholics full freedom of worship, had Jesuits to dine at his table. At the end of that year he wrote jubilantly to Podewils: 'You are the cleverest charlatan in the world, and I, Fortune's happiest favourite; our names shall never fall into oblivion.' To his friend Jordan he wrote even more ecstatically: 'My dear Herr Jordan, my sweet Herr Jordan, my gentle Herr Jordan! My good, mild, peace-loving, most affable Herr Jordan! I report to Your Gaiety that Silesia is as good as conquered and that Neisse is already under bombardment; I herewith prepare you for important projects and announce to you the greatest piece of good news that ever sprang from Fortune's lap.' Soon, with congratulatory verses from Voltaire, Frederick's cup was overflowing. The worst, he believed, was over. But he was wrong.

He was wrong, first of all, about the attitude of Europe. He had expected all would join him in attacking Austria. But France needed all her strength for the war with England in America, and England had a double motive for remaining neutral, for to attack the Habsburgs would be to weaken the only effective counterpoise to France in Europe. Despite covetous intentions, Bavaria had not dared strike at Austria without French backing. As for Russia, the best that Frederick had ever hoped for was her neutrality, and this he had achieved by dint of highly flattering letters to the all-powerful Field-Marshal Munnich accompanied by the gift of an estate in the March of Brandenburg for his son and a diamond ring for his wife. So without allies Frederick faced the Habsburg Empire, with a population ten times that of Prussia. And soon the odds against him threatened to increase. Austria succeeded in bringing about a palace revolution in St Petersburg, and, with the fall of Munnich, Russia began to contemplate a coalition with Austria, England, Holland, Saxony and Poland with the object of wresting the plunder from Frederick's grasp. At the beginning of April 1741, a treaty of alliance was drawn up and it only remained for these countries to sign it. Podewils wrote in terror to the King: 'Pandora's box is open and a heap of calamities are pouring out. We are entering the most terrible crisis which ever befell the House of Brandenburg.'

Meanwhile, Field-Marshal Count Schwerin, a highly cultivated man and a stranger to none of the pleasures of life, was commanding Frederick's troops in the field. He had spent a lifetime collecting scars under the flags of Holland, Sweden, Mecklenburg and Russia, and as a diplomat and officer had talked and fought his way over half Europe. He was not so easily disheartened and, believing the Austrians to be spread along the Sudeten mountains, was holding his troops dispersed throughout Silesia with the mass in the south in readiness for a thrust towards Vienna. Then, in those first days of April, came alarming news. Field-Marshal Count Neipperg, the Austrian commander, but recently freed from imprisonment, had crossed the Sudetens and was marching towards Ohlau, thus threatening to cut off the main Prussian army from its supplies and reserves. But Neipperg, as it turned out, was a slow mover and the King and Schwerin were able to concentrate their forces and confront the Austrians – facing, admittedly, the wrong way, with their back to Vienna and the enemy between them and Berlin – at Mollwitz, not far from Brieg. The Austrians were in the act of cooking a meal, and if the Prussians had attacked at once not one of them would have reached the saddle. But Frederick the novice took two hours to array his forces and by that time the Austrians were ready for him. As they mounted their horses the officers told the villagers to keep the soup warm for them; it would not take long to knock the saw-dust out of the Prussians. And they were right. The Austrian cavalry simply swept the Prussian horse from the field. The King was caught in the mêlée. Cursing at his men, swearing it was not worth even troubling the Devil to fetch them, he barely had time to send an officer to tell the Prince of Anhalt-Dessau that the battle was lost before he had to look to his own safety.

But Schwerin stood firm, and as the disordered remnants of the Prussian dragoons fled past him his gaze turned to the foot soldiers. With them he believed he could turn the tide of battle, provided the agitated Frederick surrendered him full command. So he urged the young King to save his person while he could and make for Oppeln and at four o'clock on the afternoon of 10th April, the King rode off in bitter mortification accompanied by two officers and a page. They reached Oppeln at nightfall and found the gates closed. One of Frederick's companions beat on them with the pommel of his sword – and was answered by a volley; a few hours before, the town had been occupied by Austrian huzzars. If they had found the gates open the King would have rode through and been captured and history would have taken a different course. But he reined in, pulled his grey mare round on her haunches and galloped away, followed by his friends. After fifty miles in the saddle they stopped at a place called Lowen. To the King this must have seemed the end of all his hopes. The dream of glory was over. How the world would laugh. . . . And the Prussian army? For all he knew it no longer existed.

Meanwhile, with drums beating and bayonets at the charge, Field-Marshal Schwerin had sent the Prussian foot soldiers marching in drill order towards the enemy. As they advanced over the corpse-strewn battlefield they were watched with admiration by an Austrian officer. A week later he wrote: 'I can well say, I never in my life saw anything more superb; they marched with the greatest steadiness, their front in a dead straight line as though they were on the parade ground. The sun shining on the bare steel made the most splendid effect and their fire sounded like nothing less than a continual roll of thunder.' This sight, coupled with the fire of the superior Prussian artillery, proved too much for Neipperg's powder-shy recruits and, unaware that some of those doggedly advancing Prussians had already expended their ammunition, they began to flee, whole bodies of infantry and cavalry abandoning the field while Neipperg cursed his 'flock of sheep' and his subordinate, General Berlichingen, clove the skulls of two deserters and cut many more from the saddle in a vain effort to stop the rout. An hour after Frederick had left the battlefield, Schwerin was able to send an estafette to report that, with God's help, he would yet win the battle. The news reached the King at two o'clock on the morning of the 11th. He never forgave Schwerin this victory, nor, though frank in other respects, did he ever mention the flight to Oppeln. But he had humour enough to think at once of a text for the victory sermon: 'But I suffer not a woman to teach, nor to usurp authority over the man, but to be in silence.'

Superiority in numbers – 22,000 to 16,000 – and the better training of the Prussian infantry had won the victory. Over half the Austrian foot soldiers had never fired a shot, the Imperial War Council having seen fit to decree that powder should not be used for training purposes. Moreover, with suicidal economy, the cheapest possible firearms had been bought for the troops, and for a time the Council had even banned army exercises on the grounds that it exhausted the men. The result was 3,000 Austrian dead on the battlefield of Mollwitz, among them the Pragmatic Sanction.

In view of Austria's decisive defeat, the States of Europe now felt obliged to review their commitments. Louis XV's Minister of State, Cardinal Fleury, on the threshold of his tenth decade

and daily applying rouge to conceal the corpse-like pallor of his
face, had throughout his life acted on the principle of never
incurring obligations that he could not get out of in case something better turned up. On the death of the Emperor Charles,
Maria Theresa had reminded Fleury of the cession of Lorraine
and besought him to honour the Pragmatic Sanction and ensure
that the Imperial Crown remained in the Habsburg dynasty.
Somewhat unctuously Fleury had replied that 'your dear husband
has been richly rewarded' for the cession of Lorraine 'by the good
fortune of possessing Your Majesty,' and went on to assure
Maria Theresa that the sole reason why France had not yet
officially recognised her was that the archives had so far failed to
reveal a suitable form of address for the Queen of Hungary. At the
same time, Fleury had written to another cardinal: 'One finds so
little integrity and good faith that the realisation of this deficiency
weighs on me infinitely more than the burden of my work.' Yet at
that moment Fleury was lavishing threats and bribes to ensure the
defeat of the 'dear husband's' candidature at the Imperial Elections. . . .

Before the battle of Mollwitz Fleury had confined his efforts to
preventing the Imperial Crown falling to the Habsburgs, but had
not contested the Pragmatic Sanction guaranteeing the Queen of
Hungary's succession to the Habsburg territories. Now, spurred
on by the war party headed by France's best general, Marshal
Belle-Isle, Fleury chose to contest the validity of the Pragmatic
Sanction and began to explore the possibility of forming a coalition to crush France's hereditary enemy once for all. Belle-Isle
was sent to seek out Frederick at his army headquarters in
Mollwitz and suggest an alliance. Soon Fleury was reading, no
doubt with pleasure as well as surprise: 'The King not only
exercises general command over his army, he takes charge of all
those matters which with us devolve upon the quartermasters and
the staff officers; victualling, the artillery and the artificers'
equipment. He planned the attack on Brieg himself. He rises at
four o'clock and rides round the whole encampment inspecting
sentries and outposts. He gives all orders to his officers, including
the lowest ranks, personally; all reports and messages go straight
to him; spies and enemy deserters as well as prisoners go to him
for interrogation – I witnessed that myself last evening and again
this morning. This Sovereign remains booted from the moment he
gets up until he goes to bed, wears the ordinary blue uniform distinguished only by his insignia and rather more elaborate
epaulettes than those worn by his adjutants.'

7

As for the alliance, Frederick felt he was in a strong bargaining position and wanted first to see whether Britain had more to offer. But compared with the British, Fleury was an artless greenhorn. At the same time as Uncle George was proclaiming a crusade in defence of the Pragmatic Sanction as King of England, as Elector of Hanover he was proposing to his nephew that England and Hanover should remain neutral on the understanding that Hanover acquired Mecklenburg, Hildesheim and Osnabrück and urging Saxony and Russia to declare war on Prussia.

This sleight-of-hand outraged Frederick, and in a mood akin to Fleury's he wrote to Podewils: 'To preserve the role of honest man amongst knaves is a highly dangerous affair and to outsharp deceivers is a desperate undertaking with an extremely doubtful issue.' However, Frederick felt up to the task, for he continued: 'If there is anything to be gained by honesty then we shall play the honest man, but if deception has to be, then it is the knaves who will be deceived.'

Being unable to reach agreement with Uncle George, Frederick concluded an alliance with France. Fleury guaranteed him Lower Silesia and undertook to give the Elector of Bavaria military support against Austria. A French army of 40,000 men would cross the Rhine within two months. Foreign Minister Podewils was amazed that the Anglophile Frederick should conclude this agreement with France. Mistrusting Fleury and finding an alliance with France strange to German ways of thought, he delayed the formal drafting of the treaty until, exasperated, the King accused him of accepting money from England – an understandable suspicion seeing that as Crown Prince Frederick himself had never been known to refuse bribes from any quarter. The King added: 'I warn you; play no games with me, but carry out my orders to the letter or your head will surely fly.'

Podewils asked to be relieved of his post, but Frederick had by now almost forgotten the incident, for the French treaty had been signed and, full of enthusiasm, he was writing to Fleury: 'I challenge you to be a better Frenchman than I.' As soon as news of the Franco-Prussian alliance reached London, the British Ambassador in Vienna, a florid Yorkshireman by the name of Robinson, was instructed to do all in his power to persuade Maria Theresa to offer Frederick the Austrian Netherlands in exchange for Silesia, thereby bringing the war to an end before France could join Prussia. Early in August 1741, having at last obtained Maria Theresa's consent, Robinson hastened to Frederick's headquarters in Silesia and proposed that the King withdraw from the province in return for £200,000 from His Britannic Majesty and the whole of Austrian Guelderland. According to Frederick, the Englishman put forward this offer 'in a wordy, high-pitched drone as though he were speaking in Parliament.' Confident of his military prowess and the prospect of French support, the King was not impressed, and, answering rhetoric with pathos, told Robinson that if he accepted the proposal the ghosts of his noble ancestors would rise from their graves and cry: 'Blush for shame, thou wretch! Thou betrayest thy subjects, the good name of Prussia, thy own fame, thy manly honour. . . . No more art thou our son, no more our kin; go hide thee in some desert place where the meaning of virtue is unknown and where only thy equals, the dishonoured, live.' Whereupon, reported Robinson, the King lifted his hat in salutation and retired precipitately behind a curtain masking the back of the tent.

Meanwhile, having signed the Pragmatic Sanction guaranteeing the Austrian territories and having only recently intended going to war to protect them, France, Spain, Bavaria and Saxony now agreed to partition the Habsburg Monarchy into four. To give Cardinal Fieury his due, he did not find it easy to break all his pledges and he only salved his conscience by refraining from a declaration of war; the French troops were to march through Germany wearing blue-and-white armbands as auxiliaries of the Elector of Bavaria. But as far as the division of the booty was concerned, Fleury managed to control his scruples; France was to obtain the Netherlands and Luxembourg; Bavaria was to have Bohemia and the Imperial Crown; Saxony, Moravia; and Spain, the Habsburg possessions in Italy. Russia's neutrality was assured by a Swedish declaration of war. When George II saw how things stood with his Austrian ally, he changed his mind about the Pragmatic Sanction and promised to vote against the Habsburgs at the Imperial Elections; in return, the allies undertook to respect the neutrality of Hanover.

With this formidable confederacy arrayed against her, what hope had Maria Theresa? Robinson, the British Ambassador, reported: 'On hearing, beyond possibility of doubt, that Prussia, France and Bavaria had combined, the whole Aulic Council fell back into their chairs like dead men.' The Austrians now offered Frederick the whole of the Austrian Netherlands and the Habsburg possessions in Italy – tempting baits containing one or two buried hooks – and even Silesia if he would take the field against France and Bavaria. Maria Theresa had no intention of surrendering these territories permanently and hoped, no doubt, to recover

99

at least Silesia when the immediate danger had passed. But Frederick replied that he would never abandon his faithful ally and the Queen of Hungary would have no alternative but to bear the whole burden of her fate. When Robinson tried to mediate between Prussia and Austria, Frederick wrote to Podewils: 'It would be shameful for me to enter negotiations with Austria and England. And also I should be taking a great risk. Get rid of that blackguard Robinson. If he stays another twenty-four hours in Breslau, depend upon it I shall have apoplexy. If I meet him on the road I will scratch his eyes out. May his whore the Queen of Hungary and his jester the King of England let themselves be deceived, the one by her arrogance, the other by his stupidity.'

The burden of Maria Theresa's fate was, indeed, a heavy one. She had no army of any kind to send against the Franco-Bavarian advance, and in no time Karl Albert, the Elector of Bavaria, was at St Polten, little more than thirty miles from Vienna; the population welcomed him with enthusiasm. The Habsburgs seemed doomed. Frederick urged a thrust to Vienna, hoping that his allies would thereby draw off Neipperg's army from Silesia. But the Bavarians thought an attack on the capital too risky, while the French were against it as being all too likely to succeed: they had no desire to see the Wittelsbach Karl August become *that* strong.

CHAPTER ELEVEN

*

The Chameleon

AUSTRIA SEEMED LOST. Then Maria Theresa was suddenly saved by none other than Frederick himself. For the King was having second thoughts about his alliance with France. If Austria were dismembered, the French would become the arbiters of Europe, and the idea would never have occurred to Frederick as it did to statesmen of later centuries that anyone could gain by upsetting the balance of power. Thus, twelve days after he had signed the treaty with the French he was engineering pretexts to abandon them. At the same time he renewed negotiations with Austria through the English envoy Lord Hyndford – in good-humoured moments he called him Lord *Hundsfott*, Lord Dogsbody. Less than a month after he had cursed the interfering Robinson, the King met Hyndford and the Austrian Generalissimo at Kleinschellendorf in Silesia and in strict secrecy, without informing his ministers, concluded a verbal treaty with them which Hyndford was allowed to put on paper but none of the parties signed. They agreed that genuine hostilities between Prussia and Austria should cease at once and Neipperg should withdraw his army into Moravia, in fact, unmolested, but in appearance harassed by Prussian skirmishers. To strengthen the impression that the two countries were still at war, Frederick should carry out a mock investment of Neisse, the fortress capitulating after fourteen days. By a formal treaty of peace to be ratified within a year the whole of Silesia up to the River Neisse was to become Prussian territory. Finally, it was agreed that this convention, as it was called, was to remain strictly secret, otherwise it would be deemed to have lapsed. Thus Frederick, as he himself confessed, would be able to disregard it whenever he chose. On 9th October, 1741, the same day as he perpetrated this betrayal of his French allies, the King wrote to the commander-in-chief, Marshal Belle-Isle, closing a letter overflowing with loyal enthusiasm with the words: 'Louis XV was destined to arbitrate between kings and M. de Belle-Isle to be the instrument of his power and wisdom.'

Frederick's most important biographer, Reinhold Koser, and with him most modern historians, condemn the Convention of Kleinschellendorf as a bad political mistake. Not once in the next forty years, they say, did he have Austria so at his mercy. But in 1741 he could have settled in his favour the whole struggle for the division of Germany. 'Throughout his long life the mistake of Kleinschellendorf could never be made good, it had to be paid for with immeasurable suffering.' But this judgment of Koser's is based on a misappreciation of Frederick's political aims. He was not concerned to solve the 'German question'; he wanted Silesia at the cheapest possible price. And the idea of 'smashing' Austria never entered his head, for to him the promotion of such a cataclysm would have seemed like tempting Fate. In any case, the destruction of the Habsburg monarchy would not necessarily have been to his advantage; who can say what would have emerged from the ruins?

For Maria Theresa, the Convention of Kleinschellendorf spelt salvation, for it freed Neipperg's, her only army. The Government had already fled to Hungary and, having learned to ride specially for the occasion, the Queen had mounted a white palfrey and galloping to the top of the Königsberg had besought, with tears streaming down her lovely face, the pride of the Hungarian nobility there assembled to come to the aid of the Reich in its hour of need. Realising that their own hour had also struck, the gallant nobles had been fired with enthusiasm and cried as one man: Let Austria first exempt them from taxation, grant Hungary administrative independence and make Siebenbürgen a Hungarian province – then they would be delighted to discuss military action. After three months' sharp haggling, Austria had agreed to these concessions and the Hungarians to provide a corps of auxiliary troops, which unfortunately turned out to be no better than a rabble.

Thus Neipperg's army remained Austria's only hope, until the Grand Duke Francis took over command and then this last weapon lost its cutting edge. As Francis watched the French and Bavarians capture Prague without stirring Frederick began to wonder whether he should not change sides a third time. If Austria were stricken he must be in at the kill. So, three weeks after Kleinschellendorf he claimed that Austria had failed to keep the convention a secret and took up arms, leaving the door open for a renewal of good relations by sending reassuring messages to the Grand Duke at the same time as he marched his troops into Moravia.

So once more Austria was surrounded by overwhelming enemy forces and the Prussian, Bavarian and French armies could have Vienna for the asking. There was no doubt this time the situation was truly desperate. After an all-night conference the Austrian ministers recommended to Maria Theresa that Silesia, Bohemia, Moravia and Upper Austria should be sacrificed in the hope of saving her other territories. One of the ministers said later: 'If anyone had suggested at that time that we might worm our way out of such pressing afflictions he would certainly have been laughed to scorn.' But the Queen never wavered; she wrote to one of her advisers: 'Now, Kinsky, is the time when courage is needed to save the country and the Queen, for without my country I am only a poor princess. . . . My mind is made up: we must stake everything on saving Bohemia. I do not say that I intend to lay waste the countryside so that it cannot recover in twenty years, but what I have I intend to hold, and all my armies including the Hungarian army shall be destroyed before I will abdicate anything. What you cannot get voluntarily you must drag from the people by force. You will say that I am cruel; I am. But I know that one day I can make good a hundredfold all the suffering I must now inflict in order to save my country. And I will make it good, but at this moment my heart is closed to all pity.'

Maria Theresa summoned her last remaining troops from Italy, sending their commander, the aged Field-Marshal Khevenhüller, her picture with the words: 'Dear and faithful Khevenhüller, here thou seest a Queen with her infant son abandoned by the world. What, thinkest thou, will become of this child? Let thy actions be such that thou canst answer for them before God and the world. . . . Be assured that thou and thy family shall receive from us and our heirs, now and for evermore, all grace, favour and gratitude, but in the eyes of the world, fame. This we swear thee by our Majesty. Fare thee well and fight bravely, Maria Theresa.'

Deeply moved the Field-Marshal read this letter to his troops. Within a few weeks he threw the Franco-Bavarian army out of the country, advanced into Bavaria and occupied Munich on the same day that the Elector was being crowned German Emperor in Frankfurt. '*Et Caesar et nihil*,' they mocked in Vienna when news arrived of Charles Albert, comparing himself on his coronation day to Job because he was afflicted with gallstones and had to pull the gloves from his fingers with his teeth during the ceremony as he could no longer bear them on his gouty hands. At first the Bavarian peasants had attempted to resist the Austrians, until the Austrian Colonel Menzel had threatened to cut off their ears and noses and hand them over to the executioner.

Frederick now advanced until his cavalry patrols reached the outskirts of Vienna and obliged Khevenhüller to recall part of his troops for the defence of the capital. Then Frederick, weakly supported by the French and Saxons and in difficulties with his supplies, withdrew to Bohemia; later he said that all 'thrusts', and under them he included all big advances, were useless in war. The continual fluctuations of the campagin were now beginning to exasperate him. Once his booty had been secured he longed to make peace. But there were, of course, his allies to think of. True to habit, he jotted down the pros and cons. The first point against abandoning them read: 'It is bad to break one's promise without reason; hitherto I have had no cause to complain at France or my other allies. A man who frequently changes sides acquires the reputation of being fickle and frivolous.' But the arguments in favour of making peace were much more specific: Maria Theresa would soon have the Hungarian army to assist her, the aggrandisement of Saxony was not in Frederick's interest, the war was proving expensive, the French were becoming increasingly less effective as their supply route lengthened, a single reverse might deprive Frederick of all he had gained, and his treaty with France made no mention of the number of troops he was to put in the field. So, forewarning the French that he might have to withdraw from the war (and adding what he believed to be the Latin for 'blessed are the peacemakers' – *beatus est posedendi*), he decided to round off the campaign with one more battle. The Austrian army had recently been put under the command of Maria Theresa's brother-in-law, Prince Charles of Lorraine. He was reluctant to commit his troops and only an express order persuaded him to fight. Despite a slight superiority in numbers he was beaten at the battle of Chotusitz. It was the first victory Frederick had won by himself, and, full of pride, he wrote to his old tutor: 'And now your friend is victor for the second time in thirteen months. Who would have believed a few years ago that your pupil in philosophy would play a military role in the world? Who would have thought that Providence had chosen a poet to overthrow the system of Europe?' And more cynically to Voltaire: 'Could one have imagined, my dear Voltaire, that a nursling of the Muses was destined, in company with a dozen pompous fools called statesmen, to set the great wheel of European affairs in

104

motion? And nevertheless the fact is incontestable, though not much to the credit of Providence. And that reminds me of the story of the parson, and the peasant who was talking with over-credulous respect of the Lord God. "Come come!" said the parson, "You picture him on too grand a scale. I, who make and sell him by the dozen, know better what he's really like." '

After the victory of Chotusitz both Frederick and Maria Theresa were ready to make peace, the latter because she realised she would have to come to terms with the strongest of her enemies in order to beat the rest. At the Peace of Breslau (June 1742) Podewils succeeded in obtaining almost the whole of Silesia for Prussia. The Austrians feared from past experience that Frederick might even then not keep the peace, but he wrote indignantly: 'From the moment that all is concluded and signed, no consideration or pretext in the world will persuade me to break the agreement reached. Rather, on my part, it will be looked upon as sacred and unbreakable.'

On one point his demands were modest: he sought nothing for his allies. An excuse to break with them was not hard to find. 'France and Prussia', he wrote to Voltaire, 'formed an alliance as one concludes a marriage contract: I promised to make war just as a husband undertakes to satisfy the amorous demands of his wife. But in the same way as the woman's wishes frequently exhaust the energies of the man, so in war the weak support of one partner may impose too heavy a burden on the other. And to complete the simile: when a husband has clear proof of his wife's inconstancy, there is nothing to prevent him from divorcing her!'

The King had never spoiled his allies, but this separate peace came as a heavy blow to them. Fleury knew that he could not win the war without Frederick, so he stormed at Prussia and cringed before Austria. His diplomats were ordered to conclude peace at any price; at the same time, he wrote to Vienna that the war with Austria and the alliance with Prussia had been forced upon him. Maliciously Maria Theresa published this flattering recantation, but declined to negotiate so long as French troops were on Austrian soil, for her ambitious plan was to reconquer Alsace, Lorraine and Burgundy, give these territories to the Bavarian Wittelsbachs and compensate herself for the loss of Silesia by taking Bavaria. All the greater was Fleury's need of Prussia, but when he tried to reproach Frederick he received an acrid reply: it was not Frederick's fault that the French General-issimo was no Turenne, and the King could hardly be blamed for withdrawing from an alliance which the Cardinal himself had said he had concluded with regret.

As for Frederick, he had every reason to feel satisfied. At the cost of 5,000,000 talers and 20,000 men, dead, wounded and deserted, he had acquired a province of 1,200,000 inhabitants with an annual tax capacity of 4,000,000 talers. As for the broken alliance, writing soon afterwards in his *History of My Time*, the King found words to justify his action. 'It is the duty of our office to watch over the welfare of our peoples. As soon as we discern some danger for them in an alliance we must abandon it rather than expose them to that danger. In this, the Sovereign sacrifices himself for the good of his subjects.'

CHAPTER TWELVE

*

Silesia, Bone of Contention

FLEURY'S FEARS PROVED JUSTIFIED: Austria was hardly free of the war with Prussia than Maria Theresa's troops threw the French out of Bohemia, reoccupied Bavaria, forced Saxony to make peace and with English help defeated another French army which was advancing to meet them. A year later they were standing on the Rhine. The Emperor Charles VII, the 'Imperial Vagabond', as he called himself, had nowhere to lay his head and the Habsburg double eagle was once more spreading its wings over Europe.

But it was not until September 1743 that Frederick became seriously alarmed. In that month, England, Austria and Sardinia made a treaty at Worms which recognised Austria's frontiers as they had been five years previously – in other words, when they had included Silesia. Was this, Frederick wondered, the start of an Austrian attempt to recover the province? What should he do? Should he shock the world yet again by breaking the Peace of Breslau? Taking a large sheet of paper, he drew a line down the middle and analysed the situation, putting the arguments in favour of going to war on one side and those against on the other. For instance: 'It is entirely perverse for a statesman invariably to act the knave; he is quickly seen through and despised.' But the danger of Austria making peace with France and then turning against Prussia seemed to him too great to justify inactivity. So, against the advice of his ministers, Frederick decided for war, and in the summer of 1744 took the preliminary step of concluding an alliance with France and a subsidiary agreement with Bavaria whereby Bavaria was to be restored to the Emperor Charles VII and France and Bavaria guaranteed Silesia to Frederick. Prussia was to supply the Emperor with 80,000

107

'auxiliary troops' and in return receive part of Bohemia.

But Frederick was only prepared to honour this bargain if he could be certain that Russia would not seize the chance of invading Brandenburg while his troops were in the south, for, as the English Minister wrote, the King feared Russia more than God. Fortunately, he stood on excellent terms with the Empress Elizabeth; a conspiracy to bring about a palace revolution had recently been uncovered in St Petersburg, and after a certain amount of persuasion some of those involved had named the former Austrian Minister as the chief conspirator. 'Are there no honest means to achieve political ends?' Frederick wrote in high indignation. 'Must all honour and integrity be suppressed in the pursuit of a selfish and, what is more, an illusory goal?' The Empress demanded that the Austrian Minister be punished, but Maria Theresa declined on the grounds that the charge was unproven. As her popularity with the Empress declined, Frederick's increased. Elizabeth asked for a German Princess for her nephew and heir to the throne, the Grand Duke Peter. She suggested Frederick's sister Ulrike. But though hardly a sentimentalist, Frederick could not bring himself to launch his own sister into the murderous jungle of the Czarist Court, and while Ulrike married instead the Swedish heir apparent, he recommended a distant relative, Catherine of Anhalt-Zerbst, for the Grand Duke Peter. The suggestion was approved, the marriage celebrated and in due course Catherine became known to historians as the Great.

Under the terms of the French alliance Frederick had reserved the right not to start hostilities before the end of August. But in July Maria Theresa's brother-in-law, the Grand Duke Charles of Lorraine, crossed the Rhine and captured two towns in Alsace. At once Frederick wrote to Louis XV that he would be in the field with 80,000 men by the middle of August, aiming for Bohemia. That would force Charles to evacuate Alsace and hurry home with his army. Let the French keep close on his heels, Frederick urged, and try to reach the Rhine crossings before him. Any Austrians that escaped could be dealt with later by himself. 'We may have Bohemia and a beaten Austria this very autumn!' he wrote, and again stressed the need for swift and energetic action. On 17th August he began to move towards the Bohemian frontier, one column approaching from the north-west through Saxony and another from the south-west from a starting-point in Silesia. When the news reached Maria Theresa, she at once recalled her army from Alsace, and the Grand Duke Francis wrote to his brother urging him to fall upon the King of Prussia and

108

destroy him. So he deserved, continued Francis, for he possessed neither faith nor honour nor religion: 'It would be a great achievement if this devil could be crushed at one blow and so reduced that we need never fear him again.'

But meanwhile the Habsburg banners still fluttered on the Rhine and Frederick reached the walls of Prague without firing a shot. The military commander chivalrously offered not to fire at the King's headquarters if he could be shown where they were; Frederick replied, the whole camp was his headquarters. Next day an Austrian cannon-ball tore his cousin's head off as he was riding beside him. The King was unmoved; he had never thought much of his relations. Prague fell, the whole of Bohemia was occupied, and the King wrote in triumph to Podewils: 'Without sailing through the clouds and flying like Mercury with my troops, I have continued my operations to the frontiers of Austria, and anyone who does not call that energetic action is a – '

But Frederick rejoiced too soon. The obese King Louis had only gone to war because his mistress, the spirited Duchesse de Châteauroux, wanted her lover to be a hero. But the transition was too abrupt: Louis contracted fever in Metz, his spiritual confessors pretended to believe that his slight illness would transport him to the Judgment Seat and they refused him absolution until he got rid of the Duchess. Louis obeyed, and, delighted he was no longer the victim of her uncomfortable ambitions, returned with alacrity to his harem. So the French made feeble war and allowed the Austrian army to escape. The King expressed his annoyance to the French Minister: 'My corpulent Valory, your Frenchmen are playing at war.' In October the Austrian army under Field-Marshal Traun reached Bohemia. Alsace was saved for France: but now began the struggle for Silesia.

Frederick's position was precarious. The inhabitants of the country were against him. He could get neither food nor news. The peasants buried their corn and fled into the forests. His lines of communication had been cut; starvation was approaching. For a moment it seemed as though Fate were coming to his aid: Grand Duke Francis wanted to take over command of the Austrian forces from his brother. But love for her husband did not blind Maria Theresa to his futility as a general, and in a letter to her sister she described how she managed to dissuade him. 'I had recourse to our usual weapons – caresses and tears; but after nine years of marriage what effect have they on a husband? Even on mine, the best of all husbands in the world, they achieved nothing.

109

Finally, I got into one of my tempers, and that was so effective it made us both quite ill.'

So Francis stayed at home and Frederick now seemed lost. Avoiding a pitched battle, Traun remained in unassailable positions and sat on Frederick's communications. The King was forced to abandon Prague and evacuate Bohemia. In addition to the enemy, torrential rain and illness harassed the troops, who having been drilled rather than seasoned were better equipped to fight battles than the elements. Seventeen thousand deserted. When the remainder reached the far side of the mountains they were no longer an army, but an undisciplined rabble. Their confidence in the King had melted away. What, after all, had he achieved? At Mollwitz he had fled from the field, his thrust into Moravia in the previous year had miserably failed and now he had destroyed his army without fighting a battle. There was only one man who would not have been surprised at this failure: his father, Frederick William.

Then, in January 1745, came another blow: the Emperor Charles VII died. He died in Munich, his capital, because his opponent, Maria Theresa, had taken pity on him and ordered her troops to spare the city so that the sick man might die in peace. From every pulpit in the country the dying Emperor had the clergy beg his Bavarian subjects' forgiveness for the sufferings he had brought upon them. Then Maria Theresa made peace with his son and left him his territory intact, for she was now bent on regaining Silesia and had only one enemy – Frederick.

For a time Frederick hoped for peace with England. The Opposition under William Pitt had accused the Government of conducting a Hanoverian rather than an English policy. The only supporters of the Government, he asserted, were the 16,000 Hanoverian troops in English pay. The Government resigned and the new Government under Pitt at once discharged the mercenaries. But it raised the subsidy to Austria by exactly the same amount as had been spent on paying them – £200,000 – and Austria thereupon re-engaged them. A Member of Parliament dared to suggest that the situation seemed to have remained the same, but Pitt thundered that this measure was necessary in the national interest and represented a totally different policy from his predecessor's. Was it really suggested that England should outlaw those unfortunate troops from every State in Europe? No one dared to contradict Pitt, the invalid who came limping to the House thickly swathed in woollen bandages and was in the habit, when cornered in debate, of apostrophising the Opposition on these tokens of his patriotic self-sacrifice. In effect, then, England stayed in the war, George II even suggesting that his nephew should be outlawed and the Electorate of Brandenburg given to his brother.

Furthermore, Frederick was in desperate financial straits. At dead of night, twelve retainers had to transfer the palace silver, including chandeliers and cutlery, by boat to the mint. Preparations began to transfer the Court to Stettin. Moreover, Frederick considered selling Emden to the English, thereby giving them a base on the Continent. This period of misfortune taught him important lessons. The French Minister stated that he was becoming less arrogant and showing more delicacy of feeling in his utterances. 'No general,' wrote Frederick in his contemporary history, 'made more mistakes in this campaign than the King. Good fortune is more fatal to princes than bad, for it intoxicates and blinds them; bad fortune teaches them caution and modesty.' In melancholy moments he was already telling Podewils that in the following spring he would be obliged to tread the path to Avignon where the last of the Stuarts lived in exile.

Nevertheless, Frederick never weakened in his efforts. To his minister Podewils, 'the wet hen', he wrote: 'Become as good a philosopher as you are a politician and learn to confront misfortune with a brow of granite and go through this life renouncing possessions, honours and vain trinkets, for they cannot follow us beyond the grave. . . . What ship's captain is so cowardly, when he sees himself surrounded by the enemy and no means of escape, as not to cast the tinder into the powder magazine and cheat the enemy of his prize? . . . I am playing for high stakes . . . a trial of arms is the only possible thing for me. This medicine will decide the fate of the patient within a few hours.'

But Frederick would probably have lost the game if Maria Theresa had not now made a mistake: she transferred Field-Marshal Traun from Bohemia to Italy, where the Franco-Spanish armies had been advancing continually. Her brother-in-law, Charles of Lorraine, was to command the army of Bohemia in his stead. On hearing this, Frederick sighed with relief, then drew up a plan of campaign which he would never have dared to offer Traun.

The crux of the plan was to entice the Austrians across the mountains into Silesia and there bring them to battle. To achieve this, Frederick gave the impression that his 90,000 men were spread in a thin line along the 125 miles of the Silesian frontier, whereas in fact two-thirds of his army was concentrated in a central position. Once they had crossed the frontier, the other part of the plan was to lure the Austrians towards the main Prussian army, and this the King aimed to ensure by personally briefing 'deserters' to spread rumours that he intended to withdraw his forces across the River Oder. So, towards evening on 3rd June, 1745, having brushed aside slight – deliberately slight – resistance on the frontier, the Austrians saw the Prussian campfires burning 'as normal' below them. And they were burning, but the tents were empty. Soundlessly the 60,000 Prussians had left by carefully prepared routes for Hohenfriedberg, to await the enemy there. The wheels of the gun-carriages were muffled, no pipes could be lit, strict silence was enjoined. On arrival the army concealed itself behind folds of ground. In the early-morning mist, when visibility was no more than ten paces, the Prussians attacked. Half asleep still in his bivouac at Hausdorf, Prince Charles heard the cannonade and felt pleased that his men had started the battle so early; when six o'clock came and at last he jumped into his trousers, one-half his army was already defeated; when the church clock struck eight the whole was in full retreat. At Hohenfriedberg for the first time Frederick showed that he was a master of war.

The victory converted at least one country: England. If the Hanoverian troops now in Austria's pay were ever to be employed against the arch-enemy France, then Austria must cease fighting Frederick. So England and Prussia concluded the Treaty of Hanover, which recognised the Prussian occupation of Silesia and promised Brandenburg's vote for the Grand Duke Francis at the Imperial Elections. George II undertook to gain Austria's concurrence to these terms. But he did not know Maria Theresa. The prospect of seeing her husband elected Emperor through Prussian support was not attractive, she said, but repellent. Without Silesia, the Imperial prestige would be empty and valueless. Of her English ally she demanded a respite until October so that she could fight one more battle. The English envoy objected that one battle, even if victorious, would not recover Silesia. Trembling with hatred of Frederick, the Queen replied: 'And if I had to make peace with him tomorrow, I would still fight him today.'

This time it was Prince Charles who planned to attack Frederick in the mists of dawn – at Soor in Bohemia, with 40,000 men against 22,000 Prussians, who were, moreover, wedged in a valley. The Austrian assault began at five o'clock. But Frederick was an early riser and the hour suited him admirably; his generals were, as usual, assembled in his tent for the daily conference when news of the enemy was brought. The Austrians were expecting the King to withdraw immediately down-valley and had an ambush waiting for him farther back. Instead, Frederick broke all the rules of war and ordered his cavalry to attack uphill. The battle was stubborn. The King's horse was shot from under him and his wife's brother, Prince Albert of Brunswick, fell at his side. The battle raged all day under a warm September sun, the Prussian cuirassiers sweeping all before them in the initial charge, the Austrian line re-forming on the heights, the Prussian infantry surging up under heavy fire, recoiling, pressing forward again with reinforcements until the Austrian cavalry were routed, the infantry on their right wing cut into small groups and scattered, and the day – at heavy cost – was won. Prince Charles had grouped his forces on a narrow front in broken country where their numerical superiority was of no effect; this error allied to Frederick's bold decision to exploit it had given Prussia the victory. But on both sides the losses were heavy, and the King ended the day with only the clothes he was wearing; in flight some Austrian hussars had looted his baggage train.

In a note to his chamberlain, Fredersdorf, Frederick reported his brother-in-law's death with the laconic words: 'The good, brave Weddell is dead; Albert, too – not much loss! . . .' A few days later he wrote to his wife: 'You will probably know what occurred the day before yesterday. I mourn the dead and pity them. They say Prince Louis is wounded. I am, with much esteem . . .' Louis was another of the Queen's brothers who had been fighting with the Austrians. Frederick also wrote to his old tutor in Berlin asking him to replace the volumes plundered from his library. Cicero, Horace, Lucian, Voltaire, Bossuet, Montesquieu. And then, despite his victory, the King had the rare good sense to order the retreat. He had risked enough.

At this time, Frederick lost the two last surviving friends of his youth, Jordan and Kayserling. It was a heavy blow. 'In under three months I have lost my two most faithful friends, people I have lived with every day, delightful company, admirable men and real friends. For a heart that was made as sensitive as mine it is hard to fight down the sorrow.'

The Prussian victory at Soor (30th September, 1745) struck a discordant note at the solemnities then taking place in Frankfurt, where Maria Theresa's husband, the Grand Duke Francis, was being crowned German Emperor after his election by seven votes out of nine. In his capacity of Arch-Chamberlain of the Reich, Frederick himself should have been present at the cere-

8   113

mony to offer Francis a silver basin containing water for symbolic ablutions. Maria Theresa had declined to be crowned Empress on the pretext that she was pregnant, but in reality because, as Queen of Hungary and Bohemia and Archduchess of Austria in her own right, she was unwilling to accept this further title deriving from her husband. So she watched his coronation. When her Franzl emerged from the city hall in his resplendent robes she was the first to flutter her handkerchief from the balcony, crying '*Vivat!*' again and again and removing her gloves so as to clap louder. Then the new Emperor raised his sceptre to her in salute and, with face beaming like the full moon, held up the Imperial Orb. That was too much for Maria Theresa and she burst into peals of indulgent laughter in which the whole company joined. When Frederick heard of this performance he gave a peevish frown, for the mixture of spontaneity and queenly pride in his illustrious opponent, her inflexible will allied to her bourgeois enjoyment of life, her uninhibited womanly ways were an incomprehensible mystery to him, and as such to be hated.

After his victory at Soor the King had hoped that Maria Theresa would abandon the struggle, but instead his spies reported that she had a new plan. In the coming winter Saxon troops were to thrust forward to Berlin while Prince Charles pinned Frederick's army in Bohemia and – a fresh enemy – 10,000 Russians mobilised on the Prussian frontier. Disregarding the Empress Elizabeth's threat to invade Prussia if he attacked his neighbour, the King now ordered the patriarch of the Prussian army, old Dessau, to invade Saxony with the reserve army of the Elbe and defeat the enemy before they could unite with the Austrians or Russians. But Prince Leopold of Anhalt-Dessau, one-time trusted adviser of Frederick's father and Field-Marshal of the German Reich, was not a fast mover. When he went to war he liked to proceed calmly and methodically. So he let a Sunday slip by because it was the day of rest, spent another whole day baking bread for the commissariat, and a third in arranging cover for his flanks. Frederick was hopping with impatience. 'The old man crawls and I have to keep driving him on,' he complained to Fredersdorf, and to Dessau himself, whom he had always hated and accused of possessing many great qualities but few good ones, he wrote in tones which the old warhorse had never yet heard in all his seventy-six years of life:

I know that I explain myself clearly, for no officer in my army has ever complained of not understanding me, and I also know that my Field-Marshal is the only one who cannot or will not comprehend my explicit orders. I cannot see the reason and I am greatly displeased for

114

you rob me of both honour and reputation. . . . This is not intended to be a joke, and will it please your Highness not to treat me as a petty princeling, but carry out my orders to the letter.

This reprimand may be said to have won the war, for it put the old man in his fiercest fire-eating mood. Some days later, when he discovered the Saxons installed on impregnable, ice-covered heights at Kesselsdorf he was determined to show his young King what that same Dessau was made of who had carried the Prussian banners to the walls of Turin when Frederick was still in his nappies. Before the battle the old warrior prayed aloud:

Lord God, help me. And if you won't do that, then at least don't help those scoundrels the enemy, but watch and see how the battle goes. Amen.

Then Dessau stood up and waving his hat cried: 'In the name of Jesus – march!' Then the God of Battles saw how Dessau set forward his life's work, the Prussian grenadiers, to scale the heights while the music thumped and the men sang the Dessau march: 'And so we live, and so we live, so live we every day!' – saw the men go trampling up the icy slope, helmet to helmet with disci-plined contempt for death; saw how thousands fell under a sudden hail of grape-shot, and how others, carried with them as they plunged to the bottom of the slope, began to climb again, hands clutching, boots sliding, breath misting the frosty air: and how, as the jagged iron tore again through the ranks, they fell back, and tears of desperation stood in old Dessau's eyes: was this how a long and glorious career was to end – in the mud and blood of utter defeat?

But then, at that moment, as though by a miracle, the whole situation changed. Madness seemed to take hold of the enemy. Abandoning their secure positions, the Saxon greencoats came storming down the slope after the disorganised Prussians. Quick as thought, old Dessau threw in his cavalry and with drawn sabres the Prussian dragoons galloped uphill in a cloud of snow against the oncoming Saxons. In a moment all was confusion. On the heights the enemy gunners had to hold their fire for fear of hitting their own people – slowly the struggling mass of men and horses moved upwards . . . the summit was gained . . . the artillery cap-tured . . . and two hours later the Saxon army was in wild retreat. Proudly old Dessau sounded a fanfare; in reporting to the King he called them his 'Sodom's trumpets' (he meant Jericho). A few days later the Prussians occupied Dresden and the Russian Chancellor Bestuchev was saying fearfully: 'God grant the King may hear nothing of our warlike preparations or he will deal with us as he dealt with the Saxons.'

At Kesselsdorf the Saxons had fought their last battle as a nation and from that day onwards – 15th December, 1745 – Frederick, aged thirty-three, was known as 'the Great'.

At first, Maria Theresa refused to accept defeat or make peace with Prussia. Count Harrach, whom she sent to Dresden, was to discuss terms, not with Frederick, but with the French. But the French were emboldened by the victory of Kesselsdorf to overbid their hand, and rather than cede parts of Flanders and her Italian possessions to them Maria Theresa ordered Harrach to approach the King of Prussia. And though his army, not the French, had won Kesselsdorf, his terms were modest: all he asked was to retain Silesia. On the morning of Christmas Day, 1745, Frederick and Harrach signed the Treaty of Dresden. Three hours later a courier arrived from Maria Theresa. She had changed her mind – Harrach was first to make peace with France. Too late. . . .

But both opponents were exhausted, and the treaty with the King of Prussia having been signed Maria Theresa said she was resolved to observe it scrupulously. As for Frederick, he told his reader Darget he would not attack a cat henceforth except in self-defence. He would not budge even if Prince Charles were at the gates of Paris. 'And would your Majesty see the French before Vienna with equal indifference?' asked Darget. 'Darget, I swear to you, at long last I want to enjoy my life. We wretched people! Is it the purpose of our existence to make plans costing so much blood? We want to live by letting others live.'

But this was disingenuous. Frederick knew that with Silesia he had gained the permanent mistrust of his neighbours. He knew there could be no peace as long as he retained the fruits of war, and three years later even, when the long war of the Austrian Succession ended and every Power in Europe, every signatory to the Treaty of Aix-la-Chapelle, recognised his ownership of Silesia, his watchword remained: *On guard*.

*

CHAPTER THIRTEEN

Frederick the Administrator

THE CLOCK OF THE GARRISON CHURCH strikes four, but the man lying on the camp bed is already awake. As usual, he has tied a pillow to his head with a towel. A corner hangs down over his face and gives him a rakish appearance. At the last stroke of the clock a trooper of the King's Own Hussars enters the room, the King gets briskly out of bed – a slight figure, he is only five feet six inches tall – and the trooper helps him into breeches, stockings and boots. The King goes over to the fire, puts on his shirt and housecoat. No women are allowed in the palace and the trooper has sewn on some missing buttons with white yarn. Now he hangs the bedclothes to dry in front of the fire: the King sweats so heavily in bed that in the morning everything including the mattress, is wet through. Meanwhile, the King has seated himself at a table where the post has been laid, and while the trooper makes his queue Frederick opens the letters and sorts them swiftly into two piles: one which he will answer himself – letters from the nobility or senior officials – and the other for his private secretary to make extracts for his later perusal. A good few of the letters get thrown half read into the fire. Then the King stands up and wipes his face and hands with a wet cloth, but as he takes a lot of snuff and sometimes eats with his fingers and throws morsels to his dogs, these ablutions still leave him looking, as he says, 'a bit of a pig.' Now the trooper adjusts his wig and Frederick dresses it himself, plants a shabby three-cornered hat on his head which usually stays there for the rest of the day and goes into an adjoining room where the Adjutant, the 1st Battalion the Life Guards is waiting to read the garrison report. The King listens to the details of the strangers who have entered or left Potsdam during the last twenty-four hours, gives the officer one or two instructions, then drinks several glasses of water followed by a cup of coffee into which he stirs a spoonful of white mustard. All this has proceeded steadily and without pause.

After coffee Frederick takes his flute and wanders up and down for a couple of hours, practising and improvising while his mind starts to grapple with the problems of the day. Sometimes an idea strikes him and he forgets what he is playing. But his fingers twiddle on, making their own music, stopping only to pick up a chocolate bun occasionally or a cherry which get hastily swallowed before the cheeks start puffing and the fingers twiddling again. After this musical breakfast, the private secretary arrives with extracts from the previous day's correspondence. The King reads twenty or so, then without looking at them again dictates his replies. Sometimes he just scrawls his decision or a comment in the margin. The post which he has reserved for himself is dealt with in the same way. Appeals for money are his bugbear – *'non habeo pecuniam'*, 'am as poor as Job', gets scrawled against them. The paperwork done, the King doffs his housecoat, the trooper pomades and powders his hair and he puts on his uniform, the same winter and summer, waistcoat yellow, coat blue with scarlet facings, three-cornered hat edged with Spanish lace with a white plume running horizontally round the brim – the uniform of the Life Guards. The King is now ready for parade. At the stroke of eleven he mounts his charger and rides out to take the salute and watch the troops being drilled. Dinner is at twelve, punctually. If there is time beforehand he may attend an officers' lecture or read official reports. Dinner lasts until two or three; two courses, eight dishes: the whole of the catering is put out to contract at 12,000 talers a year (about £1,800). But Frederick watches the details. Beneath a note from the royal kitchens that a certain meal cost 25 talers, 10 groschen and $1\frac{1}{2}$ pfennig he writes:

Thieving! There were about 100 oysters at table – cost 4 talers; cakes, 2 talers; eel-liver, 1 taler; the fish 2 talers; the rest – stolen. As there was one course extra today, herring and peas, say 1 taler, anything over 10 talers is barefaced robbery. – Frederick.

After dinner the King plays the flute a while or works at his treatises and poems. Then he signs Cabinet orders or returns them with pungent comments. At four o'clock his reader appears, but his role is usually to listen while Frederick declaims Racine or recites his own verses. At seven there is often a concert, wind instruments mostly, the performers among the best in Europe. The King plays with them; if his teacher coughs it means he has made a mistake. Then at eight-thirty comes supper – he himself usually eating nothing – and not long after supper – bed.

.   .   .   .   .

The war was hardly over than Frederick turned his mind to home affairs and decided to reform the Prussian legal system. A few days after his return to Berlin he sent a memorandum to the Minister of Justice on 'the corrupt administration of the law', demanding that justice should be 'swift and solid, fair, reasonable and cheap' in the interests of the country and its people. The old jogtrotting methods must be abandoned. Fortunately, despite forty years' experience of these methods, the Minister of Justice, Samuel Cocceji, had all his life been a firm believer in the principles of equity and was in full sympathy with the King's views. But when he attempted to put them into practice he encountered tenacious opposition. One of his colleagues asked: 'If litigation is to be shortened and simplified where are the lawyers' fees to come from?' And even after Frederick had made Cocceji Grand Chancellor some of the nobles were disinclined to accept his authority; Graf Schaffgotsch for one, who wrote: 'A man of noble blood like myself should not be confused with a person of such poor extraction as the Grand Chancellor.'

But the Chancellor acted with energy. Lawsuits that had been dragging on, in some cases for two hundred years, were abruptly wound up; judges were paid fixed salaries; lawyers were not allowed to charge fees until after the conclusion of a case. Verbal were substituted for written pleadings and procedure was regularised by a legal code in which the King abrogated all right to interfere as Sovereign in civil cases, declaring 'all orders emanating from the King to be null and void which if carried out would conflict with the established law.'

On the other hand, all sentences were to be submitted to the King for approval, but here again he ordered the courts not to pay 'the least attention to my instructions if there is anything in them subversive of established law.' His intention was not to deprive those subjects who felt they had a grievance of 'access to our royal heart.' The King also wrote a memorandum on the principles of legal administration in which he opposed the savage punishments for infanticide and abortion. Like all contemporary rulers, he retained the punishment of death on the wheel for certain offences as a deterrent. But in requiring the offender's social position to be taken into account in all criminal cases he was far ahead of his time.

* * * * *

It might have been deduced from Frederick's intellectual interests that the principles of justice would concern him, but hardly commercial affairs. Nevertheless, when his Minister died, he managed himself the whole of Prussia's trade. His principles were those of his time: as far as possible imports were to be confined to raw materials and exports to finished goods. Manufactures were therefore fostered and the attempt even made to produce raw materials – for instance, silk – at home instead of having to import them. But the King was not satisfied with overall principles. 'Take care of the details,' he preached, 'they are not unrewarding.' Thus, having discovered that mulberry leaves with the dew still on them disagreed with silkworms, he made it an offence to offer them any but dry leaves.

In his political testament of 1752 Frederick stressed that manufacturers were not usually the best people to sell their own products and therefore needed the assistance of a salesman. The testament listed a number of manufactured goods which were not, but ought to be, made in Prussia: sewing needles, paper, scissors, leather goods, bootlaces . . . The paragraph closes with the suggestion: 'The printing trade can be furthered by a line of business not yet thought of in the North – I mean, reprints. By buying a single copy of a book and reprinting it, the dealer saves his fellow citizens from having to send their money abroad, for they can then buy the book at home. Thus all good books wherever they are printed can become manuscripts for our own printers.'

Frederick enforced his mercantile laws with the utmost severity. The import of velvet, for instance, was prohibited, and he wrote to an official: 'My dear good faithful fellow! It is not enough merely to dismiss customs officers and tollmen who have failed in their duty; wherever a man has allowed in even a single piece of foreign velvet, he must in addition be sentenced to fortress-work for life.' It was the general practice in those days to levy extortionate dues on goods passing through the country, but Frederick was unique in prolonging their passage and hence the dues payable by deliberately allowing the Prussian roads to fall into disrepair. The result was merely that most foreign carters and bargemen tried to avoid entering Prussian territory.

The King's agricultural policy was simple. Nothing must be

done to diminish the rights of the nobility, for on them the whole life of Prussia depended. Army officers, senior administrators, diplomats – all were drawn from their ranks. They had the monopoly of wealth, of education and, in Frederick's opinion, of the qualities required for military leadership. Therefore their estates were made inalienable, secure from purchase either by the Crown or by the middle classes. On the other hand, the peasants provided a good proportion of Frederick's soldiers, apart from being the actual producers as distinct from the organisers of wealth. Therefore neither nobles nor State officials could treat them as they pleased, but were to deal with them 'in a Christian manner' and not to use 'unwarrantable harshness.' The King promised to make a rigorous example of anyone guilty of 'ungodly conduct towards His Majesty's subjects.' Before the tenant of a royal domain could renew his lease, the peasants were encouraged to report whether he had treated them properly. If he had tried to get the maximum profit out of them regardless of their welfare, however good a husbandman he might be, his lease was not renewed. If he had maltreated his men physically he became liable to six years' detention in a fortress. If someone offered to pay a higher rental than the previous tenant he was required to state how he intended to increase the profits, and if he could not do so convincingly the King told his officials to turn him down as a *windiges Subjekt*, a giddy creature. Thus whereas Frederick William had always tried to 'make a plus' out of his subjects, in the case of his son the humanitarian principles which characterised all his home policy came first. 'The plus,' he said, 'is accursed when it is achieved through suffering.' But though the King made life more tolerable for the peasant, the economy of the country was still based on the feudal system and the peasants were still serfs obliged to work so many days a week for their lord and free only to cultivate the ground they held from him in what time remained. This system Frederick never attempted to abolish, as before any such revolution could take place Prussia had to be secure and the existing economy made to work with maximum efficiency. How far Frederick was ahead of his time in realising that injustice and oppression were the main obstacles to efficiency may be gauged by comparing his policy with the nefarious regulations that still governed the system of land tenure in Ireland a hundred years later. Meanwhile, one of his great achievements was to cure the Prussian aristocracy once for all of the belief that they were a law unto themselves. 'Justice,' he said, 'exists for all and everyone without exception; therefore when

121

persons of rank commit an offence they must expect to be punished for it in accordance with the law' – and he wrote this to one of his best generals appealing against a sentence of six years' detention imposed on his wife for ill-treating her servants. Nobles who exacted more then the statutory dues from their peasants were liable to loss of title and hard labour for life; those who accepted bribes were punishable with hanging. Finally – the first monarch in Europe to do so – the King abolished sale of office and kept down peculation, which was then the rule throughout Europe, by means of repeated surprise checks on funds and accounts.

But the country could not be ruled entirely from a desk; if the King intended to bring all backsliders to book he would have to seek them out. So every spring Frederick set forth in his coach to tour the provinces. In his pocket he carried a small leather-bound volume containing all the statistics he might need: population figures, numbers of cattle, summaries of provincial and area accounts, lists of factories with figures of production, even the names of local officials. Before his visit, local administration boards would receive questionnaires listing perhaps a hundred items on which precise information was to be prepared so that every official would be ready with a 'prompt and accurate answer.'

Besides amassing a formidable amount of information on these tours, the King gained certain general impressions. One of these he expressed in a letter to d'Alembert: 'It angers me to see the trouble taken to persuade pineapples, banana-trees and other exotic plants to thrive in this harsh climate when so little care is taken with human beings. Whatever may be said, Man is more valuable than all the pineapples in the world. He is the plant that we should cultivate.' What did the King mean by 'valuable'? Was he thinking of educational reform? Hardly, though he did indeed make improvements: the first teachers' seminary in Germany was founded by Frederick; and he founded 170 new schools, mostly for Roman Catholics, in Silesia. Schoolmasters were forbidden to retail beer and spirits when off duty or play the fiddle in inns, though they could still do tailoring in their spare time. Apart from this, the King did little for education, largely for financial reasons. Most of the national revenue he needed for the army and his war chest. During his reign the size of the army was nearly trebled and military expenditure more than doubled. What funds remained were required to develop agriculture and industry, and if economies were needed in Frederick's view education was the most suitable field. Thus he wrote to his cultural minister: 'For the country people it is enough if they learn to read and write a little; if they know too much they will run off to the towns and want to become secretaries.' And again: 'What need has a fireman's son of learning? He ought to learn fire-fighting from his father.' As for the universities, on his accession Frederick had fetched men of learning from far and wide to fill professorships, but the annual grants to Halle, Frankfurt and Königsberg were not increased.

As a despot Frederick inevitably came to believe that he knew everything. This led him at times to make foolish decisions. For instance, a certain learned gentleman wanted to write a book about the species of fish to be found in the inland waterways of Prussia and had asked the provincial boards to inform him of any rare specimens that came to their notice. Before even this innocent request could be granted it had, of course, to be referred to the King. Clearly bored with the whole subject, Frederick commented: 'We here already know pretty well what sorts of fish there are in the country. Roughly, they are the same everywhere, except in Glatz where they have a fish which they call Ruff, or something of the kind. Otherwise the fish here are all pretty well alike and there is no need to write a book about them, for no one would buy it.' In all branches of learning the King underrated the talents of his countrymen and overrated those of foreigners, especially Frenchmen. When Winckelmann, one of the master-minds of the eighteenth century whose *Geschichte der Kunst des Altertums* opened the eyes of all German-speaking Europe to the simplicity and grandeur of classical art, applied for a pension of 2,000 talers, the King arbitrarily declared: '1,000 talers are enough for a German.'

Like all autocrats, Frederick was an enthusiastic builder. The Berlin Opera House and the Roman Catholic church called the *Hedwigskirche* were commissioned by him. But his favourite building was Sanssouci, the charming one-story rococo mansion on the outskirts of Berlin designed in part by Frederick himself and completed by the architect Knobelsdorf in the summer of 1747. For the next forty years Sanssouci was to be Frederick's favourite residence. The name – which for some reason still unexplained he had inscribed over the portico thus: SANS, SOUCI – is said to be derived from a remark he made one day referring to his tomb: 'Once there, I shall be free of care' – '*Je serai sans souci.*' In his later years he often referred to the house as 'Cents Soucis'.

The King's greatest interest was reserved for the theatre, and particularly opera. The fact that he called all actresses 'whores' was not intended to reflect on their dramatic capabilities, as he applied the epithet to most women, and, like all members of their sex, he ordered actresses about with small regard for their feelings. When a Venetian dancer called Barberina tried to break an engagement to appear in Berlin because she was preoccupied with one of her fifteen lovers the King arrested the Venetian envoy and held him as a hostage until the dancer turned up. He then paid her an annual salary of 12,000 talers, three times that of a minister. It is said that Barberina became Frederick's mistress. It seems unlikely. According to Voltaire, she only appealed to him because she had the legs of a man.

Meanwhile, Frederick was not neglecting Silesia. He had conquered the province, but he still had to gain the hearts of the people. They had not been spoilt by the Habsburgs: no Austrian monarch had set foot in Silesia for 130 years. Frederick visited it once and sometimes twice a year, staying for a fortnight each time. Affable, gay and informal by the standards of his age, it would have been hard not to like him. Excessive servility – a relic of Austrian rule – was discouraged and the King positively forbade his subjects to kneel to him in the street. When he went to church, which was not often, he made a point of sitting with the congregation instead of apart from them in the royal chair. He instructed his officials to avoid the harsh tone customary with underlings in Prussia. Those arrested for making remarks hostile to the King were quickly pardoned. Even declared enemies of Prussia were not persecuted. Lost sheep, the King ordered, were to be led gently back to the fold. He did his best to endear himself and his officials to the people. But deeds spoke louder than words.

The population of Silesia was almost equally divided between Catholics and Protestants. Before the Prussian administration had got into its stride the Protestants had naturally looked forward to better times under their co-religionists, and in Breslau when the rumble of the cannonades at Mollwitz had been carried to them on the east wind they had prayed for a Prussian victory. The Catholics, on the other hand, had been hostile from the start, and, when the victory was achieved, in that same city of Breslau more than half the congregation had left the Catholic cathedral rather than join in a hymn of thanksgiving. But now, both Catholics and Protestants were disgruntled, first, at the efficiency of the Prussian tax-collectors, who, unlike Maria Theresa's, demanded full and punctual payment and, second, at the introduction of compulsory military service. Thousands of men were crossing the frontier into Austria rather than serve in Frederick's army, and the rest of the populace were expected to stop them! There were now, it was said, not ten commandments, but thirteen, and the new ones were: thou shalt pay thy taxes, thou shalt not argue, and thou shalt apprehend all military deserters.

But though the Protestants might grumble, memories of the Counter-Reformation were still strong, and Frederick felt he could rely on their loyalty. It remained, therefore, to win over the Catholics. The task was made more difficult by the fact that relations between the King of Prussia and Pope Benedict XIV were strained; although Prussia had been secularised for the last 200 years the Pope persisted in regarding the country as under his spiritual jurisdiction and accordingly addressed Frederick as the Margrave of Brandenburg; Frederick called Benedict XIV the Bishop of Rome. To bridge this gulf the King felt it necessary to show an unmistakable bias in favour of his Catholic subjects in Silesia. Though four-fifths of the parish churches already belonged to the Catholics, despite the fact that in many cases the entire population of the village, bar the priest and the sacristan, were Protestant and the church itself had been seized from the Protestants during the Counter-Reformation, Frederick allowed the Catholic ritual to continue, while in predominantly Catholic parishes Protestants, to their great indignation, were still obliged to pay baptismal, marriage and burial fees to the priest. But Frederick also used more positive measures to gain Catholic goodwill. The Prince-Bishop of Breslau, Cardinal Sinzendorff, was loaded with royal gifts until the old man was reported to be weeping with emotion. The modest Catholic chapel in Berlin was replaced by a large domed church in the centre of the city and the King made a generous grant for its upkeep. These ostentatious favours no doubt helped to divert attention from another of the King's measures which was directly opposed to Catholic interests. As the Silesian nobility received part of their education from the Jesuits and the Silesian Jesuits were fanatically pro-Austrian, the King countered their influence by importing members of the Order from abroad.

Benedict XIV, who had been watching these events, was now mollified and was reported as saying that the King of Prussia was a true protector of the Catholic Church. Soon, those who failed to appreciate Frederick's motives were lending credence to the rumour that he himself was about to become a Catholic. For a time, Frederick did nothing to disabuse them, until an episode occurred which revealed him in a very different light. Among the canons of Breslau was a wealthy, handsome young man by the name of Graf Schaffgotsch. Though educated by the Jesuits, he derided his Church and had more than once been severely reprimanded by his ecclesiastical superiors. This zestful, ribald young man Frederick now invited to Sanssouci, put a suite of rooms at his disposal and showered such favours upon him that the Prince-Bishop declared his canon must have given the King a love potion. This seemed to be confirmed when, out of the blue, Frederick asked the Bishop to make Schaffgotsch his coadjutor, that is, his assistant entitled to succeed to the bishopric when Sinzendorff died. The old man was timorous by nature, had already had some experience of the canon's conception of decorum, and so was disinclined to accept the suggestion. But Frederick was pressing, and in return for an upward adjustment of his income, the conferment of a Prussian Order and a commandery in Malta for one of his favourites, Sinzendorff finally agreed to seek the Pope's approval of the appointment. Meanwhile, as an earnest of better things to come, Frederick made Schaffgotsch Abbot of an Augustinian monastery. The post was extremely lucrative.

Time passed and no word came from the Pope. Having declared his will, Frederick expected to be obeyed, or as he put it to the volatile Abbot: 'Either you shall be coadjutor or it will be said that I am not master in my own house.' Sinzendorff now received a warning that the same Prussian grenadiers who made the Elector of Brandenburg Sovereign of Silesia would no doubt find it within their capacity to appoint a coadjutor. The canons of Breslau who would be called on to elect their one-time colleague were also advised that if, when the time came, they did not perform the King's will with cheerful alacrity, they would be lodged below-ground for the rest of their lives. Cardinal Graf Sinzendorff also received this letter:

The Holy Ghost and I have mutually agreed that the Prelate Schaffgotsch shall be elected coadjutor of Breslau and that those of your canons who oppose him shall be treated as souls made over to the Court of Vienna and the Devil, which as foemen of the Holy Ghost merit the highest degree of Damnation.

To which the aged Cardinal replied:

This great concord between the Holy Ghost and Your Majesty is something completely new to me. I did not even know that you were acquainted. I trust that the former will inspire the Pope and the canons to act in accordance with our wishes.

126

But still the Papal breve was not forthcoming; moreover, it was now discovered that the minimum age for a coadjutor was thirty, and as Schaffgotsch was only twenty-six it would be four years before he became eligible. So Frederick announced the appointment himself, at the same time conferring on Schaffgotsch the title of Prince. Three years later, when the Prince-Bishop of Breslau died, Frederick made his favourite the temporal ruler and after another year Schaffgotsch was appointed Bishop of Breslau by the Pope. That was in 1748. In 1758, the curly-headed charmer was fighting against Frederick with the Austrians.

· · · · ·

In May 1744, when Barberina was on her way to Berlin, the hereditary ruler of the small State of East Friesland on the north-west coast of Germany had died without issue. This contingency had long been provided for. A Reich treaty of fifty years' standing decreed that the country should now pass to Prussia. But East Friesland was not Silesia. The people were self-governing, each Estate – the burghers of Emden, the nobility and the reigning prince – being represented by its own party in the East Frisian Parliament. The people were extremely proud of their flourishing and acrimonious political life and had sought to protect it from both external and internal overthrow by inviting neighbouring States to garrison a contingent of troops in their country. Thus, in May 1744, beside a Prussian battalion stationed in East Friesland, there were Dutchmen, Danes and a polyglot body of troops representing the German Reich. Although the Reich treaty had been confirmed in 1732, Frederick thought it advisable to prepare the ground before entering into his heritage. Placards announcing the transfer of East Friesland to Prussian rule were prepared and held ready in Emden. Before the Hereditary Prince died, the major commanding the Prussian battalion was instructed to act when the time came on his own initiative to ensure an orderly transfer. The King sent his Grand Chancellor Cocceji to win over the political parties – with the result that the Town Council of Emden discharged their Dutch bodyguard and on the morning after the Prince's death the astonished townspeople awoke to find themselves subjects of the King of Prussia. Having taken possession of East Friesland, Frederick then hastened to hand back the entire administration to the inhabitants in return for an annual payment of 40,000 talers.

But despite the fact that East Friesland continued to be self-governing, quarrels multiplied between the people and their

Prussian masters until, in 1748, the King ordered the whole system of government to be revised. But he did so in remarkably cautious terms: '. . . But I must declare to you that I put forward these ideas merely as speculations for you to decide whether or not they are suited to the local conditions, for not being familiar with them myself and never having seen the country, I am unable to judge at this distance.' In the result, an amicable and lasting arrangement was made which so pleased the far-off seafaring people that when Frederick visited them in 1761 they welcomed him with banners inscribed:

> O King, that mighty art
> To bless and understand,
> More father in our heart
> Than monarch of our land.

*

CHAPTER FOURTEEN

The Genius and the Autocrat

In 1743, between the two Silesian wars, the French Government had been particularly anxious to discover more of the King of Prussia's intentions, and to that end had conceived the idea of commissioning Voltaire as their agent. To make it appear that he was in disgrace and a fugitive from his own country he agreed that a last-minute ban should be imposed on the performance of his new tragedy, *La Mort de César*. Meanwhile, all unsuspecting, Frederick was pursuing no less tortuous paths to hasten Voltaire's arrival in Berlin, sending to his minister in Paris an extract from a letter to himself in which Voltaire had called the newly appointed tutor to the Dauphin, the Bishop of Mirepoix, an ass. By a round-about way, the Prussian Minister was to bring this expression of opinion to the Bishop's notice with the object of making it so hot for Voltaire in Paris that he would have to come to Berlin. Finally, Voltaire himself wrote an effusive letter to Frederick, saying that whenever he felt inclined to weep at the decay of the arts in Europe he consoled himself with the thought that there was at any rate one monarch who loved and cherished them. The letter ended with: 'You, Sire, are my great passion.'

In view of all this, it was not long before Voltaire was in Berlin. His first action was to present the King with a political question-naire. Frederick declined to look at it: 'To talk politics with you would be like offering a glass of medicine to one's beloved.' Then Voltaire asked the King to write him a letter saying that of all the descriptions he had heard of the King of France, Voltaire's was the most favourable: this the poet hoped to use to financial advantage on his return. Again Frederick declined, and less than six weeks after his arrival Voltaire was on his way home, empty-handed. 'It is a pity,' wrote the King to Algarotti, 'that such a fine intellect should be allied to so base a soul. He has the pretty tricks and the malice of a monkey. But I shall pretend I know nothing, for I need him for my French studies. One can learn even from a knave.'

Two years later, after the Peace of Dresden, Voltaire received a second invitation to visit Berlin: 'Come and visit me here. I promise you shall have a fresh crown of our finest laurels, a virgin for your use and verses in your honour.' But it was five years before Voltaire arrived; meanwhile his love for Madame de Châtelet, a married woman in her forties living apart from her soldier husband, kept him in France. Then, in 1748, Voltaire surprised his 'divine Emilie' with a lover and in the New Year she told him she was pregnant. Taking all with philosophic calm, Voltaire rose to the emergency. Establishing the principle, *Pater est quem nuptiae declarant*, he persuaded Madame de Châtelet to contact her husband with all speed and invite him to stay. Meanwhile, Emilie being an authoress in her own right, 'we shall include the child under her miscellaneous works.' The husband arrived. Coaxed by his wife's tenderness and indifferent to the fact that in those days such behaviour was considered ridiculous in a man who had been married for over twenty years, he was soon courting her anew. As he advanced, she retreated, luring him on until, weeks later when she confided her tender secret, Monsieur de Châtelet never doubted that the forthcoming event entitled him to congratulation.

All this Voltaire retailed to Frederick, though postponing his visit on grounds of ill health. The King replied: 'The body can be taught to obey the will. If the mind says "March!", then the body will move. That, let me remind you, is one of your own precepts. So Madame de Châtelet is to be brought to bed in September – but you are no midwife, therefore she can very well do without you.' Genuinely indignant, Voltaire wrote back: 'I am not the father, not a doctor, not a midwife. But I am her friend and I will not, even for Your Majesty's sake, abandon the wife who in September may be destined to die.' And when September came, his premonition was fulfilled. Madame de Châtelet died a few days after giving birth to her child. Full of sorrow and self-pity, Voltaire penned a long letter to the King, whose only comment was: 'Voltaire declaims too much – which makes me think he will soon get over it.' To hasten the great man's recovery, Frederick then invited an obscure young poet to take his place in Berlin, saying that the French Apollo was in his decline.

This finally fetched Apollo from retirement. The visit to Berlin was arranged, Voltaire ready to set off the moment Frederick granted his request for an advance of 40,000 talers for travelling expenses. The King gave him the money, accompanying it with some verses to his Danaë, who in Greek legend was said to have been visited by Jupiter in a shower of gold. 'The aged Danaë loves her Jupiter and not his gold,' wrote Voltaire, and pocketed the gift.

So, in June 1750, Voltaire came for a fifth time to Berlin and shone, outshone in wit and repartee all the clever, cynical minds assembled round the King's table at Sanssouci. He knew how to captivate, and soon he was basking in the adulation of the Court. To Frederick he poured out the ultimate in flattery, writing of the King's boring *History of the House of Brandenburg*: 'This work, unique of its kind, combined with your others, not to speak of your victories, makes you the most extraordinary person who has ever lived. Sire, you are worthy of adoration. . . . You are perhaps the greatest monarch that ever sat upon a throne.' The greatest monarch then made Voltaire his Chamberlain and conferred on him the highest decoration in Prussia, the *Pour le Mérite*, a free household and an allowance of 5,000 talers a year. Five weeks after his arrival, Voltaire wrote to a friend: 'Either he is the best or I am the most stupid man in the world.' Three months later: 'I live here as in France. Only French is spoken; German is for soldiers and horses – you only need it when travelling. As a good patriot, this small tribute paid to France 300 miles away from Paris flatters me, I find people who have never left Königsberg know my verses by heart. . . .' And after a year: 'The King's great blue eyes, his charming smile, his seductive voice, his five battles, his pronounced taste for seclusion in which to work at verse and prose, tokens of friendship to make one swoon, a delicious gift for conversation, freedom, complete social equality, a thousand courtesies and attentions which would be captivating even from a private citizen – all this has turned my head. Dazzled and impassioned, I surrender myself to him completely and without question. . . . This is how I have been living for the last year.'

But, in fact, the milk of paradise had begun to curdle after the first six months. The genius and the autocrat, each as vain, aggressive and temperamental as the other, had been unlikely to get on from the start. Voltaire could not restrain his witticisms at the King's expense, and however well the malice or irony was

131

disguised the King was not the man to overlook it: 'Majesty! How do you manage it? In the last few weeks, I have written 150 verses, but you, four or five hundred on the subject of Rome Delivered!' As Voltaire's household expenses began to soar, Frederick's gall rose with them: a minor humiliation perhaps, but he cut down Voltaire's coffee and sugar, whereupon the philosopher burnt more candles in his apartments. . . .

As often in such circumstances, a comparatively small incident set the quarrel blazing. Under the Treaty of Dresden, Saxony had undertaken to redeem her Exchequer Bills held by Prussian citizens at par. Since then the bills had fallen heavily in value and, pending their redemption, Prussian speculators were buying all they could lay hands on. For three years Frederick had turned a blind eye to these transactions until, at the request of the Saxon Government, he had made them illegal. Now Voltaire arrived on the scene and, coming from a country where the privileged were exempt from such laws, he commissioned a certain Herr Hirschel to buy 40,000 francs' worth of the bills. Pending their delivery and as security for the purchase money, Voltaire obliged Hirschel to deposit some jewellery with him. In due course, having discovered that no bills has been bought, he stopped payment of the purchase money and returned the jewellery to Hirschel. The latter then complained that some of the original stones had been replaced with fakes. Voltaire denied it and took Hirschel to court. By forging one document and committing perjury several times over, he succeeded in winning his case – and Hirschel had to pay a fine of ten talers. The King was scandalised. He wrote to Voltaire congratulating him on his victory, but added: 'I hope you will have no more quarrels. . . . Such entanglements are dishonouring and even the finest intellect in France would not erase the stain which such conduct would eventually leave on your reputation. . . . I write this letter with the robust good sense of a German who says what he thinks.'

Voltaire hastened to reply, 'Your Majesty is absolutely right,' and that being so, felt doubly humiliated. He had let the King down and the King had shown that there were limits to his indulgence. Both men were now on their guard. Each waited for the other to show the cloven hoof. Courtiers thrust into outer space by the French satellite seized the opportunity to make trouble, and before long Voltaire was waxing indignant over a remark attributed to the King. The King had said he needed Voltaire at the most for another year. 'One squeezes the orange,' he had said, 'and throws away the skin.' To Frederick a chance remark of Voltaire's was reported. On being honoured with a batch of the royal verses for correction, he had yawned and said: 'More dirty linen to be washed. . . .' By the end of his second year in Berlin, Voltaire was writing to his niece: 'I shall compile a small dictionary for the use of kings. "My friend" equals "my slave." "My dear friend" means: "you are less than nothing to me." "I shall make you happy": "I will put up with you as long as I need you." "Sup with me this evening": "I shall make a fool of you this evening." '

But still there might have been no rupture if Voltaire had not chosen to publish an anonymous pamphlet attacking the French geographer and natural philosopher Maupertuis, whom Frederick had appointed President of the Berlin Academy of Science. The occasion was the high-handed expulsion from the Academy of a Dutch scientist who had challenged the President's claim to have been the first to discover a new law of mathematics. The Dutchman was a friend of Voltaire and the caustic tone of the pamphlet was unmistakably his. Angered by the exposure of Maupertuis, Frederick himself then took up the poisoned pen, with a large crown, sceptre and eagle on the title page, anonymously attacking Maupertuis's anonymous assailant, hacking with a blunt sword where Voltaire had used a rapier: 'Crass infamy,' 'criminal ignorance,' 'impertinent slander' were some of the terms. 'The language,' said Voltaire, 'was French; the coarseness German.' And still the two philosophers smiled at one another over the supper table at Sanssouci. . . .

But to Voltaire ink was an intoxicant and when the luckless Maupertuis once more laid himself open to attack by suggesting that a hole might usefully be bored through the centre of the earth, a city founded where only Latin was spoken and doctors only paid so long as their patients remained well, yet another anonymous pamphlet with Voltaire written all over it was born. This time, Maupertuis was torn and trampled on. Blameless physicians were made to complain that he was trying to starve them – 'he treats us as though we were his publisher.' Frederick was furious. Voltaire denied authorship, then admitted it. The King forbade him to publish the pamphlet. Voltaire brought it out in Leipzig, under a licence issued for another book. The King ordered all copies to be seized and publicly burnt. Voltaire promised never to attack Maupertuis again, and had the pamphlet reprinted in Dresden. 'Your effrontery astounds me,' wrote the King. 'If you pursue this matter further, I shall publish everything and the world will judge; your works deserve monuments, but your conduct – chains.'

'*Ah! Mon dieu, Sire!*' wrote Voltaire, realising he had gone too far. '*Dans l'état où je suis! Je vous jure encore sur ma vie, à laquelle je renonce sans peine, que c'est une calomnie affreuse. . . . Quoi! Vous me jugeriez sans m'entendre! Je demande justice et la mort.*'

The King demanded the return of the *Pour le Mérite* and the Chamberlain's Key. Voltaire sent them 'as a lover in the extremities of his ardour returns the portrait of his mistress,' accompanied by a grovelling letter which ended 'my fate is in your hands.' The King relented and, to avoid a public scandal, returned both Order and Key with an invitation to stay on another few months.

So, feeling now like Damocles watched by Dionysius while a naked sword dangled from a single strand of hair above his head, Voltaire stayed. For one week he supped nightly with Frederick. Their conversation was friendly, but the sparkle had gone, and waiting only until he had drawn his quarterly allowance and arranged to smuggle his considerable savings out of the country, Voltaire resolved to go, too. He asked for sick leave, and was told it was not a question of leave, he could go whenever he liked. But first he was to return the Order, the Chamberlain's Key and a small volume of the King's verses which Frederick had given him. Voltaire went – on 26th March, 1753 – taking Order, Key and the poems with him. In Leipzig *en route* for Frankfurt he republished his original pamphlet against Maupertuis in a more venomous form. In the King of Prussia apprehension fought with rage; clearly Voltaire was unregenerate. Soon he would be attacking the King himself, with his own ammunition – the poems. Most of them were dully inoffensive, but there was one lengthy burlesque epic which was both impious and obscene. Of the twelve copies in existence, one was in Voltaire's luggage, and with it the King's reputation. Without delay Frederick wrote to his minister in Paris: 'You can let everyone know that I felt obliged to get rid of the man as his villainy, malice and knavish tricks were making him universally hated. If he comes to France, you must demand the return of a book which I gave him, as well as all my letters. You should also approach the Government to stop him publishing any further impertinences.'

Next, Frederick ordered one Freitag, the Prussian Resident in Frankfurt, to confiscate the book as soon as Voltaire reached the city. Voltaire arrived on 31st May. Next morning Freitag presented his demand. Voltaire handed over the *Pour le Mérite* and the Chamberlain's Key. And the poems? They were in a trunk which had been left behind in Leipzig. Convinced that Voltaire was lying, the Prussian then spent eight hours searching the traveller's luggage. The book was not there. Could Voltaire proceed? He could not. He would have to wait until the luggage arrived from Leipzig. Meanwhile, Free City or not, he would have to stay in Frankfurt, giving his word of honour not to stray beyond the garden of the Golden Lion Hotel. A fortnight later the trunk with the poems turned up. Having pocketed the book, Freitag had fulfilled his instructions. But still he refused to let Voltaire go, pending confirmation from Berlin. But Frederick was no longer in Berlin. Fredersdorf was now managing the affair. . . . Meanwhile, agog for a joyous reunion, Voltaire's niece, Madame Denis, had arrived in Frankfurt – and been sent to join the prisoner in the Golden Lion. After two days spent examining the wallpaper, they decided to leave. Unfortunately, they were caught as they were climbing into a hackney coach. Freitag fumed about insults to the King of Prussia and clapped the rash philosopher and his innocent niece into close confinement. It was not until 6th July, five weeks after his arrival in Frankfurt, that Voltaire was free to continue his journey. As a parting insult, Freitag made him pay for five weeks' board and lodging.

Eight months later, Voltaire published anonymously a book describing with venomous relish and much coarse detail the King of Prussia's alleged relationships with officers and pages. Frederick told his minister in Paris that he did not propose to refute the book or demand punishment of its author, as his own conscience had always been the sole arbiter of his conduct and he despised the judgments of the public. 'I serve the State,' wrote the King, 'with all the ability and purity which Nature has given me, and although my talents are feeble I am none the less quits with the State, for no man can give more than he has. . . . I would have to be vainer than I am to be angered by such idle gossip and less of a philosopher to think myself perfect and above criticism.'

Frederick and Voltaire never met again, but their correspondence was resumed by Voltaire in March 1754 and continued until his death in 1778. Of the letters he wrote in this period, 654 have survived. That the correspondence was resumed at all was due to Voltaire's desire to recapture the King's esteem; it continued because Frederick could not bring himself to bear a permanent grudge against a kindred spirit. But though the King was ready to forget the past, Voltaire never could. The indignities he had suffered – through his own fault – in Frankfurt and the loss of the honours Frederick had bestowed on him rankled almost to the last, and the tone of his letters alternated between fulsome flattery and whining complaint. Frederick was patient, but pained by the spectacle of so great an intellect allied to such defects of character. 'I have forgiven you,' he wrote in one of his letters, 'and I shall even try to forget. But if you had not been dealing with one who was madly in love with your genius, you would not have got off so lightly.' For an absolute ruler whose hospitality had been scandalously abused, this was generous. But Voltaire was incorrigible. 'Remember,' he wrote on another occasion, 'how you behaved towards me. For your sake I lost the favour of the King whose subject I was born. For your sake I was banished from my country. I loved you. I entrusted myself to you. My only wish was to end my days in your service. And what was my reward? Deprived of all you had conferred on me – the Order, the Key, the pension – I was forced to flee from your territories. I was hounded like a deserter from your grenadiers, arrested, insulted, robbed. Your soldiers dragged my niece through the mire of Frankfurt as though she were some wretched camp-follower. You possess good qualities and great talents. But you have one odious fault. You love to humiliate your fellow men. You have brought shame on the name of philosopher. You have supplied evidence for the bigots' assertion that there is no relying on the justice or humanity of those who reject the Christian Faith.' Frederick's reply was equally bare-fisted: 'You know that you behaved shamefully in Prussia. You richly deserved to see the inside of a dungeon. Your talents are no more widely known than your disloyalty and malice.'

But it would be perverse to leave Frederick and Voltaire wrangling like scullions, as though their stormy relationship was no more than an empty bubble sustained by a blast of mutual flattery. For beneath the quips, the poses, the mannered verbosity each saw in the other a man after his own heart, a lover of life and all that enlarged its bounds, a hater of all that restricted it: bigotry, superstition, cruelty, oppression. Both men were fighters. Both cherished friendship. Both worshipped at the shrine of intellect and, in an age when accidents of birth too often set folly to rule over genius, both men took pride in standing as equals beneath the universal sun of Reason. Thus, in his last letter to Frederick, the eighty-four-year-old Voltaire wrote: 'You have vanquished prejudices like your other enemies. . . . You are the conqueror of superstition as well as the bulwark of German liberty. May Frederick the Great become Frederick the Immortal.' And in a funeral oration composed by Frederick and delivered

136

by the new President of the Berlin Academy after Voltaire's death, the King declared: 'Had he done no more than champion the cause of justice and tolerance, he would still deserve a place among the small number of Mankind's true benefactors.'

. . . . .

Wilhelmina called Sanssouci 'the monastery.' No woman was ever allowed to cross the threshold. 'Solomon had a thousand wives and felt they were not enough,' Frederick had once said. 'I have one, which is one too many.' Of the male company which the Abbot, as the King sometimes called himself, entertained in his 'refectory', the core consisted of learned Frenchmen; besides Voltaire and his butt, Maupertuis, there was the witty but superstitious hypochondriac the Marquis d'Argens, who blanched with fright if he upset a salt-cellar at table, and La Mettrie, a writer and physician who had been expelled from France for preaching materialism in his book, *L'Hommemachine*. La Mettrie died young after eating a gigantic truffle pie for a bet. And then there was Darget, whose official duty it was to read aloud to the King. He became a close friend, how close can be judged by the style in which Frederick ended his letters: 'Piss well and be cheerful; that is all you can do on earth,' or: '*Mes hémorroides saluent votre vérole.*'

The usual tone at Sanssouci was one of acrid cynicism. It found expression in a series of pranks and practical jokes varying from the doltish to the malevolent. When d'Argens excused himself from supping with the King on the grounds of illness, but in reality because he wished to spend the evening with his mistress wearing a gold-embroidered housecoat which she had just presented to him, Frederick dressed himself and his friends as monks, and tinkling a hand-bell led them in procession to d'Argens's bedroom. The Marquis just had time to jump into bed before they appeared and gathered round him. Frederick mumbled some prayers, then lifted the covers and emptied a bottle of oil over the patient, ruining the treasured housecoat for ever. Augustus William, the eldest of the King's three brothers, had a similar idea of fun. At a party he gave for his sister Amalia when she was made Abbess of a nunnery in the Harz, he dressed all his staff in ridiculous clothes and named the female servants to her as she passed through the hall: *la marquise de Pissenlit, la vicomtesse de Cul-Tendre*, and the person named sank into a deep curtsy. At the end of the evening, when Amalia went to her room, she was confronted with an immense chamber-pot the size of a wine-cask inscribed: 'For the Mother Superior.'

As for Frederick, his ability to charm was matched by a perpetual urge to humiliate and outrage. One day he accused his minister Podewils, who had become Grumbkov's son-in-law, of entering a brothel in broad daylight. 'I have never understood,' said the King, 'how a man of Grumbkov's intelligence could marry his daughter to such a blockhead.' At a supper in Potsdam before mixed company Frederick let fall the amiable remark that all the attractive ladies of the Court seemed to have found husbands; only the ugly ones were left: 'You can smell them for ten miles around.' The moment the meal was over, the guests fled the King's venom 'as though from an earthquake, each thinking only of his own safety.'

Yet among his few close friends Frederick could both feel and inspire devotion. One of these was the Chamberlain, Fredersdorf. Fredersdorf had been an oboist in a military band and one of Frederick's attendants when the eighteen-year-old Fritz had been immured in the fortress at Küstrin. 'Young and handsome,' said Voltaire, 'he had served the King in more than one capacity.' Later, Frederick made Fredersdorf his valet, and on his accession presented him with a small estate which he managed so skilfully that he became a wealthy man. Meanwhile, the King rewarded his devotion and ability by making him Keeper of the Privy Purse. Finally, Fredersdorf became Theatre Superintendent with the title of Chamberlain. Towards the end of his life he was considered all-powerful at the Prussian Court. After his friend's death the King recovered most of the letters he had written to him, but those that survive reveal sincere affection. Fredersdorf suffered from constant ill health. The King watching over him with unaffected devotion, proffering advice, warning him against quacks and sending him the royal physician, Cothenius. Fredersdorf was uneducated and the King's letters were written in German, or, rather, contained phonetic transcriptions of the language he had heard spoken in a dozen different dialects, as Voltaire would say, 'by servants and horses.' In places the letters are almost unintelligible:

I thought you cared for mee, and wont giv mee the chagrin off tiking your own life; now I dont kno wat to belief! You must belief my intentions are really goode and that nothing is prescribed in diert and medcins but is essenshul to the recovery of your health. I begg you, be goode and follow out the prescription – remembre, you promissed me faithfully . . . You can tek my word, I cud not be more concurnd for myself than I am for you.

138

And again: 'I am realie sorry that the feever wont leave you yet. I wud gladly have it instead. I keep chasing Cothenius all I can. . . . I will kiss the Doctor if he makes you well. . . . '

Some letters are full of barrack-room humour; this, for instance, about a fifteen-year-old page: 'Charlie has a rash on his forehead. i say its the french and he shal have 6 weeks in the *Casterole*' (the hospital for syphilitics). 'He is terrified.' Another note from Frederick reads: 'I am sending you a Rare Eliksir that Comes from Theophrastem Paracelsio. It has done marvels for me and al who have teken off it. Teke some of this medecin, but no quack remedis beside, otherwise it will take away your Mannly Pauers of love. . . . '

Sometimes Fredersdorf became too eager a correspondent. Then the King wrote: 'You write mee 20 lettus a day! I Cannot possiply answer al that stuf!' At others, Frederick asked him to write less so as to spare his strength – a note two or three times a week to say how he was progressing would be enough. But beneath all the trivialities and the fuss burns genuine affection:

If the sunn is shining at noon tooday I will ride out. Com to the window wont you, I shud much Like to see You. But the window mus stay tight-shut; an there mus be a Good fire in the Chamber. I wish with all my hart you may improof from daytoday. Yestreday I celebrated your improvement with 2 bouteilles of Hungarian wine. Charlie sqeakd with tickling and after that fine harmoni Matshenko purformd his bear-Dance – God preservus!

A number of Frederick's letters have survived, but almost all Fredersdorf's have been lost. When he died in 1758 the King was grief-stricken, for, as he had once told his brother, his ex-valet was among the six friends he loved best in the world.

CHAPTER FIFTEEN

Facing the Music

FOR TWO HUNDRED YEARS the Seven Years War (1756–63) and the diplomatic revolution which preceded it have been browsed and brooded over by historians. Yet they still can not agree how this war came about. If we open Pierre Gaxotte's brilliant biography we find the categorical assertion: 'It is enough to follow events in their chronological order to be convinced that England was the prime mover in everything, for she alone was determined to make war in all circumstances and whatever happened.' The British historian Norward Young maintains that the war was imposed on a peace-loving Europe by France. Prussian historians have tried to show that a combination of Maria Theresa's thirst for revenge, the Empress of Russia's pathological hatred of Frederick and Frederick's indifference to the sultry charms of the Marquise de Pompadour, *née* Poisson, was responsible. Professor Gooch assures us that Frederick's 'ultimate responsibility was beyond challenge. The Seven Years War . . . was the direct outcome of his seizure of Silesia.' Earlier, Sir Charles Oman had said that no one was to blame – 'the quarrel was the result of natural causes which made it inevitable.' Finally, Thomas Mann declared that the question was too complex to be answered with a simple Yes or No.

There is another problem. How was it that, in that fateful year of 1756, Frederick found himself in the very situation which for eight years he had been striving with all the vigour of his mind and will to avoid, found himself fighting almost alone against half Europe? Surely, it was not Fate but Frederick himself who was responsible, by taking the initiative in concluding the Convention of Westminster with England, hoping thereby to check Austrian plans to regain Silesia and ensure the neutrality of Russia, but instead binding France, Russia and Austria in a coalition to destroy him? Striving for peace, Frederick blundered into war. And why? Because, it is said, he was behind the times. He failed to realise that England had superseded Austria as the arch-enemy of France and hence ruled out the possibility of a Franco-Austrian *rapprochment*. But was he striving for peace? Those who cannot accept this judgment on their hero, among them two well-known and highly esteemed German historians, Professors Lehmann and Delbrück, say that he was not. We are not, therefore, entitled, however damning the appearances, to call Frederick 'a complete fool' before we have considered his actions in relation to their true end. The Seven Years War began by Frederick invading Saxony, the gateway to Austrian Bohemia, with the object, as most historians maintain, of forestalling a combined attack by Russia, Austria, Sweden, Saxony and France on Prussia. In other words, war was inevitable; Frederick merely got his blow in first to have a better chance of winning it. But the Professors disagree. They maintain that Frederick took the offensive in order to conquer Saxony and West Prussia. Undeterred by the hostile plans of countries with a total population ten times his own, he was out for booty. His war of aggression and theirs just happened to coincide and go down to history lumped together as 'The Seven Years War.' To those protesting the complete lack of documentary evidence for this theory, Professor Delbrück explains that Frederick always kept his plans to himself; witness the familiar quotation: 'If I thought it possible that my shirt, yes, even my skin knew anything of my intentions, I would tear them to shreds.'

The Seven Years War gave rise, then, to the War of the Historians; and this still rages round three main questions: firstly, did Frederick start the war to forestall attack or in order to conquer Saxony and West Prussia? Secondly, would there have been no war if he had not started it? Thirdly, how was it that Frederick had to fight at such overwhelming odds? There are clear answers to all these questions, but first, what are the facts?

• • • • • •

The Treaty of Aix-la-Chapelle (1748) had guaranteed Silesia to Frederick and Maria Theresa had sworn to respect the provision. The King would have been only too glad to believe her, but he could not: 'Though she swore before God she was my friend, I

141

would trust her only so long as she found no opportunity to injure me.' Meanwhile, resolved to commit no unfriendly act, Frederick felt bound to take precautions.

The King knew that Austria would never act alone against him, hence all depended on keeping her isolated – from Russia, from France, and from England. 'Of all our neighbours,' wrote the King, 'Russia is the most dangerous, because of her power and geographical position. Those who come after me will be well advised to cultivate those barbarians, for they could ruin Prussia without fear of reprisal. Their nearest territories are in extreme poverty and to reach the Ukraine would involve crossing a desert.' The lustful, zestful Empress Elizabeth had at one time admired Frederick and been on bad terms with the Court of Vienna. 'I stand well with the King of Prussia, what else matters?' she had been in the habit of declaring. On his advice she had married her son to Catherine of Anhalt-Zerbst. But even a tortoise, says a Turkish proverb, is not impervious to contempt, and Frederick's witticisms about her weakness for strong waters and strong men ended by annoying the Empress considerably. Moreover, with short-sighted economy, he had proffered no less an insult to her all-powerful Chancellor Bestuschev by failing to bribe him, and having married his daughter to one of Elizabeth's natural sons Bestuschev ranked on private occasions as one of the family. He had already formed a close attachment to the gold sovereigns that reached him periodically from England, hence the King of Prussia's meanness struck him as doubly sordid and the aggrieved Chancellor and the aggravated Empress found no difficulty in agreeing that Frederick was both odious and dangerous – a powerful and land-hungry neighbour who bribed members of the Diet to thwart her Polish plans and even tried to stir up the infidel Turk against her. Maria Theresa, on the other hand – what a noble woman! A trifle priggish perhaps, but so generous in her gifts of Tokay wine and so right in her detestation of Frederick. . . . Soon after the Peace of Dresden the Empress Elizabeth suggested to Maria Theresa a joint assault on Prussia. But fearing France's reaction, the latter preferred to conclude a defensive alliance only; a secret article provided that if Prussia attacked Austria, Russia or Poland the Austrian renunciation of Silesia should lapse. Frederick had neither the skill nor the tact to detach Russia from this alliance. Assuming that sooner or later the Chancellor would fall from grace, he made no attempt to win Bestuschev and, instead, lavished attentions on a minor emissary of the Tartars in the

142

belief that the Russians could be more easily bullied than wooed. In due course, these mistaken tactics achieved their result: a complete rupture of relations between Prussia and Russia.

Thus, though wide awake to the Russian danger and anxious to isolate Austria, Frederick helped to bring about an understanding between his two most powerful neighbours. As for England, he could not hope to influence her policy in any direction. Diplomatic relations were temporarily suspended and a time-hallowed animosity existed between him and his uncle George, whom he described in official documents as 'The Junior Elector,' because Hanover had been the last German State to become an Electorate, while he carelessly flouted English susceptibilities by making the outlawed Scottish rebel Keith his minister in Paris. 'What will your uncle say?' Podewils had timorously inquired. But it hardly mattered. King George was already on record as saying that his nephew was 'a malevolent rogue, a bad friend, bad ally, bad relation, bad neighbour – in short, the most dangerous trouble-maker in Europe.'

Frederick's ten-year treaty with France had not yet expired, but the French had not forgotten his threefold betrayal during the War of the Austrian Succession and cordially detested their ally. Though aware of his unpopularity, Frederick thought it of no consequence as he was convinced that France would remain the hereditary enemy of Austria and so continue to have need of the Prussian army, the dagger perpetually poised above Austria's heart. This was his first disastrous miscalculation. The second was his belief that a bankrupt State cannot make war. War cost money – at least 5,000,000 talers a year. Where could Austria or Russia find such a sum? It was impossible for either to increase taxation at home, or raise an internal loan. There remained England. They might be able to borrow the money in London. Until then, Frederick felt certain there could be no war. So he stood, alone but unapprehensive, criticised but uncompromising, surrounded by a boundless mistrust.

Mistrust would have turned to panic if his neighbours could have read his first *Political Testament* which he wrote in 1752. But it was not published in its entirety until 1920 after the Hohenzollerns had ceased to be Kings of Prussia. In a chapter headed '*Rêveries Politiques*' which had been read by Bismarck in 1880 and marked 'to be kept permanently secret,' Frederick described how Polish Prussia, i.e. West Prussia, and Saxony could be annexed by his successors. West Prussia, he wrote, must be consumed 'like an artichoke, leaf by leaf,' each portion being the reward for Prussian non-intervention in Polish affairs during the period of chaos which would inevitably follow the death of an elected Polish King. This, with luck, would be a bloodless process. Saxony could only be acquired by capturing Bohemia from the Austrians and then returning it at the peace in exchange for Saxony. But that would only be possible if Russia and Austria were at war with Turkey and France, and this would hardly come about unless Bestuschev were out of the way and an ambitious statesman were at the helm in France. Moreover, the neutrality of England must be assured; in other words, George II must have died and the country be weakened by political faction during the minority of his son, Frederick Prince of Wales. Even then, it would still be advisable for the King of Prussia to wait and not reveal his intentions until the belligerents were exhausted. Frederick had called this a political dream, thinking that one day it might come true. But it never did, for soon France and Austria were to become allies.

Immediately after the Peace of Aix-la-Chapelle, the Austrian Foreign Minister Kaunitz had written a 252-page memorandum recommending a reversal of the traditional policy of hostility to France. For 250 years Habsburg and Bourbon had fought one another, and who had profited? Not they, but the small States: Sweden from the Thirty Years War and Brandenburg from the War of the Austrian Succession. While lion and tiger were mauling one another the jackal had made off with the prey. Now, Austria wanted to regain Silesia and France sought territory in the Low Countries. As enemies they had small chance of succeeding, but if they united each could attain her object without harm to the other. In return for French help, Austria might even, if necessary, sacrifice the Austrian Netherlands.

This memorandum made a deep impression on the Aulic Council, which resolved 'cautiously, step by step,' to pursue the policy it recommended. Kaunitz was sent to Paris to propagate the new doctrine. He preached it solidly for a year but to no avail. To French eyes, behind a strong Austria loomed Germany united under Austrian leadership, and no Frenchman would risk conjuring that spectre. So Kaunitz wrote a new memorandum: the loss of Silesia would have to be accepted. Austria must forget the past in an attempt to woo Frederick away from France. Maria Theresa said no. If she could not recover Silesia, then it would be up to her son when he succeeded her. Another year passed; Kaunitz was recalled from Paris, Maria Theresa still dreamt of

Silesia and the prospect of recovering the province still seemed as remote as ever. Then events occurring thousands of miles away on the other side of the Atlantic set the stone rolling that was to start an avalanche.

In the 1750s France had begun to link her North American possessions of Canada and Louisiana by advancing along the valleys of the Ohio and Mississippi. The English were slow to realise that if France succeeded their colonies would be confined for ever to the eastern seaboard, and it was not until 1754 that a military expedition was sent out to arrest the French advance. But meanwhile the unofficial war at sea was bringing in rich prizes and 300 French merchantmen with a freight worth 30,000,000 francs and 6,000 French sailors were captured by the English. Soon, as 'the surest way to get something out of that *Schweinehund*,' Frederick was urging the French to invade his uncle George's Hanover. The French asked why Frederick did not despoil his uncle himself. In his *History of the Seven Years War*, Frederick tells us that he was indignant and replied that such a proposal would be better addressed to the notorious highway robber Mandrin. His real answer, however, was to demand tangible benefits in return for obliging the French, until, weary of haggling, they dropped the Hanover project.

Meanwhile England was taking steps to ensure the safety of the Electorate by suggesting to the Russians that, in the event of a continental war between England and France, they should provide 80,000 troops for the defence of Hanover in return for an English subsidy. The Empress Elizabeth saw at once that, as the troops could not fly, they would have to pass through Prussia to reach Hanover and that would mean war with Frederick – a war after her own heart, for which, moreover, she was going to be paid! She agreed with alacrity, asking and being granted a mere £500,000 annually if her troops were called upon to fight, otherwise £100,000 a year to keep them in trim. In addition, to clinch the bargain, Bestuschev got £10,000 down and £2,500 a year, the other ministers correspondingly less, and Elizabeth herself £50,000, while her heir, Catherine, had to be satisfied with £25,000.

When the Austrian ministers heard of this they felt sick with envy. All that money for services which the Russians would have been delighted to perform for nothing! 'It is beyond compute,' groaned Kaunitz, 'of how many facts an English diplomat can be totally ignorant.' But there was some advantage in this for Austria, for now she could start to discuss joint action with

Russia against Frederick. Soon the Saxon Minister in St Petersburg was reporting to his Government:

It has been decided to attack the King of Prussia without further discussion not only if that monarch attacks an ally of this Court, but also if one of those same allies attacks him.

A month later this letter together with details of the Anglo-Russian Treaty were being read by the King of Prussia. The ring seemed to be closing.

But England was not aiming to squeeze Prussia out of existence and did not envisage Frederick as the potential invader of Hanover, but France. France was England's enemy overseas and France would be her enemy in Europe, if it came to a continental war. In that case, Frederick would be a valuable ally. How could he be gained? By allowing him to believe that the Anglo-Russian treaty was aimed against him, then he would come running to his uncle. Thus the treaty was used by the English, not to crush enemies, but to gain another friend. In December 1755, Newcastle's Secretary of State, Fox, sent for the Prussian Minister in London and asked him whether, in view of the treaty, Prussia would not prefer to guarantee Hanover herself. Then England and Prussia could agree to exclude all foreign troops, including Russian, from Germany. The King of Prussia, said Fox, was in a commanding position, holding a sword in one hand and an olive branch in the other. Let him but speak the word and all outstanding differences between the two countries could be settled. . . . And though, by this description, Frederick already had his hands full, England was prepared to slip something further into his palm as compensation for Prussian ships sunk in the late war.

Frederick hesitated. If he rejected this overture, sooner or later he would probably have to face a coalition of England, Russia and Austria, with as sole ally the ineffective and unreliable French. But if he accepted it, it was at least possible that he would be rid of the Russian threat, and so of the Austrian threat also, for Maria Theresa would never risk attacking him alone. On the other hand, his treaty with France still had three months to run and it obliged him not to oppose but to support a French attack on Hanover. However, the French had missed their chance in the previous summer, and if they attacked Hanover now they would start a general war. All things considered, they ought to be grateful, thought Frederick, if he came to an arrangement which neutralised the threat of 120,000 Austrians and Russians combined. So he decided to accept the English offer, and on 16th

January, 1756, the fateful Convention of Westminster was signed whereby the Kings of Prussia and England agreed to oppose with their combined forces the entry of foreign troops into Germany.

Frederick now believed that the danger of an Anglo-Russo-Austrian coalition had been removed. But in signing the convention he had underestimated the Russian and French reactions. When the British Minister in St Petersburg suavely explained that the convention merely reinforced the Anglo-Russian Treaty in that both were designed to preserve the peace of Europe, Bestuschev was, as ever, open to financial persuasion. Not so the Empress. The purpose of the treaty, she declared, had been to place the forcible restraint on Prussian ambition. If the English did not accept that interpretation then the treaty could lapse, and to prove that she meant it she declined for a while to accept the first £100,000 instalment of the subsidy. In all Russian history nothing like this had ever happened before, and when Frederick heard of it he realised that he had miscalculated. He had failed to take the imponderables into account; in this case, the hatred which his ruthless campaigns and reckless insults had aroused in the Empress Elizabeth.

And what had Paris to say to the Convention of Westminster? Assuming Franco-Austrian enmity to be a law of Nature, Frederick had not worried. The French might feel hurt, but he had been convinced they would remain his friends. Moreover his minister in Paris had told him that Madame de Pompadour was in control of foreign affairs, and as her influence depended on services to King Louis which could not easily be rendered on a battlefield, she was on principle opposed to war. So, when the French offered to renew the Franco-Prussian Treaty, Frederick was in no hurry to reply. French troops would, admittedly, be more useful to him than English ships, but he felt he could continue to rely on the friendship of France even without a formal alliance. To the Duc de Nivernais, who came to Berlin to offer him the West Indian island of Tobago in return for a renewal, Frederick replied angrily that France could find someone else to act as Governor of Barataria – Barataria being the island ruled by Sancho Panza in *Don Quixote*. Then the King showed him the terms of the Convention of Westminster; the Duke pointed out that the Franco-Prussian Treaty had not yet expired. But it only had three months to run, retorted Frederick, and altercations over a mere three months were better confined to posthumous children. He said he had been afraid of the Russians

147

and had taken steps to protect both himself and France against them. In any case, he assumed that France herself did not want to occupy Hanover. Then, saying that he could easily find a pretext to terminate the Convention of Westminster, Frederick opened a map of the English coast and pointed out the best places to effect a landing. Finally, he assured the Duke that if France started to make serious trouble he would conclude a formal alliance with England.

But neither excuses, threats, witticisms, nor even logic could diminish the consternation and resentment of the French Government. If it had come as less of a surprise, they might in time have accepted the Convention of Westminster as a sensible arrangement. But Frederick had deserted France three times; a fourth was once too often. Moreover, talks had in the meantime been resumed between Paris and Vienna.

In Vienna, the conflict between France and England had revived hopes of coming to terms with the age-old enemy so that Austria could be free to deal with Prussia, for 'Prussia', declared Kaunitz, 'must be crushed if the Imperial House is to stand' – and Maria Theresa would have added: 'if Silesia is to be recovered.' But to achieve these aims, French help, not merely French neutrality, was needed, and in the summer of 1755 a concrete though somewhat cynical proposal had been sent to Paris. In return for French financial assistance, Maria Theresa was prepared to cede the Austrian Netherlands to France and use her influence to ensure the election of the Prince de Conti as King of Poland. This offer was made direct to Louis XV's mistress and procuress, the butcher's daughter Madame de Pompadour.

The Pompadour, *née* Poisson, was favourably disposed in that she, like the Empress Elizabeth and Maria Theresa, had been the victim of Frederick's malice. Careless of who might hear and report him, the King of Prussia had called them 'the three sovereign strumpets of Europe,' a description which only Maria Theresa could ignore as inept. Moreover, the Pompadour had not forgotten Frederick's curt 'don't know her' when at her request – 'if the King of Prussia will pardon me such a liberty' – Voltaire had conveyed a friendly message of esteem on his last visit to Berlin. Louis XV's preference for private pleasure before public duty had also not escaped comment in Potsdam, and he, like his mistress, had good reason for personal animosity against Frederick. But it was not Frederick's insults which mattered to France so much as the injuries his army might inflict, and if the

French financed an Austrian effort to regain Silesia it seemed all too probable that they would be investing in a fiasco. So the French Government reminded Maria Theresa that they were bound to him by treaty and declared themselves ready for discussions only on the basis of Frederick retaining Silesia. Then came the Convention of Westminster. The French abandoned faith in Prussia and turned to Austria as the means of preserving peace in Europe. 'Westminster,' wrote Kaunitz later, 'was the decisive event in the salvation of Austria.'

Meanwhile – as popular history books assure us – Kaunitz had persuaded Maria Theresa to write to the Pompadour, addressing her as *ma chère cousine*. This incident provoked the English historian Macaulay to thunderous indignation:

> Though the haughtiest of princesses, though the most austere of matrons, she [Maria Theresa] forgot in her thirst for revenge both the dignity of her race and the purity of her character, and condescended to flatter the low-born and low-minded concubine who, having acquired influence by prostituting herself, retained it by prostituting others. Maria Theresa actually wrote with her own hand a note, full of expressions of esteem and friendship, to her dear cousin, the daughter of the butcher Poisson, the wife of the publican D'Etioles, the kidnapper of young girls for the harem of an old rake, a strange cousin for the descendant of so many Emperors of the West!

When he wrote this, Macaulay was no doubt relying on Carlyle, who had said: 'there exist in writing, at this very hour, various flattering little notes . . . '; and Carlyle, as he told his readers, was relying on Preuss, the nineteenth-century editor of Frederick's works, and Preuss had the story from one Hormayr – nevertheless, to this day, no one has ever set eyes on a single word written by Maria Theresa to the Pompadour. All she sent was a writing case with her portrait.

On 1st May, 1756, France and Austria signed the defensive Treaty of Versailles promising to go to each other's assistance with 24,000 men in the event of either being attacked. The Pompadour claimed the credit for this alliance. The French then went further, inquiring of the Austrians what their attitude would be if France attacked Hanover. Maria Theresa professed high indignation. 'It is past comprehension how the unblushing suggestion could be made that His Imperial Majesty should, as Supreme Head of the Reich, permit the free passage of French troops through Germany for the purpose of attacking Hanover.' Realising what lay behind the outburst, the French then unblushingly proposed discussions to partition Prussia. On Maria

Theresa's instructions, Kaunitz at once agreed.

In April, Kaunitz had informed Russia of his promising negotiation with the French. The Empress Elizabeth replied warmly approving, but insisting that, with or without the French, the attack on Prussia must be launched that year (1756). A draft agreement to this end followed, providing for the inclusion of Sweden and Saxony in the onslaught. 'This is most cheering,' answered Kaunitz, ' – beyond all our hopes.' But first he insisted on reaching agreement with France that French help would be forthcoming for an offensive as well as for a defensive war. As for operations in 1756:

'At best,' wrote Kaunitz, 'it will probably be several months before our present negotiations are concluded and by then it will be too late to mobilise the army, set it in motion and co-ordinate operations. Consequently these must be postponed until next spring. Meanwhile, all will depend on keeping the game well concealed and taking energetic steps to allay the suspicions already aroused in England and Prussia; in other words, we must keep our project a secret until it has actually started.'

Kaunitz believed in thorough preparation. When the time came, he intended to make a *casus belli* out of some internal German affair, so as to bring in the small German States. His first move in this direction was to lodge a protest in Berlin over Prussian recruiting in Mecklenburg – and lodged it was, in the Berlin State Archives until 1876, in which year the letter was first opened, Frederick having preferred to remain ignorant of its contents. Meanwhile, Kaunitz preached restraint: 'As Russia is not going about her preparations in the most cautious manner, it may easily happen that Prussia will not wait much longer, but will decide to forestall us by attacking suddenly with her whole strength.' The Russians then promised to wait until 1757.

And what did Frederick learn of all this? At first, very little. He had no representative in St Petersburg. His minister in Vienna lacked initiative and intelligence. As for the twenty-six-year-old Knyphausen, Count of the Holy Roman Empire and Frederick's minister in Paris, the King wrote in one of his letters: 'I have never received from any of my ministers abroad so ill founded and frivolous a letter as yours. It teems with palpably false assertions and ridiculous bombast of the kind indulged in by young men without knowledge or experience.'

Frederick was also misled by his English allies, who concealed from him the deterioration which had taken place in their relations with Russia. Consequently, when news of Russian troop concentrations reached Berlin. Frederick at first thought they were in fulfilment of obligations incurred under the Anglo-Russian Treaty and that in the event of a conflict with Austria he would have them fighting on his side. Then, from a spy in Dresden, Frederick received the text of a letter from the Saxon Minister in Vienna to his Government. He reported that Austria, Russia and France were planning a combined onslaught on Prussia. Other sources confirmed this. Frederick's brother-in-law, the Austrian field-marshal, Prince Louis of Brunswick, told him that the Austrian intention was to attack him as soon as possible. Hungarian cavalry regiments were reported to have been mobilised and about to leave for Bohemia. Another source gave the numbers of troops to be employed: 80,000 Austrians and 150,000 Russians; and the time of the attack: spring 1757.

What should the King do? Should he try to get his blow in first? 'Better *praevenire* than *praeveniri*,' he wrote in mock Latin: 'Better forestall than be forestalled.' In June 1756 he started to mobilise. Afraid that Frederick intended to attack Austria, the British Government tried to suggest that Maria Theresa's noisy preparations for war were intended to provoke him to aggression. 'What!' replied the King angrily to the British Minister, Mitchell. 'What, sir, do you see in my face? Do you think my nose was made to receive fillips? By God, I shall not allow it.' Mitchell retorted that the King had no need to give Europe proof of his character. Mitchell had never heard patience or submissiveness mentioned as being among his many great qualities. Frederick laughed, then, pointing to a portrait of Maria Theresa, said seriously: 'This lady wants war – very well, she shall have it.'

But before committing himself irrevocably, Frederick asked Maria Theresa bluntly whether her warlike preparations were aimed at Prussia. In July she replied, reading a statement prepared by Kaunitz to the effect that they were purely a precaution and not aimed at anyone. This evasive statement, wrote Kaunitz to the Saxon Minister, was intended to keep the King of Prussia guessing so that he would either consume his strength in piling up armaments or force the issue before he was ready. About this time, the French Minister in Berlin told the King categorically that if he attacked Austria France would fight on her side.

Assuring his private secretary Eichel that he would not break the peace so long as there remained a gleam of hope, the King sent fresh instructions to his minister in Vienna. The latter was to indicate clearly what Frederick already knew of Russian plans to attack him and was then to seek an assurance from Maria Theresa that she would make no hostile move against Prussia either in 1756 or 1757. 'We must know,' Frederick wrote, 'whether we are at war or at peace. I leave it to her to decide. If her intentions are honourable, now is the moment to declare them; but if I am given an indefinite or non-committal answer in oracular style, then the Empress will have to accept responsibility for the consequences.'

When Frederick's minister, Klinggräffen, conveyed this request, Kaunitz sought to gain time by asking it to be put in writing. Simpleton that he was, Klinggräffen then referrred the matter to Berlin before complying, thus wasting ten valuable days and obliging Frederick to postpone the order to march.

In Vienna, where preparations for war were not yet complete, two of the five members of the Aulic Council were in favour of giving the assurance for which Frederick asked. But Maria Theresa had every intention of fighting Prussia, at any rate in 1757, and so, as Kaunitz suggested, it only remained to formulate an answer that would give France no pretext to stay out of the war on the grounds that Austrian lack of diplomacy had started it. The formula was duly agreed, and in August Klinggräffen was informed that the Empress had been so angered by the form and content of the Prussian request that she declined to give any reply, beyond declaring that no offensive alliance existed between Austria and Russia. Technically this was correct, as the treaty of alliance was not signed until January 1757; at the same time, the assurance that Austria did not intend to attack Prussia was not forthcoming.

The French were somewhat indignant over this form of reply. For one thing, they had not been consulted before it was delivered, and they would, in fact, have preferred Austria to give the assurance sought, thereby at least postponing the outbreak of hostilities and giving Austria time to complete her dispositions and arrange for the defence of threatened Saxony. But the French conceded that they themselves were ready – they had the men and they had the money.

In a letter to the Austrian Minister in St Petersburg, Kaunitz explained that 'in the circumstances a certain mental reservation was inevitable in the reply we gave to the King of Prussia' – in other words, it had been necessary to conceal Austria's aggressive intentions – because it was essential either to make Frederick appear the aggressor so as to be absolutely certain of the French help envisaged in the defensive Treaty of Versailles, or, assuming Frederick did not attack in 1756, to enable Austria to have her hands free in the measures to be concerted with France and Russia. 'It is nothing less than the truth,' continued Kaunitz, 'that no offensive treaty has yet been arranged between the two Imperial Courts.' Kaunitz concluded that he hoped Austria would be ready for joint action with France and Russia in 1757.

Meanwhile, Maria Theresa was telling the Saxon Minister that she had given the required assurance to Prussia. Curiously enough, when Frederick heard of this he did not jump to the obvious conclusion, that Maria Theresa had told a lie, but believed that Kaunitz must have suppressed part of her original statement. Nevertheless, on 29th August, 1756, four days after receiving the official Austrian reply, he entered Saxony with his troops. On 2nd September Klinggräffen was instructed to convey a third and last message to Maria Theresa: if she would give the requested guarantee not to attack Prussia in the current or the following year, the King of Prussia would withdraw his troops from Saxony. At the same time, Frederick sent a present of 100,000 talers to Bestuschev. But the Empress Elizabeth had made up her mind and it was too late. 'If I had known about this two months ago,' said the Chancellor ruefully, 'a lot could have been done. . . .' Maria Theresa replied on 7th September: Saxony had been invaded and she had nothing more to say. Had Frederick sincerely expected that these abrupt and belated questions would persuade his opponents to keep the peace? The answer must be 'no', or he would have asked them earlier.

．　　．　　．　　．　　．　　．

Let us return to the questions indicated at the beginning of this chapter. Firstly, did Frederick start the war because he feared an attack and wished to forestall it or because he wanted to conquer Saxony and West Prussia? Secondly, would there have been a war if Frederick had not opened hostilities? And thirdly, how was it that Frederick found himself involved in a war with half Europe? There are clear answers to all three questions.

Frederick's critics maintain that he concluded the Convention of Westminster in order to be able to attack Saxony. But he considered the conquest of Saxony possible only under four conditions: Austria and Russia must be at war with Turkey and France; an ambitious statesman must be at the helm in France; Bestuschev must be out of the way; George II must have died.

None of these conditions had been fulfilled in August 1756. On the contrary, Austria, Russia and France were Frederick's declared opponents and all had their hands free. Yes, say his critics, but Frederick did not expect to fight France. Yet the Treaty of Versailles had been in existence three months and the French had expressly told him that if he attacked Austria they would go to her aid. No doubt he hoped that aid would be confined to the 24,000 men provided for by treaty, but no one but a 'complete fool' – and Frederick, those same critics assure us, was never that – could believe in 1756 that France would not enter the struggle. The combined population of France, Austria and European Russia were at least 80,000,000 while that of Prussia was 4,000,000. No dream of conquest could have persuaded Frederick to fight against such odds, but only the conviction that war was inevitable and that he must anticipate the onslaught of the formidable coalition arrayed against him. 'Frederick's sword was much shorter,' wrote Carlyle, 'but he unsheathed it at thrice the speed.' And in speed lay his only hope of survival.

There can be no doubt, then, that in opening hostilities, Frederick's main object was not aggrandisement but self-defence. His action was based on the belief that he was about to be attacked. Was that belief justified? No tripartite offensive pact existed between France, Austria and Russia. But the quoted documents show that both Russia and Austria were determined to make war, the former at all costs, the latter preferably with French assistance. This would be forthcoming under the Treaty of Versailles if Austria were attacked and, in any event, if the French were given unopposed passage through Germany to attack Hanover, and this Maria Theresa was now prepared to grant. In the spring of 1757, therefore, Prussia would have been at war with Russia and Austria and probably also with France even if Frederick had not forestalled his opponents in 1756.

But how was it that he found himself obliged to fight so overwhelming a coalition at all? Frederick's situation after the Second Silesian War was similar in many respects to Bismarck's after the Franco-Prussian War. Both stood at the head of States whose rapid rise to power had earned them the enmity and suspicion of their neighbours. Both had to reckon with the implacable hostility of a proud State whom they had recently humiliated. Bismarck fully realised the danger of his position and wrote in a secret letter to the Kaiser that the founding of the German Reich was the utmost which the European Powers would accept without a war, that Germany must now consider herself fully satisfied and

154

that not the smallest step in the direction of further aggrandisement must be taken. Even the unfounded suspicions of neighbouring States must be tactfully treated. Bismarck was careful to ensure that Germany always had some formal understanding with two of the three Continental Great Powers, namely with Austria-Hungary and Russia, and that, in the event of war, he could count on British neutrality. He sought defensive pacts wherever he could find them, with Italy, Spain, Rumania and Serbia. His great aim was to preserve the peace by preventing the formation of a hostile coalition round the hard core of France.

No so Frederick! Indifferent to his neighbours' susceptibilities, addicted to the most insulting remarks at the expense of foreign rulers and delighted to think his words would be reported by their spies, he had no more conspicuous talent than that of making enemies. Ill informed on all countries but his own, and self-sufficient as a hedgehog, he heard little and cared little about foreign reactions to his words and deeds. Whereas Bismarck kept a first-class body of diplomats in foreign capitals and made it his business to cultivate those accredited to Berlin, Frederick was content to be represented abroad by yes-men who, if they heard them, took good care not to report unpalatable truths. And if they had, they would have made no impression, for the King saw the world as he wished it to be and not as it was. He knew that, as long as he retained Silesia, Austria would be his enemy. In view of their colonial rivalry, he knew that he could only win France or Britain, but not both. So for him, as for Bismarck, the friendship of Russia was all-important. Bismarck never ceased to strive for good relations. Frederick could have possessed them throughout the forty-six years of his reign instead of merely during the first and last decades if he had taken the trouble to cultivate the Empress Elizabeth and her Chancellor Bestuschev with gold and flattery, and if he had supported her in her Polish plans. Instead of which, viewing reality through the distorting mirror of his temperament, Frederick believed he could gain Russia by signing a pact with England. In the Convention of Westminster he believed he had won English friendship and Russian neutrality without alienating France. He was wrong on all three counts. A firm alliance with England came only later, and for different reasons, while the convention was to become a contributory cause of a war with Russia and France.

Thus Frederick's desperate situation in the autumn of 1756 sprang not from isolated errors on his part, but from the whole structure of his mind and character. At the very moment when he was marching into Saxony he wrote to his Adjutant-General, Winterfeld, that he believed the French and Russians would, after all, not come to Austria's assistance.

*

CHAPTER SIXTEEN

The Invasion of Saxony

RIDING AT THE HEAD of his troops, Frederick crossed the frontier into Saxony in the early afternoon of Saturday, 28th August, 1756 – 'neutral Saxony', some historians have said, on the grounds that the Court of Dresden had signed no formal treaty with either Frederick or his enemies. But in a letter to the Russian Chancellor, the Saxon Minister of State, Count Brühl, had declared: '. . . Nothing can be of greater service to the common cause than to determine in advance effective means of destroying the inordinate power of Prussia and the undoubted ambition of that State. But it must not be taken amiss if, in view of her neighbour's superiority, Saxony proceeds with the utmost caution.' This was in reply to Bestuschev's assurance that neither Russia nor Austria wished to expose the wealth of Saxony to Prussian attack and that there was no need for her troops to join the fray until the Prussians were beginning to weaken.

This assurance must have been welcome to Count Brühl, for his personal interests were far removed from the rough and tumble of the battlefield. Though he had been appointed General of Infantry at his own request this was solely a political move designed to impose his authority on his King's military advisers. Brühl's private ambitions lay in the sartorial field. He possessed 200 pairs of shoes, 802 embroidered nightshirts, 500 suits, 102 watches, 843 snuff boxes, 87 rings, 67 smelling-bottles, 1,500 wigs, and 29 carriages. The choice of dress which faced this unfortunate man each morning was thus a formidable one; to ease his task, he had an album prepared containing coloured reproductions of his entire wardrobe. After the basic ensemble had been selected, it was at least possible for him to get up. Then the accessories –

rings, snuffboxes, etcetera – could be chosen at leisure. Nor was his collecting mania confined to inanimate objects. At bedtime he had again to act with promptitude and decision, declaring his preference among an *embarras de maîtresses*. He lacked nothing, in fact, except intelligence. For the last ten years he had been supplying the Courts of Europe with cautionary tales of the King of Prussia's misdeeds, some true, some imaginary, but all in due course reaching the King's ears through his paid informers in the Dresden Chancellory.

As his army marched unopposed through Saxony, Frederick's opinion of Brühl proved accurate: 'Fifteen hundred wigs, but no head!' Taken completely by surprise, Brühl's only action was to withdraw hurriedly with his Sovereign to inaccessible country near Dresden, where, at a place called Pirna, the Saxon army was then slowly assembled. Nightshirts, smelling-salts, even the incriminating State archives were left behind in the capital, where the last were soon seized by a resolute Prussian general despite the Queen's efforts to hide some of the documents in her bed.

With the Prussians rapidly approaching, King Augustus of Saxony decided to withdraw with his army into Bohemia. He had got into his carriage and was ready to start when news came of enemy patrols on the road ahead. Before he would move Augustus required his generals to clear the route for him and also to guarantee the safety of his person. No 'stray bullet' must be allowed to touch him. Could they promise that? They could not. Very well, then, the King would stay with his army in Pirna. . . . The position was a naturally strong one and the troops would have been comfortable if anyone had remembered to feed them. Though Frederick himself said later that the Saxons starved 'with good grace' and despite the daily wagon-load of food which he allowed through his lines for the besieged Augustus, the 'dunghill', as the fastidious Brühl called Pirna, eventually proved untenable and Augustus then offered to observe the strict neutrality which Frederick had demanded of him on first crossing the frontier. But to their amazement the Saxon emissaries discovered that this was no longer enough. The monster Frederick now demanded nothing less than a military alliance against Austria and the incorporation of the Saxon troops in his army. 'But such terms are unheard of in all history!' exclaimed Augustus's plenipotentiary. 'I try to be original,' was Frederick's reply.

Augustus was indignant: 'How can I take up arms against a Queen who has never given me grounds to do so? My will is to take no part in this war. . . . The probity which I have preserved into my sixtieth year permits of only one reply to Your Majesty: you have arbitrarily seized my lands. Europe shall be the judge of my case and of the hostile plan you have falsely accused me of harbouring against you, plans which no Court in Europe believes ever existed.' This sounded dignified and was generally held to be true, and, soon after, when Augustus's Queen, Maria Josefa, died while under Prussian guard, Frederick's reputation reached the nadir and the whole of Europe echoed with indignation at the inhuman behaviour of the Prussian Scourge.

On 1st October, 1756, Frederick defeated an Austrian army coming to relieve the Saxons. The battle was fought round the mountain village of Lobositz, half in mist and half under a burning sun. As a result, the Saxons were forced to capitulate and accept whatever terms they were offered. Augustus's army consisting of about 18,000 men, most of whom had been born in Saxony, was compelled to swear allegiance to Frederick, and in their existing formations, but under Prussian officers, the troops were absorbed into his army. The Saxon officers were offered Prussian commissions. Few accepted. Two-thirds of the men deserted on the march to garrisons in Prussia, in some cases disappearing as an entire unit after shooting their officers. . . . The rest escaped later, many going to Austria to join the 12,000-strong Saxon army being re-formed there under the Saxon officers whom Maria Theresa had readily absolved from their enforced oath not to fight against Prussia.

Through Holland as intermediary, Frederick then offered peace to all the world, renouncing claim to any part of Saxon or Austrian soil. But his enemies were not in the mood for peace; in the coming year they intended to destroy him.

CHAPTER SEVENTEEN

*

The Purple Testament

FREDERICK SPENT THE WINTER of 1756 in Dresden, sitting for hours in the picture gallery, hearing an occasional sermon in the Evangelical church, listening to good music in the Catholic church and to Hasse's oratorios. Evening concerts were held in which he played the flute. He lodged in the Brühl palace, saw the Count's 304 pairs of breeches and said: '*C'est assez de culottes; montrez-moi des vertus!*' In January he paid a flying visit to Berlin and saw his mother. It was for the last time. She found him well and cheerful. The day before he returned to Dresden he wrote a secret letter of instructions to the Minister for Home Affairs, his boyhood friend Count Finckenstein:

> In the critical state of our affairs, I ought to give you my orders so that you may have authority to take the necessary decisions in case of necessity. If I should be killed, affairs must be carried on without the slightest change and without it becoming apparent that they are in other hands. Should I be taken prisoner by the enemy, I forbid the smallest consideration for my person or the least notice to be taken of anything I may write from captivity. If such a misfortune occurs I wish to sacrifice myself for the State and allegiance must be paid to my brother, who, together with all my ministers and generals, shall answer to me with his head that neither province nor ransom shall be offered for me and that the war shall be prosecuted and advantages exploited exactly as though I had never existed in the world.

At the same time he wrote to Wilhelmina:

> It is shameful at my age to be knocking about with four furious females. But I have got to defend my skin and persuade these ladies to lay down the sword and return to their spinning-wheels. As for me, dear sister, fear nothing from this war. Only the worthy get killed; my type always survives.

160

Two of these 'females', Maria Theresa and the Empress Elizabeth, had agreed in that same month of January 1757 to put 80,000 Austrians and the same number of Russians in the field and to wage war until Prussia capitulated. Russia was to obtain Polish Courland and Poland be compensated with East Prussia. Magdeburg was promised to Saxony. Infected by the general cupidity, Maria Theresa had wanted this province for her second son, but while her courier was still on his way to St Petersburg she had suddenly repented of her 'land-lust' and sent a second courier with instructions to cancel the demand.

By the second Treaty of Versailles in May, the third 'female', the France of Madame de Pompadour, promised to contribute not 24,000 but 115,000 troops to the common cause. The fourth 'fury' was Frederick's own sister Ulrike, now sharing the throne of Sweden and, in common with most crowned heads of Europe, at daggers drawn with her brother. Recently, however, she had been involved in a plot against the ruling Swedish nobility, the plot had been discovered, heads had rolled and it was not her influence, which stood at zero, which now persuaded Sweden to declare war on Prussia, but the tempting bait of Prussian Pomerania and a contribution to the war chest, though in accordance with long-standing tradition this was promptly converted into wassail for the nobles, with the result that – war or no war – the Swedish army insisted on food before fighting.

And what allies had Frederick? At first none, for British support was uncertain. Hanover pleaded in Vienna for her neutrality, and it was only the Austrians' folly in demanding free passage for French troops through the Electorate that finally brought about an alliance between Britain, Hanover and Prussia which Brunswick and Hesse-Kassel soon joined. Frederick suggested the Duke of Cumberland as commander of the western army, hoping that if a son of George II were appointed Parliament would vote larger supplies. In this he was disappointed, for it was an accepted dogma in Britain that British soldiers should not fight for Hanover; moreover Cumberland was the sworn enemy of Pitt, the great friend of Prussia, and in April 1757 Pitt was dismissed from office by his King. Cumberland was to prove more than averagely incompetent as a military commander, but fortunately Pitt soon returned to the helm of State with the splendid words: 'I know that I can save this country and that no one else can.'

Frederick wanted to await the enemy in Saxony, but his two best generals, Field-Marshal Schwerin and General Winterfeld, objected. Winterfeld, whose functions were a cross between those of a chief of staff and an adjutant-general, had enjoyed the King's favour for fifteen years. A cultural Philistine, he was nevertheless a fearless man of action with much natural good sense and a straightforward, upright character. Frederick called him a man after his own heart. He and Schwerin suggested that their two armies should enter Bohemia. Frederick agreed, ordering them to converge from different directions on Prague. Incorrigibly optimistic, he also told Field-Marshal Lehwald, holding 30,000 troops against a Russian attack in East Prussia, to conclude peace in the event of victory in Bohemia on the condition that Polish West Prussia was ceded to the King.

Early in March, Prince Charles, the Austrian commander-in-chief, set out to join his troops in the field. The journey was shorter than he expected, for by now they had been forced back upon Prague. Completely unnerved by the speed of the Prussian advance, the Prince's deputy, Browne, tearfully handed over the command, asking permission to lead 4,000 men to a heroes' death. This was sternly refused.

Charles's brother, the German Emperor Francis, was an experienced soldier, and before allowing him to leave Vienna had given the young Prince a pocketful of excellent advice. Owing to the forced marches imposed on them, Frederick's troops, said Francis, always reached the battlefield near to exhaustion. Therefore the longer the battle could be kept going the better. Secondly, Frederick's tactics were always the same – he flung everything he had against one flank. As soon as he had committed himself irrevocably, Charles was to encircle him on the opposite flank. This sounded easy, but Charles was to find it difficult. Soon after he reached his army at Prague, Frederick attacked.

On 6th May, 1757, the two Prussian armies came in sight of the Austrians. With nearly 65,000 men the Prussians almost equalled their opponents. But the latter were holding an extremely strong position, a horseshoe ridge with soft ground at the foot and flanks protected by rocks and chasms. The King, with Schwerin and Winterfeld, saw at once that the Austrian centre and left were unapproachable. Frederick examined the right flank, found it possible and attacked. But his troops were tired after an all-night march (Schwerin had wanted to give them a twenty-four-hour rest), and the reconnaissance had been too perfunctory. Some flat green meadows which Frederick had chosen for the line of advance turned out to be a stretch of stagnant water. The troops got stuck in the mud. Winterfeld, in the van of Schwerin's infantry, splashed through with his men and swept forward, only to meet a murderous fire from enemy batteries on the ridge. Almost immediately he fell from his horse, severely wounded. Schwerin's own regiment (army commanders led their own regiments into battle) turned to flee. The seventy-two-year-old warrior jumped from his horse, seized the colours and ran forward, crying: 'Come on, lads!' After a few paces he dropped dead, struck by five pieces of grape-shot. Watching all this, Frederick saw the attack come to a standstill, and suddenly his nerves gave way and he was overcome with nausea.

But what Schwerin's heroism failed to achieve was done by the folly of Prince Charles. As he poured reinforcements into his right flank a gap began to open near the centre of his line. General Mannstein saw it first, then the King. In a flash, Frederick threw in his reserve and the Prussian foot, superlative as always in speed and accuracy of manoeuvre, went scrambling up to seize and widen the hole. A few minutes of confused fighting and they were through and spreading out, while the entire Austrian front wavered, crumbled and finally disintegrated into groups of men, Prince Charles among the first, with only one thought – to reach the safety of Prague citadel.

The victory – if such it could be called – was remembered as the bloody battle of Prague. Prussian losses were almost as high as the Austrian: 13,000 killed and wounded. The death of Field-Marshal Schwerin was perhaps an even greater calamity. The impetuous Frederick could ill afford to lose his stalwart good sense. But Frederick's first reaction after the battle was one of triumph. 'The Austrians have as good as lost the whole campaign,' he wrote to his mother.

Meanwhile, the terror of Frederick's name was being carried far into enemy territory by a small body of men led by an Austrian-born soldier of fortune named Meyer. Attracted by the King's military fame, this man had volunteered to enter his service and been given command of a Free Corps of 1,300 foot and 200 hussars, all, like himself, volunteers for death or glory. The stocky, resourceful Meyer proved a dynamic leader. Sent by Frederick to blow up an Austrian magazine at Pilsen as the main armies were entering Bohemia, he had succeeded without losing a man and then pushed on westwards 'with his swift, wild fellows,' scattering any troops he encountered, exacting tribute, holding whole towns to ransom, and living off the country as he went. Reaching Nürnberg, 100 miles inside enemy territory, he laid siege to the city, and though unable to take it with the five small cannon he had brought with him, so impressed the city fathers that they offered to pay him 80,000 guilders and, disregarding their duty as liegemen of the Emperor, refuse to contribute a contingent of troops to the Reich army if Meyer would leave them in peace. Thereafter the bright-eyed buccaneer descended on Fürth, levied more tribute, billeted his men in the town, got each of them a new suit of clothes and then took up his quarters in the nearby manor house, where his courtesy and restraint soon endeared him to the noble owners. On the evening of 2nd June they gave a ball for his entertainment. Meyer unpacked his spare uniform; the whole neighbourhood turned up in gala dress, and the desperado, his little black eyes shining with glee, danced until long after midnight. Next morning he was off again, heading northwards with his men to rejoin the main army. Evading an enemy force of 6,000 men and twenty-four cannon as they were about to attack him, he passed through Coburg, revictualled, purloined some necessary supplies, and in early July brought his men safely back to the Prussian lines. Before the war ended, Frederick had eighteen of these marauding columns in operation.

But Meyer's success weighed little against the heavy task which now confronted the King. Part of his army would have to remain before Prague to contain the swollen Austrian garrison while the remainder faced Field-Marshal Daun, now advancing to relieve the city with a fresh army of 54,000 men. Beyond him a French force was said to be slowly approaching. Frederick could spare only 34,000 troops to fight Daun – even less if the garrison of Prague had bestirred themselves and, as Napoleon later considered was their duty, made continual sorties to tie down the maximum number of Prussians. But though Prince Charles was content to sit in Prague and watch the price of horsemeat soar, his mere presence there was embarrassment enough.

Daun was a cautious soldier and in no hurry to come to grips with the Prussians. Frederick, on the other hand, was eager for the fight. His record so far was: seven battles, seven victories. An eighth was surely within reach. Once it was achieved, France and Russia might abandon the coalition. So, on the afternoon of 18th June, 1757, 34,000 Prussians hurled themselves against 54,000 Austrians. As usual, the King attacked a flank. And the attack succeeded, although, contrary to Frederick's orders, his commanders on the opposite flank allowed a separate battle to develop with the result that he had to commit all his reserves. Still, two hours after the start, all was going well. The Prussian infantry were fighting furiously, though with heavy loss. Their will to conquer seemed irresistible, and towards four o'clock, in the fifth hour of battle, when his troops were no longer dominating the heights, Daun gave the order to retreat. Swampy ground crossed by a stream lay to his rear. If his men were to get away, now was the time to go, while daylight lasted and discipline could still be preserved. Daun took out a notebook, tore out a page and wrote in pencil: 'The retreat is to Suchdol.' This was a small town to southward. Taking the paper, his aide-de-camp galloped off to inform the Austrian generals.

The decisive moment of the whole Seven Years War was approaching. One by one, in the smoke and tumult, the aide sought and found the Austrian generals, and soon, on the right wing, the artillery was out of battery and on its way rearwards. Elsewhere troops were starting to disengage. One general had still to be found, a Saxon commander of cavalry holding his squadrons in reserve on the right flank. The aide came up with his troopers, saw a Lieutenant-Colonel von Benkendorff, gave him Daun's order. Benkendorff took the piece of paper and promised to deliver it. The aide rode off. Having found his General, Benkendorff showed him the order. They decided to ignore it. With two squadrons, soon followed by the rest of the cavalry, they wheeled and charged the exhausted Prussian infantry. The Austrian foot took heart. They, too, ran forward, bayonets at the charge. Soon, the whole mass was surging on as the Prussians gave ground. 'Rascals, would you live for ever?' roared Frederick at a retreating regiment. 'At thirteen pfennig, that's enough for today,' answered an old soldier.

But Frederick would not give in. Ordering the drums to roll, he collected forty men and marched into the cannons' mouth. But his grenadiers had indeed had enough, and he marched alone. Still he went on, till his adjutant called to him: 'Sire, do you mean to take the battery single-handed?' Only then did Frederick turn, mount his horse and, with tears in his eyes, ride from the stricken field. This was the Battle of Kolin, a disastrous defeat which cost Frederick 12,000 out of 18,000 foot soldiers, threw him back into Saxony and destroyed all hope of dealing a death-blow to Austria before she and her allies were ready for battle – all this because two Austrian officers had decided to disobey orders.

After thirty-six hours in the saddle, Frederick was with his main army again before Prague. He sent for his younger brother, Prince Henry, and after loading himself with reproaches and expressing the wish to die, told him he intended to withdraw from Prague. Henry even advised him to hand back Silesia to Maria Theresa. 'Phaethon,' he wrote joyfully to his sister Wilhelmina, 'has fallen and we do not know what is to become of us. . . . Phaethon took good care of his person and withdrew before the loss of the battle was fully decided.' But Kolin held one blessing for Frederick. From then on, Field-Marshal Daun enjoyed Maria Theresa's unwavering confidence. In the following year he became commander-in-chief of all her forces and remained so until the end of the war. He made no small contribution to Frederick's survival.

Meanwhile, Frederick had suffered another blow. On 2nd July, when encamped north of Prague and waiting for the survivors of Kolin to reach him, he received news of his mother's death. She alone had shown him tenderness as a child, only she had dared to stand between him and his vengeful father. Far from home, surrounded by enemies and facing, perhaps, the complete annihilation of his army, he felt he had lost one of the few links that still bound him to the normal world. For two days, prostrated with grief, he saw nobody.

But the King had little time in which to indulge private feelings, for the enemy in overwhelming numbers was now beginning to close in: 100,000 Austrians, 90,000 Russians, 100,000 French, 30,000 troops in the newly created Reich army and 20,000 Swedes – in all 340,000 soldiers. Against them Frederick could muster slightly over 60,000 men in Bohemia and 30,000 under Lehwald in East Prussia. Not one man could be spared to oppose the Swedes. Opposite the French stood the Duke of Cumberland with 36,000 men. 'Things are beginning to look vile,' wrote Frederick to Winterfeld. Long screeds full of rhetorical indignation were despatched to Wilhelmina:

> I am trapped like a traveller surrounded by robbers and threatened with death. It is abominable and a blot on civilised humanity. What three great princes have ever before combined to destroy a fourth who has done nothing to harm them? If three citizens dared to despoil their neighbour in ordinary life, they would be broken on the wheel. *O tempora! O mores!* Truly it would be better to live among tigers, leopards and lynxes than with the murderers and robbers that rule this poor world in a century called civilised.

But despite these heroics, Frederick saw his danger clearly: 'Fifteen minutes' bad luck could put Europe at the mercy of the Habsburg tyranny.'

In July Frederick started to withdraw his forces from Bohemia in two sections. The larger he led back himself to the frontier of Saxony. The smaller, about 18,000 men lying to northward, was to withdraw more slowly under his eldest brother, Augustus William, keeping an eye out for enemy movements towards the Silesian frontier as they went and covering the town of Zittau, which contained Frederick's forward magazine, until the Prussian garrison had withdrawn into Silesia. With 80,000 Austrians in the vicinity the task obviously required a first-class soldier. Frederick made matters worse by attaching several generals to his brother, including Winterfeld, as advisers, with the result that no major decision could be taken without a council of war. At these, Winterfeld's opinions counted for less than they were worth because the other generals were jealous.

The Prince set out westwards on 3rd July, 1757. By the 14th the Austrian Generalissimo had caught up with him and was attacking his supply train. Without waiting for orders, 3,000 Prussians rallied to defend it, at the same time sending an appeal to the Prince for reinforcements as they were facing annihilation. Though time was short, the Prince summoned a council of war at which pros and cons were lengthily discussed. Winterfeld did not attend. Finally, it was decided to abandon the three thousand to their fate and press on to Zittau, otherwise it might be too late to save the magazine. So a sixth of the entire force was left behind, and with it every wheeled vehicle the army possessed. Eight days later, Augustus William came within sight of Zittau to find the enemy had got there before him. The Austrians promptly set fire to the town. Within a few hours the heat drove out the Prussian garrison. The men scattered. Their colonel was taken prisoner. After twelve hours as an impotent spectator, the Prince was moving west again with not one crumb of bread to offer his 15,000 men – he had been relying on Zittau for supplies. On 24th July, more dead than alive, he reached safety at Bautzen, forty miles east of Dresden. Five days later, after a faultless retreat, Frederick arrived. Ignoring his brother's greeting, he summoned Winterfeld to his side and then sent a written message to Augustus William: he and his other generals deserved to be court-martialled and sentenced to death. Later, Frederick wrote his brother a letter:

Never again as long as I live will I trust you to command ten men. You can commit as many follies as you please when I am gone, but this is the last while I am alive. May your best officers make good the confusion you have wrought. . . .

'My health has been weakened by these fatigues,' replied the Prince, 'still more by these afflictions. . . .' He protested his good intentions, his loyalty, but Frederick was inexorable and Augustus William too weak to stand up for himself. Certainly, he had made grave mistakes, but so had Frederick in his time, and his heartless reproaches sprang from self-distrust as well as dissatisfaction with his brother. But Augustus William felt an indelible shame. He begged leave to return to Dresden, and was told he could go when he pleased. Frederick never relented, and within a year his brother was dead.

But once again there was no time to brood over the past. Danger was now threatening from a new quarter – the west. Two French armies totalling 100,000 men were advancing, one in the north under the Duc de Richelieu and the other under Prince Soubise in the south. Frederick thought this a good moment to ask for English help – English troops for Hanover and English warships to prevent a Russian landing in the Baltic. Neither was forthcoming, the troops because of the sacrosanct principle that no British blood should flow for Hanover, and the ships because they might disturb British trade with Russia. But at Hastenbeck on 26th July, 1757, Hanoverian troops were able to beat Richelieu's army without British help, though it took the Duke of Cumberland to turn victory into defeat. A sudden burst of firing on his left where his own troops were counter-attacking the French made him order a general retreat, in the belief that his army was about to be outflanked. Thanks to his feeble spirit the day was lost and the situation in the west became critical. Soon it was desperate.

Frederick was still joking, 'I began the war as a general and shall end it as a partisan,' when the plump and pusillanimous Duke performed his master-stroke. Having withdrawn his army to the tidal waters of the Elbe, followed without enthusiasm by the Duc de Richelieu, Cumberland and his opponent became tired of their war and appealed to Denmark to mediate between them. Whereupon Count Lynar, a pietist and somewhat of a religious crank, drew up a document and persuaded them to sign it. It was called the Convention of Kloster-Zeven and provided that the Dukes and their men should return whence they had come and perpetual peace should reign between them. Cumberland went home. The Duc de Richelieu stayed. The British and French Governments refused to ratify the convention and meanwhile French troops were occupying Hanover, Hesse and Brunswick and were threatening Magdeburg. There was nothing between them and the western frontier of Prussia. Still, Count Lynar had done his best; the convention had been a bright idea. How had he managed to think of it? 'The idea,' he said, 'was inspired by the Holy Ghost.'

The convention was signed on 9th September. On 30th August, the Russians had defeated the Prussian army east of Königsberg and occupied East Prussia. Fearful atrocities against the civil population followed, accompanied by honeyed manifestos calling on the Germans to start a new and happier life in Russia.

More blows were to follow. Detaching all he could spare from his main army, a mere 20,000 men, Frederick was preparing to meet the southern French army under Soubise while his brother-in-law, the Duke of Bevern, with Winterfeld to advise him, remained in Silesia with the bulk of the Prussian forces. Winterfeld was killed in a minor skirmish. The Duke was obliged to evacuate most of Silesia. A few weeks later a Croat leader emerged from Saxony with 3,000 men and made a dash for Berlin, found poor defences and practically no garrison, extracted 180,000 talers from the inhabitants and withdrew twenty-four hours later as Prussian troops were reported to be advancing against him. The Swedes, too, had entered the fray and were walking through defenceless Pomerania. After a year of war the greater part of Prussia lay open to invasion. The end seemed to be near. Comparing himself to Job, Frederick scattered verses and letters to Wilhelmina and indeed anyone who would lend an ear to his lamentations. He talked of suicide and of how he was 'as tired as a dog.' But this meant nothing, this was merely the by-product of stress in one whom approaching disaster did not paralyse, but keyed to the highest pitch of mental and physical activity. His voice might be breaking and sodden with pathos, but his nerves were taut. 'I shall bless Heaven,' he told Wilhelmina, 'if it grant me the favour to die sword in hand.'

At this moment of high tragedy came a farcical interlude. The supreme deliberative body of the Holy Roman Empire, the Reich Diet, decided to put the King of Prussia under the Imperial Ban, in other words, to pass sentence of outlawry against him. A summons, a *Citatio Fiscalis*, was drawn up calling on Frederick to show reason why the Ban should not be imposed, and was entrusted to the Reich Notary, Doctor Josephus Aprill, who was to deliver it to the Prussian Minister in Regensburg, Freiherr von Plotho. But Aprill, as his subsequent statement revealed, was unable to 'insinuate the Citatio into the Minister,' in plain

169

language, to deliver it, for, after His Excellency had glanced
at the document:

> . . . His face began to colour, and then to colour a little more and he
> then fell into such violent anger that he was unable to contain himself,
> but with visage aflame held both arms aloft and with trembling hands
> made to rush at me, the while still holding in his right hand the Citatio
> together with Apponendo, and burst out upon me with these words:
> 'What, jackanapes, would you insinuate?' Thereto gave I answer:
> 'This is my notarial duty, the while I am obliged to fulfil.' None the
> less, he, the aforesaid Freiherr von Plotho, then fell upon me with
> great fury and, seizing me by the front of my cloak, declared: 'I say
> thou shalt take it back!' I having declined to do so, he now thrust and
> pushed with all his force the aforesaid Citatio together with Appon-
> endo between my coat and waistcoat and, still holding me by the
> cloak, propelled me from the room, calling to the two servants who
> had witnessed the scene: 'Throw him down the stairs!' The which
> persons however, being themselves amazed by this injunction and not
> knowing what they should do, without laying a hand on my person,
> conducted me downstairs and required me to quit the house.

The Citatio was then put on file and the Reich outlaw allowed
to go his ways. Meanwhile, a Reich army of 36,000 men was
mobilising, and this had to be taken more seriously. It comprised
contingents from several hundred areas and institutions. In one
Swabian company, for instance, the town of Gmünd supplied the
captain; another town the lieutenant; the Abbess of Rotmünster
the second lieutenant and the Abbot of Gengenbach the ensign.
The troops were mostly vagrants dressed in rags. Literally dozens
of organisations were responsible for the commissariat; in other
words, no one. As one official remarked, the Reich army ought to
be on show as a curiosity, it was worth paying to see it. An
antique warrior, Prince Hildburghausen, had been unearthed
to command this force, which, together with the southern French
army under Soubise, comprised 60,000 men. Before long they
were to meet Frederick at Rossbach.

Meanwhile, Job was lamenting to his sister:

> How can a Prince survive his State, the glory of his Country, his
> own Reputation? If I had followed my inclinations I would have put
> an end to my life after the battle of Kolin. But I felt this would have
> been a weakness and that it was my duty to repair the damage. . . . But
> no sooner had I hastened hither to face new enemies than Winterfeld
> was defeated and killed near Görlitz, the French entered the heart of
> my States and the Swedes blockaded Stettin. Now there is nothing
> effective left that I can do; there are too many enemies. If I managed to

defeat two armies, the third would crush me. . . . My death will mark
the beginning of Austria's tyranny. But what matter: I shall not be
burdened with all the misery that will come upon the world, and,
though too late, people will gratefully realise that I fought to the last
against the subjugation of my Fatherland and only succumbed
through the faint-heartedness of those who sided with the tyrants
instead of with one who was fighting to defend them.

The whole letter, which was written on 17th September, 1757,
contained nearly 2,000 words and was the longest Frederick ever
penned to his sister. As regards his intention to commit suicide,
Wilhelmina replied: 'Your lot shall be mine; I do not intend to
survive your misfortunes or those of your House.' A touching
pact. . . . But before carrying out his part, Frederick set himself
a literary task. He would condense the entire letter into rhyming
verse. The finished product contained 250 lines, was dedicated to
D'Argens and began:

> The die is cast, 'tis o'er with me, my friend;
> Exhausted unto death I near my end.

Frederick promised Wilhelmina a copy if he could find time to
make one. Meanwhile the opus was despatched to Voltaire for
comments and correction. Amalia, his youngest sister, also received 300 verses from him on the subject of Chance, his brother
Henry a poem of the same length on Death. Before sending it,
Frederick had his reader recite it aloud, but the pathos was lacking
and half-way through the King took the paper and read it himself
until he could no longer see for tears. At night sometimes he
could be heard pacing to and fro, declaiming lines from Racine's
tragedy of *Mithridate*:

> *Enfin, après un an, tu me revois, Arbate,*
> *Non plus, comme autrefois, cet heureux Mithridate*
> *Que de Rome tojours balançant le destin*
> *Tenais entre elle et moi l'univers incertain.*
> *Je suis vaincu. Pompée a saisi l'avantage . . .* '

'I should like to get drunk to drown my sorrows,' Frederick
exclaimed to his reader, 'but as I cannot drink, nothing distracts
me so well as hammering away at verses. While I am doing that
I can forget my misfortunes.'

But so long as he could sink himself in some activity, even
versifying, he was not ripe for suicide. Why, then, the solemn
threats? In part, no doubt, because he could rid himself of his
griefs by writing about them. But there was another reason. Every
letter the King wrote at this time to his sister was accompanied

171

by another, in cipher. The first would be full of gloom, the second, short and factual, telling her of his plans and encouraging her not to give way to despair. For Frederick had come to the conclusion that Prussia was doomed unless he could persuade France to make peace and, if possible, become his ally. In great secrecy he made a cautious approach to the French Government through four intermediaries, of whom Voltaire was one and Wilhelmina, via her Court Chamberlain, another. Frederick hoped for a favourable response, less because he had helped France to retain Alsace than by making her ministers realise that only Prussia stood between them and a Europe dominated by Austria. And without Frederick, Prussia would collapse; she would in any case if France continued to support her enemies. Hence the talk of suicide in his letters, a theme which Wilhelmina made sure reached the ears of the French, and Frederick's own abundantly clear words: 'I make bold to prophesy that they will not find it easy to make good my loss.'

But if France were prepared to discuss peace, the King realised their terms would be harsh. 'I foresee,' he wrote, 'that even the best conditions we can expect from these people will be cruel and humiliating, but no efforts are being spared here to convince me that the welfare of the State demands it and I am bound to go so far.' If need be, he was prepared, even, to offer Madame de Pompadour half a million francs and life ownership of the principality of Neuchâtel in Switzerland, which at that time belonged to Prussia.

Both Wilhelmina and Voltaire passed on Frederick's proposals, the latter deriving malicious enjoyment from the predicament of the King, who, as he claimed, had maltreated him, and doubly so because he felt sure the *rapprochment* with France would not take place. As for suicide: 'It cost me little trouble to argue him into staying alive.' Voltaire wrote to Frederick that the French Government might take up his proposals more keenly if he was prepared to cede a province; alternatively, even if his enemies overwhelmed him, there was no need to despair. A Roman death would be unnecessary. He himself would never lack resources and in Paris society he would still find some admirers. In short: why worry? To which, on 9th October, 1757, the King made his famous reply:

> Believe me, if I were Voltaire
> I could mad Fortune's antics bear.
> A private man, my needs were small
> And I would mock Her follies all.

172

If then she smiled and now she frowned
At night I still would sleep as sound.
But all men must accept their fate,
Must suit their actions to their state.
Then let Voltaire secluded be
And live secure, in honesty,
As a philosopher and sage.
But I must face the tempest's rage,
And more, with shipwreck threatened, I
As King must think and live and die.

'*Penser, vivre et mourir en roi* . . .' So ended Frederick's literary interlude. Now once more he faced the storm. For two days the men of the Reich army had eaten no food; now, at the beginning of November, they were obliged to go forward and give battle or else retire, for the area they occupied had been stripped bare by the French. On 5th November, 1757, they were joined by the French at Rossbach and Hildburghausen persuaded Soubise to attack. Their combined armies amounted to 43,000 men. Frederick had only 22,000. But while the enemy infantry were forming up for a flank attack, Frederick burst upon them with his cavalry and they were routed. The thirty-six-year-old Major-General von Seydlitz smashed the French horse. In ninety minutes all was over. The Reich army was in flight and did not stop till it reached the River Main; the French till they were in the Harz. It was '*une bataille de douceur*', said Frederick later. Soubise wrote: 'Our dispositions were, I think, very good. But the King of Prussia left us no time to exploit them. We must now save the honour of the nation, if we can, by laying the blame for this calamity on the army of the Reich.' Voltaire was disgruntled. 'I guarantee,' he wrote to a friend, 'that instead of elegies, he [Frederick] will now be writing epigrams. This is no good time for Frenchmen abroad. People laugh in our faces as though we were the adjutants of Soubise.'

True enough, Frederick was writing epigrams, but what a subject!

'There's no finer prospect in the world
Than the fat backsides of heroes. . . .'

Even in those parts of Germany whose soldiers had fought against Frederick, such as Bavaria, Franconia and Württemberg, the people looked on Rossbach as their own victory. For months the French armies had been eating and pillaging their way across western Germany while the polyglot vagabonds of the Reich had been terrorising the Germans they were supposed to defend. Now the locusts had gone, scattered in a matter of minutes by a small body of Germans led by a German king. For the first time in centuries, wrote Goethe, 'Germans felt the joyful spur of proven strength and capability and the proud consciousness of political power.' As the Reich army retreated, the adjutant of the Hesse contingent wrote: 'With the utmost respect I would advise the Holy Roman Empire not to risk another scuffle with furious Fritz for quite some time to come; he has given us powerful proof that he understands the business of war very much better than we do.'

In his essay, *Frederick the Great*, Macaulay wrote that after Rossbach the King's fame became a rallying-point for all true Germans:

> Then first it was manifest that the Germans were truly a nation. . . . Yet even the enthusiasm of Germany hardly equalled the enthusiasm of England. The birthday of our ally was celebrated with as much enthusiasm as that of our own sovereign; and at night the streets of London were in a blaze with illuminations. Portraits of the Hero of Rossbach, with his cocked hat and long pigtail, were in every house.

But while Frederick's victory over the French provoked widespread rejoicing, he himself took care not to humiliate them. He ordered captured French troops to be treated with consideration and assured their officers that he could not get used to the thought of fighting their country.

Meanwhile, owing to supply difficulties and the fact that the Empress Elizabeth was ill, some of the sting had been taken from the Russian menace in East Prussia. Large bribes to the Chancellor Bestuschev helped for a while to remove it altogether. But in late November Prince Charles had entered Silesia with vastly superior forces, defeated and taken prisoner Frederick's brother-in-law the Duke of Bevern near Breslau, captured the city without firing a shot and then occupied almost the whole of the province.

Before the month was out Frederick was approaching by forced marches with 12,000 men, meeting 20,000 survivors of Bevern's defeated army on the way and taking them under his command. There were 60,000 Austrians waiting for him, but he was resolved to attack them. Few beside himself believed he could beat them. Many of his officers were convinced, despite Rossbach, that their country's fate was sealed. All were in a desperate mood. Rumours began to circulate: Bevern was said to have gone over to the enemy, old Dessau's son Moriz to have asked to be relieved of his command. And where was the heir to the throne? Biding his time, said some, certain that before long he would be King. And as the survivors of Breslau talked to Frederick's troops they became increasingly demoralised. Knowing this, the King put Bevern's generals under arrest, but treated their men like conquering heroes, increased their rations, gave them plenty of wine and showered promotions. At night sometimes – and it was now the end of November – he would join them as they sat round the camp-fire, sleep for a few hours by the dying embers and then make room so that another man could get warm. If they get the chance, troops are interested to study the commander who holds their lives in his hand, and these men were no exception. They liked what they saw.

On 3rd December news came that the Austrians were holding strong positions about thirty miles away. They were reported to be full of confidence, joking about Frederick's small army and calling it 'the Potsdam Guard Company.' That night he summoned his officers and spoke to them briefly, in French. His exact words were recorded by a subaltern named Retzoe.

'Gentlemen,' said the King. 'I have sent for you to thank you for the faithful service you have rendered to me and to our country in the past, a service which I acknowledge from the depth of my heart. There is hardly one of you here who has not distinguished himself by some outstanding action. It is on your courage and experience that I have based my plan for the battle which shall and must be fought tomorrow. I am going to break all the rules of war and attack an enemy who is twice our strength and well established upon high ground. I must do it, for if I don't all will be lost. That enemy must be beaten, or we perish to the last man before his batteries. That is how I see it, and that is how I shall act. But if any one of you thinks differently, let him come forward here and now and demand his discharge – and I shall grant it without the smallest reproach.'

Frederick paused, then continued with a broad smile:

'I knew it! I thought none of you would desert me! From now on I shall have complete confidence in your loyal help and in certain victory. If I am left on the field and not able to reward you for what you are going to do tomorrow, our country will see to that. Now go down to the lines and tell your regiments what I have said here. And tell them I shall keep a close eye on each of them. Any cavalry regiment failing to charge the enemy at full gallop when it is ordered shall be unhorsed immediately after the battle and made into a garrison regiment. The infantry battalion that even begins to slow up no matter what it encounters shall lose colours and sabres and I shall have the badges cut from their uniforms. And now, fare you well, gentlemen. By this time tomorrow we shall have beaten the enemy, or we do not meet again.'

By four o'clock next morning the King had his army of 32,000 men on the march towards the Austrians installed, over 60,000 strong, on a line of hills ten miles due west of Breslau between the villages of Leuthen and Lissa. By early afternoon, they had reached the small town of Neumarkt, where the Austrian field bakery was working protected by a force of 1,000 Croats. Sending two regiments of cavalry to occupy a hill on the far side, Frederick burst into the town, scattered the Croats, taking 500 prisoners, and seized the bakery with 10,000 loaves hot from the ovens. Before dawn next day – Monday, 5th December, 1757 – the Prussians were moving steadily forward again along the main highway from Neumarkt to Breslau. Meanwhile the Austrians were reported to have left their positions and be advancing to meet them. Confident in his superior numbers and fresh from his victory over the Duke of Bevern, Prince Charles had overridden the advice of Field-Marshal Daun and decided to destroy the Prussians in open battle. It was splendid news – for Frederick.

He had gone about five miles from Breslau when a triple line of cavalry suddenly appeared through the greying mist standing athwart the road. Without waiting to identify, the King fell upon them, front and flank, with his own cavalry, sent them galloping eastwards, leaving 540 men and horses to be examined at leisure by their captors. They were Saxon dragoons, the outposts of the Austrian army.

Forward again, through a small village. The van halted on the far side while the main body closed up, and Frederick with his staff officers went on to survey the countryside from a hill-top. Below them they saw the main highway to Breslau running east across a rolling plain dotted with hamlets and clumps of fir trees with marshy ground lying between low hills running from north to south. About two miles away, extended on one of these lines of hills, stood the Austrian army. Their right wing leaned on broken ground with peat bogs and was clearly impossible to attack. The left stretched beyond the village of Leuthen, about three miles to the south-east. It looked approachable. Frederick decided to attack it. For three hours he stayed on the hill-top surveying the enemy dispositions while the Prussian army was forming up in rear. Here at last conditions seemed perfect for attempting his favourite form of attack. Instead of moving his forces *en masse* southwards, parallel to the enemy's front, so revealing his intention to attack the left flank, he would approach at right-angles with the troops staggered in echelon, like a staircase rising to a ceiling. Then at the last moment, each man would turn half right, the units would close up and go into the attack. It was a manoeuvre only the Prussians, with their rigid discipline and rigorous training, could perform. Its value lay in confusing the enemy, particularly on this occasion, when for some of the time the movement would be hidden from their view.

Prince Charles was well aware that Frederick never made a frontal attack and he was carefully watching his flanks. Soon he caught sight of troops moving southwards in small groups and erratic formation. 'The good folk are smuggling themselves out,' he remarked to Daun. 'In God's name let us leave them to it.' Then an orderly came galloping up from General Lucchesi on the right wing. He had seen cavalry, what looked like the van of the Prussian army, moving cautiously towards him. He must have reinforcements. He was about to be attacked, he was certain. At first Prince Charles did nothing. Then a second and more desperate message arrived, and with the whole reserve of horse and further troops from the Austrian left wing Daun himself was sent to succour Lucchesi on the right – a good five miles from the real danger-point.

Frederick's moment had come. The time was one o'clock. The Austrian general Nadasti had chosen the positions on the left flank with skill. The right, he had heard, was already engaged. But he was vigilant, and when, preceded by a deluge of fire, the Prussian cavalry followed by infantry struck slantwise, he counter-attacked at once, sent Ziethen's horse reeling and turned a battery of fourteen heavy pieces on the assailants. But Frederick had his reserves well forward and flung them in; Ziethen charged again; the battery was taken; Austrian infantry coming to the rescue were caught among their own troops flooding back, and fighting like madmen the Prussian infantry were hacking their way steadily forward. 'That's honour enough, lads! Get back into reserve!' yelled the young Dessau. 'F – the reserve!' came the answer. 'Let's have more cartridges. More cartridges, quick!' Frederick was in the thick of it, but keeping a cool head.

With one hour of daylight remaining, the Austrians were in full retreat on their left flank, but in the centre resistance round Leuthen village was still fierce and Frederick had committed his last infantry reserves. They fought their way through a grave-yard, and beyond that the going was easier. But they were near to exhaustion, and as the battle moved forward their left flank was becoming vulnerable. Frederick saw this, and so did Lucchesi on the Austrian right. Judging that his moment had now come, he left his positions with a swarm of cavalry and came thundering

177

down on the grenadiers. He might have won the day if, waiting close by in a hollow with strict orders from Frederick not to commit himself until Lucchesi moved, Driesen had not been waiting with a body of Prussian horse. He let the Austrians go galloping past, then, with bullet and sabre, stormed into their rear. Lucchesi was killed, his horsemen scattered. Now Driesen wheeled and charged into the enemy foot struggling back from Leuthen, took them in flank and rear, and as the sun was setting sent the last Austrian reeling eastwards towards Breslau.

After dark Frederick put himself at the head of two grenadier battalions and set off with flickering lanterns to pursue the defeated enemy. Following the main road eastwards he came to the village of Lissa and a milling throng of demoralised Austrians. Leaving his grenadiers to take care of them, he went alone to the manor house standing back from the street. '*Bon soir, messieurs!* Is there any room left?' He saw a supper table, gaping enemy officers. 'I don't suppose you were expecting to see me here?' They could easily have taken him prisoner, but were paralysed by his self-assurance. The King smiled and they diffidently introduced themselves. He told them they could keep their rooms; his own officers would find billets elsewhere. Then, from the far end of the street came the sound of musketry – Frederick's grenadiers speeding the rabble on their way. The noise was heard farther back in the Prussian encampment and soon strong forces arrived in Lissa in case help was needed. When the troops saw that the King was safe and all quiet, they bivouacked in the fields surrounding the village, while 'Old Fritz', as they called him, slept in one of the houses on a bundle of straw.

It was a famous victory: 30,000 Austrians captured, killed or wounded, but only 6,000 Prussians. This battle alone, said Napoleon, was enough to make Frederick immortal and place him among the world's greatest generals.

CHAPTER EIGHTEEN

*

A Box of Pills

WITH THE VICTORIES of Rossbach and Leuthen Frederick's fame
soared skywards to its apogee. He had fought for the freedom of
humanity, wrote Mitchell to London, and from now on England
gave her victorious ally powerful support.

But 8,000,000 Prussians still faced 100,000,000 enemies;
Frederick's position was still critical and his one desire was to
make peace: a good peace with territorial compensation –
Saxony, for instance, or West Prussia – for the war which had
been forced upon him. To this end he sent a rambling letter to
Maria Theresa:

> If it had not been for the battle of 18th June (Kolin), where luck was
> against me, I would perhaps have had an opportunity of paying my
> respects to you in person; perhaps, contrary to my nature, your
> beauty and generosity might have conquered the victor, but we
> might also have found means to settle our differences. Your Majesty
> had indeed had some advantage in Silesia, but it has not been of long
> duration, and I am still horrified that so much blood was shed in
> this latest battle. I have made use of my victory and occupied Breslau,
> thus I shall be in a position to enter Bohemia and Moravia. Reflect
> on this, Cousin, and learn to know those you trust. You will see that
> you are plunging your country to destruction, that you yourself are
> the cause of all this bloodshed and that you cannot overcome the man
> who, if you had been willing to make him your friend as he was
> already your close relation, could in your company have made the
> whole of Europe tremble.... If your allies stand by you as they should,
> I foresee that I shall be ruined. But my justification will be that I
> did not contribute to the aggrandisement of the House of Bourbon
> and that I had to defend myself against two Empresses and three
> Queens.

179

Though this unsavoury letter can hardly have improved Maria Theresa's opinion of Frederick, her resources were by now severely strained and she told the French Minister in Vienna that she was prepared to renounce Silesia for the sake of peace. The French Foreign Minister, the Abbé Bernis, could only applaud: he himself considered the war lost and he wrote to Vienna that King Louis must think of saving his crown. France had no general to match Frederick. Peace, if possible a sensible peace preserving the *status quo*, was essential. But if Frederick would not leave Saxony – and there were no means of taking it from him – that should not be an obstacle to a general cease-fire. This attitude was not shared, however, by the Empress Elizabeth. No sooner was her health patched up than she had the Russian commander-in-chief court-martialled for inefficiency, banished her Chancellor Bestuschev to Siberia and reoccupied East Prussia, forcing the population to take an oath of allegiance. Her energy reunited the allies. Maria Theresa put conciliation behind her and bravely declared she would fight to the last man and the last village. France, still under the Pompadour's influence, was ready to risk one more campaign. Kaunitz breathed fire and slaughter. Rossbach and Leuthen might never have been.

It was lucky for Frederick that at this moment William Pitt, a statesman of the highest rank, came to power in Britain. The colonial war against France was galvanised by his furious energy. By land and sea throughout the world troops and ships began to move according to precise instructions pouring from the Spartan study of the gout-ridden genius. His own head was his encyclopaedia; every fact he needed was stored there, down to the seasonal variations in the width of the St Lawrence River. No detail was too small for his attention: hygiene in troopships, beer for regiments serving in India, the construction, down to the last plank and the last nail, of whaling boats. Inefficient officers were sacked, recalcitrant M.P.s bribed, the whole civil and military hierarchy compelled to furious action by fear of his blistering tongue, till even the Turkish doorkeeper at the British Embassy in Constantinople sensed that a new spirit was at work in the world. In the House of Commons no one could resist this man who, with right arm in a sling and joints swathed in flannel, dragged himself on crutches to the chamber and then rose to speak, gradually taking fire from his theme, until suddenly he would wrench free his fist to point in massive accusation at the waverers, the faint-hearted, all those who could not see, as he did, that England's hour had come to build the greatest empire in the world. Impossible? When an admiral complained that the task set him was too difficult, Pitt glanced at his crutches and said: 'Sir, I walk on impossibilities.'

Pitt was determined to crush France so that she would never rise again. To defeat her in America was, therefore, not enough; French power would also have to be broken in Europe. In this task the King of Prussia was his natural ally. Pitt had offered him a subsidy after the Battle of Kolin, but Frederick had declined for fear of prejudicing the peaceful arrangement he was then hoping to make with France. Now, after Leuthen, those hopes had been abandoned and he was greatly in need of money. So, in April 1758, he agreed to accept an annual subsidy of £675,000 which would enable him to put another 50,000 troops in the field and in return agreed to loan a general to command an Anglo-German army being formed to fight the French in the West. He sent his brother-in-law, Prince Ferdinand of Brunswick, a soldier as far above the average as the Duke of Cumberland had been below it. In the spring of 1758 Ferdinand was to defeat a much larger French force and drive it from the Elbe to the Rhine.

Meanwhile, in December 1757, Frederick had written a pleading letter from Breslau to his hypochondriac friend, d'Argens:

> My divine Marquis, When things are quieter could you not bring yourself to spend the winter with me in Silesia? It would be a deed of charity. I have no company. We will banish all draughts and wrap you in cotton wool. Bring Madame d'Argens if you like. I look forward to your answer as a prisoner awaits sentence or acquittal.

The Marquis duly arrived, escorted by a body of light horse sent specially to fetch him from Berlin, after a journey divided, on Frederick's instructions, into a number of short stages so as to lessen the strain. The winter was spent in pleasures, but also in stern business: several generals were sentenced to fortress detention for failure to oppose the Austrians vigorously enough before the Battle of Leuthen. Officials who had sworn, though under compulsion, an oath of allegiance to Maria Theresa were fined or deprived of office. Frederick's one-time favourite, Schaffgotsch, having fled to Austria, the Prince-Bishopric of Breslau was declared in abeyance. Silesian Protestants were exempted from the obligation to pay baptismal and other parish fees where the incumbent was a Catholic. This and Frederick's confirmation of a death sentence passed on a Jesuit for alleged confessional condonement of military desertion earned him the bitter enmity of Silesian Catholics.

Early in 1758 Frederick realised it was destined to be another year of battles. 'If everyone looked at things as philosophically as you and I,' he wrote to d'Argens, 'we would have had peace long ago. But we are dealing with people cursed by God, for they are consumed with ambition. Therefore I wish them all to the Devil.' He wrote in similar terms to Wilhelmina: 'Those ruffian Emperors, Empresses and Queens are going to make me dance the tight-rope again this year. I console myself with the hope of fetching one or other of them a good swipe with the balancing bar; but, that done, I shall truly have to think of peace. What sacrifice of human lives! What fearful slaughter! The world in its blindness calls these bloody deeds heroic, but seen close to they are always ghastly.'

But before he could enter the field Frederick needed money. Up till 1757 he had estimated his annual military requirements at 4,000,000 talers. But that year had cost him 20,000,000 and now he had only 1,500,000 left in ready money. As taxation could be screwed no higher he decided to raise 7,000,000 talers from Saxony and Mecklenburg and a further 1,000,000 from Silesia, mostly from the Catholic Church. All this added to the English subsidy made nearly 15,000,000 or the equivalent of 140,000 men.

As the Russians would hardly be ready before the summer and Frederick's army was superior to the Austrians in numbers and equipment he resolved to beat them first. But the plan failed. Having advanced unopposed as far as Olmütz in Moravia, he failed to capture the fortress and failed to bring Daun, the new Austrian commander-in-chief, to battle. Meanwhile, Loudon, the most skilful of the Austrian generals, was creating havoc with Frederick's lines of communication, and in June 1758 he was forced to abandon the siege of Olmütz and withdraw, cursing his engineers for having failed to blow up the fortress for him, to Silesia. Loudon was a Lithuanian. As a young captain of cavalry he had applied to join the Prussian army, but Frederick took an immediate dislike to his arrogant hatchet-face and turned him down – a decision he was destined to regret.

While on the retreat from Olmütz Frederick received news of the death, at the age of thirty-six, of his brother Augustus William. His military disgrace in the previous year had struck the heir to the throne a mortal blow. Of no more than average intelligence and less than average fortitude, he had refused medical assistance during his last illness and seemed almost glad to die. Frederick wrote his younger brother Henry an involved letter which began:

182

'I have received some very sad and serious news from Berlin. It is the death of my brother, for which I was completely unprepared. It touches me the more in that I always loved him dearly and always ascribed the trouble he caused me to his weakness in following bad advice and to his choleric temperament which he was not entirely able to control.' Frederick advised Henry to accept the blow philosophically; the latter replied shortly that his grief and the respect he owed the King made it impossible for him to go into such matters and, in any case, he could see no virtue in parading an assumed indifference.

In August 1758 the Russians had appeared at Frankfurt-on-Oder, and in a series of forced marches, 'excessive in length and speed' as Daun professionally noted, Frederick hurried with 14,000 men to the aid of his small eastern army. He arrived as the Russians were about to attack the weak Prussian forces at Zorndorf near Küstrin. Having manoeuvred so that he could drive the Russians into the River Oder, Frederick spent the evening before the battle at a mill on the Mützel, one of the tributaries of the Oder. It was Thursday, 24th August, 1758. The Prussian vanguard had crossed the Mützel during the afternoon, followed by the rest of the army after dark. All night long, guns and troops could be heard rumbling and trampling over the wooden bridge near the mill. What were Frederick's thoughts? How was he occupied? His *Lecteur*, a young Swiss named de Catt, can tell us. Attracted by his tact, modesty and good sense, Frederick used him during these war years as a kind of sounding-board for his opinions, an audience for his recitations and a critic and editor of his verses. Whenever he had the time, in the afternoons or evenings, he would summon him for a chat and de Catt kept a record of their conversations. 'When you look at it in later years,' the King told him, 'you will say: this is what that garrulous old warrior told me who was always bemoaning his lot, always in a fever-heat, wondering anxiously how matters would end and shouting at me, his life was no better than a dog's. . . .'

That evening, on 24th August, de Catt was summoned to the King:

. . . I found him writing busily in a very small room in the mill. I thought he was making his plans for the battle. Not at all. He was writing verses. 'Verses, Sire? And tomorrow Your Majesty intends to fight a battle!' 'What's so unusual about that? My thoughts have been on the main business all day, my plan is ready, I have made my decisions. So now I think I might be allowed to scribble verses like any other man.' . . .

The King then remarked that Racine's odes were not nearly so good as his tragedies. The record continues:

'I think, Sire, it would be very difficult to write verse in the style of Racine, starting, for instance, with: *"Celui qui des flots assouvit la fureur ..."* ' 'You are right, that would be difficult. But, *mon cher*, suppose I try?' He had seized his pen when the generals were announced. 'Wait a moment in my room. I want to give them their instructions. Everyone must know exactly what he has to do....' The King went out and returned after talking to his generals for half an hour. 'Well, all's said. Now, what can I say about *"Celui qui des flots ..."*?'

In a quarter of an hour he had finished the verses, which he allowed me to keep. 'Now, my friend,' said the King, 'let us eat these grapes, for who knows who may eat them tomorrow. We move at dawn.'

Next morning, Frederick's servant told de Catt that the King had slept so soundly he had had difficulty in waking him.

Frederick despised the Russian army, which consisted largely of serfs and criminals. Some units were led to the battlefield in chains. He was confident of destroying them with small loss. But though half the slightly larger Russian army succumbed to the violence of the Prussian onslaught, the remainder stood firm and for a time it seemed the Prussians would have to retreat. The King came galloping up to his right flank with the cry: 'May God in heaven have mercy!' Fearing a panic, Prince Moritz von Dessau threw his hat in the air, shouting: 'The battle is won! Long live the King!' and, pointing to the green-clad lines of Russians advancing on the opposite wing: 'Those are prisoners being led away. Courage, lads! Forward!' The battle raged for ten hours. At a critical moment Frederick seized the colours of a grenadier battalion and charged forward under a rain of bullets. But it was a savage attack by his youngest general, Seydlitz, nicknamed 'the horsed hurricane', that decided the battle. Almost everywhere the end of the long day saw the Russians still in their original positions, but, according to one of their generals, they were either 'dead, wounded or drunk.' The battle, said an Austrian, was like a heavy box on the ear which spins a man round, but leaves him standing. It seemed at the time to be a drawn battle, but it was, in fact, a Prussian victory, for the Russians withdrew next day and did not risk another encounter with Frederick for a whole year.

Meanwhile Daun, with a resurrected Reich army, was feeling his way towards Dresden with instructions to ccoupy Saxony in Frederick's absence. The only opposition was an army one-quarter his strength under Prince Henry. But Daun lost time arguing tactics with the Aulic Council and had still reached no agreement with Vienna on a plan of attack when news came that Frederick was marching towards him. Daun at once dropped all idea of taking Dresden and withdrew to strong positions in the hills. 'One would imagine,' wrote Frederick, 'that Austria re-recruited her generals in the Caucasus or the Cordilleras; no sooner do they see a mountain than they have to climb it.'

A week later Frederick decided to march into Silesia, where the Austrians were besieging several fortified towns. At Hoch-kirch, on the way, he chose an extremely dangerous site for his encampment, spreading his army over a series of hill-tops with the Austrians occupying the ground below. 'They deserve to be hanged if they don't attack us here,' said Field-Marshal Keith. Frederick replied: 'They fear us more than the gallows.' But while the King spent his evenings reading letters intended for Wilhelmina, who was ill, to de Catt, Loudon was trying to per-suade Daun to attack. After three days he succeeded. At five o'clock on the morning of the fourth day, after a slight bombard-ment which the Prussians took to be nothing unusual, they sud-denly saw Austrian infantry climbing towards them through thick fog. No sooner were they engaged than more Austrians emerged from behind the Prussian tents and took them in the rear. By now the whole army was aroused, and fighting desperately hand to hand with rifle butt and bayonet, the darkness and fog making it almost impossible to distinguish friend from foe. Keith was killed, Moritz von Dessau severely wounded and taken prisoner, Frederick, his charger streaming blood, was leading a counter-attack, an officer was handing round his snuffbox: 'Gentlemen, a pinch of sangfroid?' – and the next moment was rent asunder by a cannon-ball. But the troops had rallied and were now closing the ranks; after four hours of fearful carnage they were able to disengage in recognisable order.

Summoned that evening to the King, de Catt was met by Frederick the Tragedian, declaiming with tears and pregnant pauses Racine's *Mithridate*, altered slightly to meet the occasion:

> *Enfin, après un an, tu me revois, Arbate,*
> *Non plus, comme autrefois, cet heureux Mithridate*
> *Qui de Vienne (Rome) toujours balançant le destin,*
> *Tenais entre elle et moi l'univers incertain.*
> *Je suit vaincu. Daunus (Pompée) a saisi l'avantage*
> *D'une nuit qui laissait peu de place au courage.*
> *Mes soldats presque nus, dans l'ombre intimidés,*

Les rangs de toutes parts mal pris et mal gardés,
Le désordre partout redoublant los alarmes,
Nous-mêmes contre nous tournant nos propres armes,
Les cris que les rochers renvoyaient plus affreux,
Enfin toute l'horreur d'un combat ténébreux:
Que pouvait la valeur dans ce trouble funeste?
Les uns sont morts . . .

And here, undoubtedly, the actor must have paused, for Racine continued: '. . . *la fuite a sauvé tout le reste.*' But that would never do. So Frederick paused; then, one can imagine, laid hand on heart, looked up and, fixing proud eyes on an invisible gallery, gave the ringing cry: '*moi-même j'ai sauvé tout le reste!*'

The faithful de Catt must have been deeply moved. Two hours later, at five in the morning, he was again summoned. This time, Frederick undid his collar and drew from under his shirt a small gold box attached to a cord. De Catt records:

'Here,' said the King, 'is all that is needed to put an end to the tragedy.' He showed me the box. It contained eighteen pills, which we counted. 'These pills,' he said, 'are opium. There are more than enough to transfer me to that dark shore from which there is no return.'

The King little knew as he said this that the tragedy was a double one. On the same day that the Austrians had surprised his army at Hochkirch his sister Wilhelmina had died. Despite the wrangling that occurred whenever they came face to face they had been devoted to each other. Before Hochkirch Frederick had written to her: 'If you love me, give me some hope of your recovery. Without you, life would be unbearable to me. That is not just a figure of speech, but the truth. Think what would become of me if I lost you. Oh, my dear, my divine sister, do the impossible and get well. My life, my happiness, my existence lie in your hands.'

The news of her death reached him on 17th October, three days after the battle. When de Catt was summoned in the early hours of the morning he found the King in tears. 'My sister has gone,' he said. 'I shall never see her again. Soon I shall have no friends, no relatives left. Death is taking them all.' Five days later, Frederick had resumed the march to Silesia, re-equipping his depleted army from Dresden, watched by Daun and harassed by Loudon. They thought he was heading for Glogau: instead, he turned suddenly south-eastward for Görlitz, occupied the town before they realised their mistake and was astride the main highway with nothing between him and Neisse before they could stop him. Ten days later, the three-month siege of Neisse was over – the Prussian garrison awoke to find the Austrians had gone, vanished overnight at the news of Frederick's approach. The same happened at Kosel, and at other places. The mere whisper of Frederick's name had driven the enemy siege forces from Silesia. At once Frederick returned to Saxony and Daun backed away into Bohemia. Silesia and Saxony were now firmly in the King's possession again.

But what of the future? Prussia had been bled white in money and manpower. Frederick was at his best when retrieving disaster, but some of the disasters had been of his own making. Olmütz was his mistake; Hochkirch his inexcusable blunder. He was plugging the leaks, but the boat was still slowly sinking. Victory was now beyond his grasp. Survival was all he could hope for. That he had survived so far was due to the enemy's cowardice as well as to his own powers of endurance. But they would not last indefinitely. 'If you could see me, you would detect no trace of my former self. You would see a man turned old and grey, minus half his teeth and quite without gaiety, fire or imagination, in brief, a shadow.' So he wrote to d'Argens, and to von Finckenstein: 'How is all this going to end? We may parry a few more blows, but we still face ultimate defeat.'

CHAPTER NINETEEN

*

The Limping Skeleton

AS THE BELLS RANG in the New Year Frederick started to plan his campaign. The first preliminary was finance; once again he would need 20,000,000 talers. But the problem was, how to raise them. The war treasure had been spent, the limit of taxation reached, and though the King was prepared to fleece the occupied territories, Saxony and Mecklenburg could not provide a quarter of the sum required, whatever pressure was applied. There remained one alternative; depreciation. Frederick instructed his Court bankers, Ephraim, Itzig and Isaac, to mint new talers slightly lighter than the old. As in all his undertakings, Frederick acted with thoroughness and guile. Not only talers were minted, but Polish, Russian and Hungarian coins as well, to be exchanged in their respective countries for undepreciated currency. At first the new coins contained slightly less than half their weight of copper; before the war ended they were minted in three parts copper to one of silver and a dull bluish tint was visible beneath the surface. The Berliners joked:

> Outside bright, but inside dim,
> Outside Frederick, inside Ephraim.

But though prices soared and their savings melted away in the inflation, being Berliners they could relish to the full the thought of the King's enemies financing their own destruction.

But this wizardry could not provide Frederick with an army of more than 110,000 men, and of such poor quality that, on his own admission, they were only 'fit to be shown to the enemy at a distance.' By brute force and cajolery the Prussian recruiting officers had scraped them together from every part of Germany, including enemy countries. Tempted by the offer of a commission, the would-be officer would volunteer, only to find himself a private soldier as soon as he reached Prussian soil. Thereafter force, if not enthusiasm for Frederick, would keep him to the colours. Not surprisingly, such men made unreliable soldiers. When under fire, recruits threw away their cartridges and fled, obliging Frederick to keep a reserve of ammunition in bullock carts and issue the following savage order: 'As I have seen that after they have been under fire a while the fellows pretend they have run out of ammunition, they are to be warned that the first man who throws away cartridges during a battle shall be made to run the gauntlet thirty-six times immediately afterwards, and if, when the ammunition carts reach them, the fellows refuse to take cartridges, anyone found guilty of such conduct shall be shot.' But even if such threats were successful, how could battles be won with men like these, men whose songs, even, breathed the spirit of defeat?

> Say farewell to me, my dear,
> For I march to fight the foe.
> When the enemy draws near
> Frederick then will disappear,
> Melting as the winter's snow.
> Numberless as stars at night
> Or the sand on ocean's shore
> Come the enemies we fight.
> So then if we judge aright
> Say farewell for evermore.

But in the West the situation was hopeful: here, reinforced by 10,000 British, the troops of Hanover, Brunswick, and Hesse faced the badly led, ill-disciplined and poorly equipped French with confidence. The Swedes, or the 'Hottentots' as Frederick called them, were not a serious menace, either; they could be held in check by territorial troops. Finally, though the new Pope, Clement XIII, was supporting Prussia's enemies more actively than his predecessor, Frederick treated the matter lightly. A Dutch newspaper reported that the Pope had bestowed a consecrated hat and sword on Field-Marshal Daun, and though this was denied in Vienna and the story may even have come from Frederick himself he then published a parody of the type of letter that might have accompanied the gift:

> May this sword which we send you serve to destroy for ever those heresies whose pestilential breath rises from the Bottomless Pit. May it drink the blood of rebels. May the axe be laid to the root of the tree that bore the accursed fruit.

189

D'Argens translated this into Latin, and many people took it for the words of Pope Clement himself. Frederick then composed a letter allegedly from Soubise to Field-Marshal Daun:

It is a pity that the Holy Father did not confer these gifts on you earlier. At Rossbach I was badly in need of a consecrated hat and sword, and I don't think they would have done you any harm at Leuthen.

From now on Frederick always referred to Daun as 'the consecrated creature.' What would the creature do in the New Year? The Austrians and Russians now realised that to beat Frederick they would have to attack him jointly, and Frederick was hoping to beat Daun before they could unite their armies. But though outnumbering the Prussians by two to one, Daun, said Frederick, must have had 'sixty pounds of lead in the backside,' for he refused to move from prepared positions. The King then ordered his eastern army to attack the Russians before they had time to concentrate and sent his Adjutant-General Vobershnov to support and advise the army commander. But here, too, the enemy refused to commit himself. Frederick laid all the blame on Vobershnov, recording disgustedly that 'a mediocre general in his cups could not have handled an army more erratically.' Now General Wedell was sent out as 'dictator' with orders to stop officers complaining on pain of being cashiered, court-martial deserters and at all costs – bring the enemy to battle. Wedell carried out his orders to the letter. With 26,000 men he attacked 70,000 Russians at Kay on the River Oder on 23rd July, 1759, and was beaten. On the following day a fresh order arrived from the King telling Wedell not to attack if heavily outnumbered. When he heard of the defeat, Frederick was generous. 'I had the feeling,' he wrote to Wedell, 'that things would go wrong . . . the troops were overawed . . . we must not dwell on this defeat . . . it was not your fault that the rascals fled so shamefully.' Fortunately, Daun did not move with his main army to join the Russians, but detached only 20,000 men under Loudon.

Leaving his main army under Prince Henry in Silesia, the King now marched north with 50,000 men to intercept Loudon before he could join the Russians. But Frederick failed, and on 12th August, 1759, he faced the combined armies of over 70,000 men at Kunersdorf, near Frankfurt-on-Oder. As usual, it was Frederick who attacked, striking at the Russian flank and overrunning it. All his generals, including Seydlitz, then begged him

190

to rest on his laurels. The enemy had suffered heavy loss and would be certain, they said, to withdraw in the morning. But Frederick was determined to strike such a blow that the Russians would never dare tread on Prussian soil again, and, disregarding his generals' sound advice, ordered the attack to continue. By now his men had been on their legs for fifteen hours and were nearing exhaustion. Their progress slowed up, then stopped altogether, then Loudon's fresh cavalry counter-attacked and the Prussians began to waver. Soon they were retreating, flooding back. Frederick was in the fray, trying to stop them, had two horses shot from under him; a ricochet flattened his snuffbox. 'Will none of these blasted bullets hit me?' He looked round. The remnants of his army were flying, panic-stricken, into a gathering mist. No Prussian army had ever been seen in such a state before. It was time to leave. But Frederick still stayed, gazing . . . He had his bodyguard with him and some of Ziethen's hussars under Captain Prittwitz. A moment later, the sound of galloping hooves made him turn – Cossacks! 'Prittwitz, I'm lost!' Was it a cry of fear? Or a statement of fact? Or was it, perhaps, an expression of hope? *'Nein, Makestät!'* And leading the Prussian horse, Prittwitz just managed to hew a path, an adjutant seized Frederick's bridle, turned his horse's head and galloped with him from the field.

That evening Frederick wrote to von Finckenstein in Berlin:

> My coat is riddled with bullets. My misfortune is that I am still alive. Our losses are very considerable; of an army of 48,000 men I have, as I write this, not 3,000 left.
> All are in flight and I have lost control of my men. You would do well to look to your safety in Berlin. I have no more resources and I will tell you no lies: I think all is lost. I shall not survive the downfall of my country. Farewell for ever. Frederick.

This time the pathos was genuine. Frederick was on the brink of ultimate despair. Sitting in a peasant hut amidst the wounded and the dying, tortured by gout in one arm and both feet, spitting blood, he decided to relinquish command to one of his generals. He wrote out the order in German. One can almost hear his feverish breathing:

> General Finck gets a hard commission. The luckless *armée* such as I hand to him is no longer in a condition to Fight the Russians, Hadek will press on to Berlin, perhaps Loudon too, if general Finck goes after they both, the Russians will take him in rear, if he stops on the Oder, he will gett Hadek thiss side, but I think iff Loudon tri for Berlin

191

he cud attack and beat him on the way, Thiss, iffit go well, would put a good face on missfoortun and hold things up. Time gained is very mutch in thees Desperat circumstances . . . he must keep my brother [Prince Henry] whom I appoint Generalissimo informed of everything, to make good the misfoortune completely is impossible, but my brother's orders mus be obeyed, the army mus sware allegiance to my *Neveu* [the young Prince Frederick William]. In these unfortunate circumstances thiss is the onnly advyce I am able to give. Iff I still had any resources I wood hav staid.

If his enemies had followed up their victory, Prussia would have been doomed, but the mere name of this 'limping skeleton', this 'piece of luggage that burdened his army', was enough to paralyse them. The Russians refused to advance farther. Daun was ordered to avoid at all costs another battle with Frederick and attack Prince Henry instead. The Russian commander-in-chief reported that the victory had been dearly bought: 'Another such and I shall have myself to bring the news to St Petersburg staff in hand.' The French military plenipotentiary spoke the truth when he said: 'We are all too afraid of the King of Prussia.'

Meanwhile the Russians had marched off into Poland and the King of Prussia had resumed military command. His first thought was to make peace with France. 'My position,' he wrote to Voltaire, who acted as intermediary with Choiseul, 'is not so desperate as my enemies imagine. I am not disheartened, but I realise that peace is necessary' – and as these sentiments had to reach Choiseul, and Voltaire would not bother to pass them on without his due meed of flattery: 'what a unique tribute if it could be said in the nineteenth century this famous Voltaire so forcefully rebuked princes for going to war that he dictated the peace terms. Voltaire, it will be said, tutored kings as well as Europe.' But Choiseul could expect no concessions from Frederick: 'I am dealing with such simpletons that I am bound to triumph in the end. But they will find me a spirit stronger than lemonade; if I were a private citizen I would yield anything for peace, but a man must act according to his station.'

Voltaire's name for Frederick was 'Luc'. Some say it should be spelt backwards. 'Luc,' he wrote to a friend in Paris, 'is the same as ever – getting himself and others into trouble, astonishing Europe, inundating it with blood, reducing it to poverty and producing verses. Luc wants peace. Would it, after all, be so great a calamity if it were granted, and a counterpoise to Germany maintained? Luc is good for nothing, I know. But is it worth ruining ourselves to do away with a ne'er-do-well whose existence is a necessity?'

The new Foreign Minister Choiseul agreed with these sentiments. France had been beaten by Pitt in the colonial war and was bankrupt. The desire for peace was mutual. England and Prussia both suggested a conference. Then Frederick made a blunder which destroyed hope of a settlement.

He had returned to Saxony – in a sedan chair as he could not stand being jolted on horseback or in a carriage – with the intention of manoeuvring Daun out of the province. For this purpose he had sent Finck with 15,000 men to take Daun in the rear, overriding his objections with the words: 'You know I can't stand having difficulties; be off!'

Frederick had a low opinion of the 'consecrated creature' and intended that Daun should not leave Saxony 'without some forceful boots in the backside.' But his entire staff disapproved of Finck's errand; Prince Henry even threatened to resign. When their protests failed, de Catt, the *Lecteur*, undertook to speak to the King:

> I was called at four o'clock in the morning. I found the King busy writing a Voltairean parody of the Song of Solomon. He composed several lines in my presence and read them to me.

After a lengthy poetic discussion, the worthy de Catt managed to steer round to the subject of Finck. He raised his objections to the King's plan, but Frederick answered:

> No, my friend, no. You have nothing to fear. You will see that the sacred hat and his companions will be delighted to have a chance of getting back to Bohemia. Now I'll read you my lines again. . . .

On the following day de Catt tried again, with no better result. All the same, Frederick was anxious, for he knew well enough that it was himself Daun feared, not General Finck. On 21st November, 1759, Daun attacked the Prussians at Maxen with superior forces and compelled them to capitulate. After the war Finck was cashiered and sentenced to one year's detention for having acted without due caution and resolve. No doubt this was true, but all Frederick's generals agreed that he himself had been chiefly to blame. Prince Henry wrote venomously: 'From the day he joined forces with my army, he has spread disorder and disaster. All my efforts in this campaign, the luck which favoured me, all have been thrown away by Frederick. He plunged us into this terrible war; only the valour of generals and soldiers can get us out of it.'

Depressed by knowledge of his fault, the King recalled the harrowing scenes of his youth. 'Consider, my friend,' he said to de Catt, 'how unfortunate I have always been! Hard treated by my father, shut up alone in the same room for three months where I suffered much ill treatment, unlucky in every respect in this war, I have only seen the face of happiness for one brief period in Rheinsberg.' De Catt continues:

He showed me some verses which he had been trying to write – I say, trying, for the lines were unfinished. The sight of them, which revealed the turmoil of his mind, distressed me deeply. 'I jotted these down as a diversion, *mon cher*, but I find it impossible to write anything with the least sense in it.'

On the following afternoon I went again to the King. 'Look. I wrote this after you left. It's not good, but what can I do? I keep seeing Finck at the tip of my pen.'

The disaster of Maxen lost Frederick eight generals and 10,000 men, killed, wounded or captured, together with all their equipment. In weakening his military prestige it contributed to the breakdown of the peace negotiations with France, for Pitt was now more than ever determined to crush French power in Europe and he rejected Choiseul's offer of a separate peace. But if Pitt continued the war against France, Frederick alone could not make peace, for he could not afford to lose the English subsidy. As it was, his popularity in England was waning. Three years before, the hero's name had been known throughout the length and breadth of the country, even though some of the simpler folk might have thought he and Pitt were the same person. Now the Tories were talking of sending the 'King of Küstrin' into retirement on the Ohio.

Early in 1760 a volume of Frederick's poems was published in Paris under the title *Oeuvres du Philosophe de Sanssouci* with the spurious heading 'Potsdam' on the title page. These were the same verses that, seven years before, Frederick had been at such pains to recover from Voltaire's luggage. Voltaire may well have had a hand in their publication now. They were full of scurrilous witticisms about his enemies and allies, amongst others George II. As soon as Frederick could get hold of a copy, he suppressed some passages, altered others and, declaring the Paris edition to be spurious, republished the verses headed by an ode against slander. But the damage was done, and feeling in England ran high against the perfidious Frederick who publicly derided the allies on whose subsidy his survival depended. Such trifles made

194

no impression on Pitt and he continued his powerful support, but they gave welcome ammunition to his Tory enemies, and in that same year they were to return to power.

*

CHAPTER TWENTY

Skirting the Abyss

THE YEAR 1760 started badly. Frederick spoke of a 'film of sadness' overlying all he did or wrote. 'The Wandering Jew, if he ever existed, never led such a vagrant life as I. We drift homeless through the world like a troupe of village players, performing our bloody tragedies wherever the enemy chooses to set up the stage.' He had no money to pay his officials, civil administration was collapsing. But still he refused to contemplate peace if it meant sacrificing his conquests.

In June Frederick's boyhood friend Fouqué with 13,000 men was attacked at Landshut on the Silesian frontier by three times that number of Austrians under Loudon. Fouqué withdrew, was ordered to advance again at once, was defeated and taken prisoner. Loudon then invested Breslau, demanding immediate capitulation or he would spare no one, not even mothers with child. The fortress commander replied blandly that neither he nor his troops were pregnant – whereupon Loudon raised the siege.

Meanwhile Frederick was hesitating. As his energies flagged, self-confidence began to wane. 'Last night,' he told de Catt, 'I had a curious dream. I dreamt I was in Strasbourg with Marshal Daun. Suddenly we found ourselves in Charlottenburg. I saw my father and old Dessau. "Have I done well?" I asked Dessau. "Very well." "I am glad," I said. "Your good opinion and my father's mean more to me than all the rest of the world's." – And then I woke up! Can you imagine anything more strange?' Then Frederick declaimed a French ode, complaining afterwards that de Catt did not congratulate him on knowing so many verses by heart. Then his thoughts returned to his desperate military position. 'Another month', he predicted, 'and I shall certainly be turning somersaults. . . .'

But August brought another victory over Daun at Liegnitz. Surrounded on three sides by 90,000 Austrians, with, three days' march away, 80,000 Russians hastening to join them, late in the evening of the 14th Frederick managed to withdraw his forces from the trap while peasants kept the camp-fires burning to deceive the enemy. From time to time a hussar bugler would sound a call from the deserted lines to complete the illusion. Soon after midnight Frederick had his 15,000 men resting in battle order on a crescent of hills behind Liegnitz, intending next day to march on to Glogau, where, if Daun followed him, the heavy fortress guns would assist his inferior numbers. Meanwhile, somewhere near the centre of the crescent, Frederick, wrapped in his cloak, sat dozing on a drum. All round, his men lay stretched on the grass, staring up at the glittering night sky. The time was half past two.

Suddenly an officer came running along the track that led to the army's left wing. He had been on reconnaissance, seen enemy infantry advancing in strength not half a mile away towards the Prussian flank. . . . It was Loudon with 35,000 men intending to occupy the selfsame heights where Frederick's army now lay. He had set off at about the same time as the Prussians, believing they were still in their original positions and intending to attack them in the rear at first light. He, too, had left his camp-fires burning. Now, as his men tramped silently up the hill, they were looking forward to a promised sleep before they swept down at dawn on the Prussians below. Then suddenly the hill-top belched flame as the Prussian artillery went into action. The battle lasted for two and a half hours. By 5 a.m. Loudon had lost 10,000 men; the Prussians 1,800. Two and a half miles away to the south-west and upwind of the battle, Daun had heard nothing. He had been intending to deliver a frontal attack on the morrow, shortly before Loudon took the Prussians in the rear. At 1 a.m. his scouts had discovered that the Prussian camp was deserted; Daun took note of the fact and did nothing. Some time later he had seen a column of smoke rising to the north-east and concluded that a battle was taking place. He decided to wait. When news came that Loudon had been defeated he issued his first order – for an immediate retreat.

Frederick, meanwhile, had written a letter in his own hand to his brother Henry telling him that the Austrian army was in headlong flight, Loudon fatally wounded, and that in a few days

197

he intended to smash the Russians. He gave the letter to a peasant with instructions to let himself be captured, and relates in his history of the Seven Years War that as soon as the Russians read it they withdrew their army. In fact, they started to retreat the moment they heard of Loudon's disaster, their commander, Czernichev, declaring that if Daun had not risked a battle with Frederick when his own subordinate was in trouble, then why should he? The lessons learnt on the Allied side were best summed up by a Frenchman who wrote gloomily: 'It is all very well to say that the King of Prussia is ruined, his troops are not what they were and he has no generals. All this may be true, but his spirit is still the same and it is that which brings all to life. Unfortunately our spirit too, remains unchanged.'

Though in greatly superior numbers, Daun now refused to budge. The Aulic Council urged him to attack, Maria Theresa promised yet again to accept full responsibility in the event of defeat, but Daun was adamant. He replied that if he did attack it would be 'with the self-evident prospect of failure' and the blame 'for irresponsibly shedding the blood of so many loyal and intrepid soldiers' would inevitably be his. 'I am calling upon the Almighty night and day,' he added, 'that it may please Him in His mercy to grant me more abundant enlightenment than heretofore.' And with this, Maria Theresa had for the time to be content. But in two months all that the Austrians and Russians could summon the initiative to achieve was a combined raid on Berlin in October 1760, when they occupied the capital for three days and then withdrew on Frederick's approach.

The King was not deceived by this lull in the major fighting. 'The crisis I am in,' he had written in early September to d'Argens, 'is taking another shape, but how it will develop cannot yet be foreseen. You talk always of my person, of my dangers. Need I tell you, it is not necessary that I live, but it is that I do my duty and fight to save my country, if possible.' D'Argens replied that Frederick was indispensable – which prompted the calm retort:

I have sacrificed my youth to my father and my adult years to the State; therefore I think I am entitled to dispose of my old age as I please. Some people can submit to Fate; I am not one of them, and having lived for others, at least I intend to die for myself. What the world may say leaves me quite unmoved – anyway, I shall not hear it. Brandenburg existed before I was born and will continue to exist after my death. To put an end to an unhappy life is not weakness, but good sense, for we shall be at our happiest in that place where no one ever again can harm us or disturb our rest.

198

Within a week of writing this fatalistic letter Frederick was again acting with the utmost resolve. Daun, he knew, had been ordered to hold Saxony at all costs; he was equally determined to defeat Daun and recover the country, for without it he would have neither the men, the money, nor the manoeuvring space to carry on the war. Fully aware of this, Daun had installed his army of 65,000 men (half again as large as Frederick's) in inaccessible positions protected by hills and gullies at Torgau on the Elbe. Frederick decided on a bold manoeuvre. He himself with half his army would march right round Torgau and attack Daun from the rear, while the other half would deliver a frontal attack on Daun's flank. Having long since lost Schwerin and Winterfeld, Frederick had to give command of this second body to Ziethen, a man with plenty of dash and excellent as a general of hussars, but not equipped by temperament or training to carry out a deliberate assault with a large composite force. The two attacks, with about 22,000 men in each, were, of course, intended to coincide.

Monday, 3rd November, 1760. In a cold, wet dawn Frederick set off with the flower of the Prussian infantry to march fourteen miles to his starting-point. His force was divided into three columns, each having a separate route going clockwise round the Austrian army and ending south of it. The columns were to form up in dense woods and attack due north in three waves. The march was twice as far as Ziethen's, and what with heavy going over sodden ground and the necessity of dealing with some advanced Austrian outposts *en route* Frederick's column comprising 8,000 picked troops was an hour late and did not reach the rendezvous until 1 p.m., to find no sign of Hülsen with the second column or Holstein with the third. Frederick decided to wait for them. Meanwhile, Daun had got wind of Frederick's intentions through his outposts and had skilfully swung round to meet him, building his defence round 150 pieces of artillery, the heaviest concentration yet seen in the war. He, too, was waiting.

The zero hour for the Prussian attack was long past, but there was no sound of Ziethen engaging the enemy flank. Hülsen and Holstein had still not turned up and it was now nearing 2 p.m. Then, borne on the north-west wind, came the sounds of heavy cannon and musketry fire. Ziethen! Frederick waited to make sure. The firing continued. He decided to attack, in one wave instead of three, with 8,000 men instead of with 22,000. He gave his orders and the men began to move steadily through the wood. It was snowing, a full storm. The flakes lashed their faces. The wind shrieked and moaned. They came to the edge of the wood

– and immediately every gun the Austrians possessed started pouring destruction. The crash and crack of trees, the yells of the wounded, the dark fury of the storm, the wall of flame from the massed cannon on the hill-top – it was a scene no soldier, not even Frederick, had ever experienced before. But the Prussian grenadiers, the finest soldiers then existing in the world, went on, literally into the cannons' mouth. Of 6,000, perhaps 2,000 survived to reach the infantry beyond, creating such a slaughter that Daun had to throw in a continuous stream of reinforcements. But after an hour, the Prussians began to yield. The Austrians followed them. Frederick threw in his small reserve. The enemy was flung back, and the survivors of the first attack – a bare 600 – dragged themselves back under cover of the trees.

At 3 p.m. Hülsen's column appeared, having lost the way. At three-thirty he went in with his infantry at the same point as before. A frenzied struggle ensued. At last the enemy cannon were silenced and their front was beginning to crack open when Daun – by no means a waverer once he was committed to battle – managed to plug the gap. Frederick had been in both attacks and was mounting his fourth horse. Almost his entire staff had been wounded. Now a spent piece of case-shot struck him in the chest. He fell, unconscious, from the saddle, quickly recovered, mounted, and was off to rally his men, who were falling back. But for the thick fur and velvet lining of his pelisse he would have been killed.

The second attack had also failed. Now, as it was getting dark, the last column, Holstein's cavalry, arrived. At once a third attack was organised with foot and horse against Daun's centre and right flank. Again furious fighting ensued. The enemy front sagged and bulged and, as night fell, split up into small pockets of men, some far inside the Prussian mass, others well back on the far side of the hill, awaiting their chance to slip away in the darkness. But there was still fight in the Austrian army and the Prussians were not yet in full possession of the contested ground. Leaving Hülsen the unenviable job of organising the bivouac, Frederick now left the battlefield, hoping the Austrians would withdraw during the night, but prepared if necessary to resume the battle next day. Field-Marshal Daun, who had been wounded in the leg, also handed over command and rode away, sending premature news of a victory to Vienna.

But the battle was not yet over. During that morning Ziethen had been making for the starting-point of his attack when he came across a small party of the enemy. Before turning tail, the

Austrians fired at him with cannon. Concluding they were in strength, Ziethen brought up his own guns, fired back, then – the incorrigible cavalry commander – forgot all about his timetable and gave chase. It was the sound of this skirmish which had persuaded Frederick to launch his first attack. Finding himself under fire from distant enemy batteries, Ziethen then spent an hour or two exchanging desultory shots, until at long last, when daylight was almost gone, the sounds of Frederick's battle brought him to his senses. The indecision which his unaccustomed responsibilities had laid on him then vanished, and, gathering his forces, he made at full speed towards the firing, reaching the scene at about 6 p.m., when most of the fighting was over. With reckless daring, determined to retrieve his folly, he charged in pitch darkness to the one point where intermittent flashes showed that Prussian troops were still engaged– a hill-top which was the key to the whole battle area. Ziethen swept on, taking the enemy completely by surprise. Soon, with drums beating the Prussian March, Hülsen was on the scene with his infantry. Together, after some bitter fighting, they turned the tide, and if Daun, warned by despatch riders, had not ordered an immediate retreat towards the Elbe, at right angles to the advancing Prussians, his entire army would have been destroyed. As it was, the bulk of his forces managed to reach safety on the far bank.

The rout of his army at Torgau left Daun stupefied. 'God would have it so,' he wrote to Maria Theresa, 'otherwise the day could never have ended in such disaster. God is just.' He offered to explain verbally the defeat, 'if Yr Majesty can bear to have so miserable a creature as myself before Her Supernal Gaze.' Meanwhile Frederick was being ribald. Ascribing authorship to an Austrian army chaplain, he wrote and published a memorandum arguing that the Prussians owed their victory to the Devil; one because during the night Daun's consecrated sword had suddenly lost its virtue, and, two, the Austrians had not been defeated by Prussian valour but by the sulphurous stench they brought with them from the Nether Pit.

After Torgau, France was ready for peace. 'We have no money, no resources, no soldiers, no generals, no brains and no ministers,' declared Louis XV. Through the Minister in Vienna, Choiseul inquired whether, in view of the general weariness, it would be prudent for Austria to continue the war alone, thereby incurring dangers beyond the talents of Graf Daun to master. Piqued, Maria Theresa made the feeble reply that her only alternative would be an alliance with the King of Prussia. But of course it was peace she was really considering, if necessary at the price of ceding Silesia. 'People must be surprised to see me with such feelings,' she confessed sadly. 'Three months ago I was thinking quite differently, but that is the way with women.' For lack of money the Austrian army in the field had to be reduced to 20,000 men. But the Allied gloom after Torgau was a passing reaction, and the first to realise it was Frederick. A week after the battle he wrote to d'Argens: 'Do not imagine that our enemies are so reduced that they are compelled to make peace.' And whereas in their case military responsibility rested on many shoulders, Frederick bore the whole fate of Prussia alone. Without his tenacity and resource, above all without the prestige of his name, who could doubt that Prussia would quickly succumb? Thus outward circumstances as well as his own temperament combined to make unnatural demands on his energy. Long after other men would have died of exhaustion, he drove himself on under the double compulsion of duty to the State and of the fierce resolve born of parental derision to prove himself a man. No wonder his laments were loud and anguished. 'I swear to you,' he wrote to his second mother, the Gräfin Camas, 'that only Don Quixote lived such a dog's life as I. These trials, this never-ending confusion have aged me so much you would barely recognise me. The hairs on the right side of my head have gone quite grey; my teeth are rotting and falling out; my face is wrinkled like the folds of a lady's dress, my back as bent as a fiddle-stick and my mind as melancholy as a Trappist's. I tell you this in advance so that you will not be too shocked by my appearance if we ever meet again.'

By the spring of 1761 the crimson snows of Torgau had been forgotten and the Allies now resolved to make one last effort. The French were hoping to bring Spain into the war. In Russia the Empress had once again survived an amorous and alcoholic winter and was swearing she would never make peace with Frederick. His position was now truly desperate. Somehow his recruiting agents had managed to procure another 100,000 men, but a good half were foreigners. On Daun's frank confession that a Prussian officer or soldier was worth more than an Austrian, Maria Theresa had refused to exchange prisoners with the King and his seasoned veterans were fast dwindling. A good soldier, Colonel von Möllendorf, wrote at this time: 'I do not fear the enemy as much now as our own situation. The soldier cannot live, he lacks the bare essentials. So it comes to looting, and a looter is without honour, and a man without honour is a coward.'

Meanwhile, relations between Prussia and England were continuing to deteriorate. Occasionally Frederick even bickered with his faithful friend, the British Ambassador Mitchell. After a British reverse at sea Mitchell said he hoped that with God's help the reverse would be made good. 'I didn't know God was an ally of yours,' said Frederick tartly. 'Yes, indeed, Your Majesty – the only one who costs us nothing. And look what He does for you!'

The British were, in fact, intending to reconsider the subsidy to Prussia in the light of the 1761 campaign. But the best that Frederick could hope from it was survival: the combined Russian and Austrian armies outnumbered his by three to one – and if they ever did combine his fate was sealed. For some weeks in August and September 1761, they were both within striking distance and he was obliged to await their attack near the small village of Bunzeldorf in Silesia. In a matter of days he turned it into a prodigious fortified encampment complete with palisade, entrenchments and a vast ditch in some places sixteen feet broad by sixteen deep. Half his 50,000-strong army slept while the other 25,000 men wielded pick and shovel. The work went on round the clock, the whole system of fortifications, battery positions and ramparts being planned by Frederick himself. Eyeing the result from a distance Loudon realised that Bunzeldorf was almost if not quite impregnable. He was prepared to attack it if the Russians would join him. For days he argued with Butterlin, their commander, but, partly perhaps because the Empress Elizabeth was ill again and half his mind was on his political future, Butterlin refused to co-operate and, to close the discussion, withdrew his army at the very moment when the Prussians were running seriously short of food. This negative triumph was the only kind that the King was now able to achieve. Respect for his military prowess had contributed to his salvation at Bunzeldorf, and at the end of September it saved him again. Thanks to the Prussian commander's faith in astrology rather than vigilance, Loudon had captured the fortress of Schweidnitz in Silesia. His army was twice the size of Frederick's, and thereafter he had a chance to meet him in the open field. Instead he chose a more prudent course and arranged with a Silesian nobleman named Warkotsch to kidnap the king. Though the Austrians were only two miles away, Frederick's headquarters, as Warkotsch discovered, were guarded by only thirteen grenadiers. The plot would have succeeded if Warkotsch's groom, Kappel, had not loyally taken a vital letter to the King instead of to the Austrian general for whom it was intended.

Owing to the loss of Schweidnitz, Frederick had less room for manoeuvre at the end of 1761 than ever before. Almost the whole of Saxony was already lost to him, and now the greater part of Silesia as well. East Prussia and East Pomerania were in enemy occupation and his Rhenish possessions had long since fallen to the French. Only the March of Brandenburg, Magdeburg and a small portion of Silesia remained in his hands. How was he to recruit an army, how pay them and how feed them, in 1762?

Meanwhile, in October 1760, George II of England had died, to be succeeded by his twenty-two-year-old grandson, George III. Glorying, as he said, 'in the name of Briton,' but ingloriously indifferent to Britain's true welfare, this pious, hardworking and frugal young man possessed public vices far outweighing the private virtues which endeared him to his people. Though unable to read at the age of eleven and already showing signs of mental confusion at thirteen, he had boundless confidence in his ability and was determined to use it, not as a figurehead but as a ruler, and one who on principle made his policy the exact opposite of his grandfather's, whom he detested. Whereas George II had been content to let the Whigs run the country and prosecute the war, George III was determined to oust them from office and make peace. One of his first actions was to foist on Pitt and Newcastle his ex-tutor, the pedantic and dim-witted Lord Bute, as Secretary of State. Thus the first of the King's yes-men added his bewildered bulk to one of the most vigorously active Administrations in British history. More were created from the remnants of the old Tory Party whom George trained to do his bidding in Opposition. Regardless of constitutional practice and obstinate as only those of moderate intelligence can be, for a whole year the King meddled with the conduct of affairs through his mouthpiece, Lord Bute, but failed to impede Pitt's triumphant management of the war. Then, on 5th October, 1761, after Bute had vainly opposed Pitt's Spanish policy, George III publicly denounced it and the great minister was forced to resign. Dazedly Bute took his place and, having received the royal instructions, proceeded to cancel the subsidy to Prussia.

Frederick now felt he was on the brink of the abyss. In the coming year of 1762 only 60,000 men could be put into uniform. To d'Argens he wrote: 'A skilled musician is said to have been asked: Could you play on a violin with only three strings? Somehow, he managed. Then another string was removed. Still he contrived to play. Finally, the last two strings were taken away and he was told to produce sounds from his instrument. But this time it was impossible.' One day, he sent some letters that had reached him from Constantinople to Finckenstein with the note:

'I cannot bring myself to read them. I am so despondent I am leaving business to chance.'

But the despairing Frederick was not the whole man. In that same being dwelt an indestructible will and tireless agility of mind. For some time he had been negotiating with the Turks and the Tartars of the Crimea. On both, but particularly on the Turks, he now pinned all his hopes. Twelve thousand of them were to break into Hungary in the spring, and 30,000 Tartars invade Russia. Then, he thought, the Austrians would have to send so many troops southward that he would outnumber the remainder and be able to occupy Bohemia and Moravia in one campaign. Frederick confided these ideas to his brother Henry, but the latter merely said it would be better to wait and see. Then Frederick decided that if the Turks had not declared war by 20th February, 1762, he would put an end to his life. 'What is to become of us next year, of my people, my army? I have not the faintest hope of salvation. All the same, I will do my utmost. We must conquer or die. Certainly, I shall not die a coward's death and when I see on 20th February that all has been in vain, I shall cling to my Stoics and the little box.' And even more clearly to his minister Finckenstein: 'As our wretched situation will no longer let us survive the coming campaign, we must get used to the thought of negotiation and saving for my nephew all we can squeeze out of our greedy enemies.' And to d'Argens: 'You know the pitfalls which surround me and can guess how much hope still remains. But we cannot discuss that until February. I have given myself this reprieve. Then it must be decided whether I follow Cato's advice or Caesar's *Commentaries*.'*

But by the time Finckenstein and d'Argens received these letters, they knew that their sentiments were out of date. On 5th January, 1762, the Empress Elizabeth died of a stroke and her nephew, Peter III, husband of Princess Catherine of Anhalt, ascended the throne of Russia. 'Dead is the beast, dead is the poison!' rejoiced Frederick, and wrote an epitaph:

> *O passant; ci-gît Messaline,*
> *Du Russe, et du Cossaque elle fut concubine,*
> *Et les épuisant tous elle quittes ces bords*
> *Pour chercher des amants dans l'empire des morts.*

Peter's first act of diplomacy was to ask Frederick, with whom his country was still at war, for the Prussian Order of the Black Eagle. Frederick sent it, and also an emissary to St Petersburg with

* i.e. commit suicide or continue to fight.

peace proposals. If the Russians wished to have East Prussia he would be content so long as he obtained compensation. But Frederick happened to be the young Czar's hero. Peter declared he would hold it a greater honour to be a Prussian general than the Czar, and he not only concluded peace but handed back East Prussia. 'The King of Prussia is now Emperor of Russia,' moaned the Saxon minister in St Petersburg. Immediately Sweden asked for peace through Frederick's sister, Queen Ulrike. It was concluded on 22nd May, 1762, a fortnight after signature of the treaty with Russia.

But in April the English subsidy had been terminated and soon, disregarding the interests of England's ally and the terms of that alliance, Bute was scrambling to seize the bloodless hand of France. At the same time he suggested to the Prussian Minister in London that his master King Frederick might care to open peace negotiations with Austria. Some sacrifices would, of course, be necessary; a province or two might have to change hands – the same provinces, in fact, that the armies of all Europe had failed to prise from Frederick's grasp and would now clearly never succeed, but which Bute fancied he could woo from him with avuncular words. Frederick's minister in London was rash enough to 'suggest with great respect' that the King should consider the English point of view. But with the certain prospect of peace with Russia and Sweden the King had no need to listen to the perfidious Bute and his minister received the searing reply: 'Learn your duty better and take note that it is not your place to proffer me such foolish and impertinent advice.' Bute's pacific aims did not, in fact, extend to Prussia. He hated Frederick no less than he hated Pitt, for he knew they were in touch and would jointly rejoice at his downfall. Moreover a remark of Frederick's had reached his ears that the English ministers belonged in a lunatic asylum. So Bute approached Kaunitz and suggested a renewal of the Anglo-Austrian alliance. He was willing, he said, to persuade Prussia to make sacrifices in Silesia. But Kaunitz was not amused, and neither was the Czar Peter when the ex-tutor enjoined him to keep Russian troops in the field against Frederick and refrain from encouraging the man by protestations of friendship. The Czar merely forwarded the English note to Berlin.

As an ally Frederick had never been a model of loyalty, but for that very reason perhaps Bute's treachery provoked him to shrill indignation. 'To break faith with an ally,' he wrote in his *History of the Seven Years War*, 'to hatch plots against him, to work zealously for his downfall, such enormities, such dark, disreputable deeds must be stigmatised as abominable so that those capable of such crimes may be deterred in future by public opinion.' Meanwhile, at Sanssouci a horse employed with a mule team for carting firewood was christened 'Lord Bute.'

George III's defection was, in fact, more than outweighed by Peter III's friendship. This had now ripened into an offensive alliance. At the end of June 1762 the Russians were to enter the field against Austria with 20,000 men. Appalled by this news, Maria Theresa managed to convince herself that the Russian liaison officers who now appeared in the Prussian camp were Frederick's own men in disguise – until the appearance of Cossack hordes in Bohemia soon removed all doubts. Then strange news came from St Petersburg. The Czar Peter had lived for twenty-four years, but mentally he was and always would be a child. For six months now, with absolute power over a vast empire, he had strutted and grimaced, aping Prussia down to the last button of his soldiers' uniforms, dissolving the secret police, restoring the banished to favour, exasperating the nobility, alienating the Church, and spending long hours playing with toy soldiers. His strong-minded wife, destined to become Catherine the Great, was politically if not personally insulted by his openly expressed doubts of her son's legitimacy. She decided to remove him. The plot was discovered, but Peter hesitated. Her choice was clear – either the throne or the scaffold, either act boldly or receive sentence of death. The same applied to Peter, with the difference that his feeble mind failed to grasp the fact. So he was forced to abdicate, and soon after, on 9th July, 1762, the conspirators – without, apparently, Catherine's knowledge – murdered him at a banquet.

Frederick considered that Peter should either have imprisoned his wife at once or else forgiven her completely. Fortunately, he kept this opinion to himself and his written advice to the Czar had been to seek an understanding with Catherine based on respect. On her accession Catherine found this letter among her husband's papers and it did something to mollify her attitude to Frederick. She had been intending to resume the war against Prussia; instead, she now terminated the alliance and recalled the troops which had been sent to Frederick's aid. The King persuaded their commander to stay another three days so as to tie down a part of the Austrian army, and then, on 21st July, 1762, Frederick defeated Daun in a fierce engagement at Burkersdorf. Next morning the Russian departed with his 20,000 men, taking with him a gift of 15,000 ducats and a diamond-studded sword.

Three weeks previously at Kassel, Duke Ferdinand of Brunswick had defeated a superior French army under Soubise with British and Hanoverian troops. No one was more annoyed at this victory than the British Prime Minister Bute: he advised the French to put up a stiffer resistance to his troops in future, otherwise, the war party under Pitt might gain the upper hand and crush him. Choiseul was already counting on the invasion of French territory by Ferdinand and predicting that 'our generals will be no better in Alsace than they were in Hesse;' when, in February 1763, peace was signed between England and France. France ceded Canada and many of her West Indian possessions, but many others that she had lost and had no means of recovering were restored to her. In the Commons, Pitt spoke against the peace for four and a half hours, arguing that it was too lenient and betrayed the interests of Prussia. 'America has been conquered in Germany!' he cried, and called the Treaty of Paris 'deceitful, treacherous, insecure and inadequate.'

Meanwhile Maria Theresa had realised she was at the end of her resources. In October 1762 Frederick had regained control of Silesia by the recapture of Schweidnitz, and on the 29th of that month Prince Henry had decisively defeated the combined Austrian and Reich forces at Freiberg, forcing the enemy to retreat homewards through Dresden. To Henry's letter telling him the news, Frederick replied joyously: 'Yesterday I was sixty, today hardly eighteen.' Five days later, to his sister Amalia, Abbess of Quedlinburg: 'I know your interest in our successes and my brother's victory. It came just at the right time when we must try to compel our enemies to an honourable and reasonable peace. You are in touch with heaven and can judge whether your eternal father favours or disfavours us. To me, poor mortal, unacquainted with so much as a dog in paradise, these matters are not revealed, and I can only enjoy good fortune and endure bad with patience.'

The peace between Prussia, Austria and Saxony which was signed at Hubertusburg on 15th February, 1763, was certainly honourable to Frederick. The frontiers of all three States remained as they had been in 1756, in other words, Frederick kept Silesia. For seven years Maria Theresa had fought in vain to recover her lost province. Frederick, at an untold price, had won the world's respect for his soldiers and his own military prowess. Skirting the abyss, he had reached the pinnacle of his fame. He had proved that, as long as he was King, his small country was a match for any in Europe. He had established the core of the future German nation. Yet the draft peace treaty had to be translated from German into French before he could understand it.

At the close of the long war Frederick felt no sense of triumph. Congratulating him on the day peace was signed, someone said it must be the happiest day in his life; the happiest day, he replied, would be the last. His refuge was his studies: 'In them I will find contentment until my lamp is extinguished. They impart restraint. They temper the harshness of absolute power with philosophy and tolerance so enabling one who is himself not perfect to govern imperfect subjects.'

In March, the King left Leipzig for home, on the way making a detour to visit Kunersdorf, the battlefield where he had learnt the meaning of despair.

*

CHAPTER TWENTY-ONE

The Arts of Peace

THE SMOKE OF BATTLE had hardly lifted than Frederick was at work on the reconstruction of his country. The day after reaching Berlin he summoned the District Chairmen of the Electoral March. The senior began a speech of welcome. 'Be silent,' broke in Frederick, 'and let me speak. Have you a pencil? Now write this down. You gentlemen are to calculate how much rye is needed for bread, how much for seed, and how many horses, oxen and cows your Districts require. Think that over carefully and come back to me the day after tomorrow.'

Army horses and military stores were distributed, and, to the amazement of Europe, the King of this small, devastated country even had a few million talers to spare for its ruined economy. Unlike his richer neighbours who were bankrupt, his war treasure comprised nearly 30,000,000 talers at the end of hostilities, mostly in debased 'Ephraimites' worth half of their face value. He kept two-thirds for military purposes and distributed the remainder, in the following ten years issuing a total of 20,000,000 for reconstruction. 'Princes,' he wrote, 'should be able, like Achilles' – he was probably thinking of Amfortas – 'to inflict wounds and to heal them.' A large part of the money was, of course, given to the nobility, but the middle class and the agricultural community received their share, so that the wounds inflicted by war did quickly heal. Seven thousand houses had been destroyed in Silesia; 8,000 new ones were built in three years. 'Under the Habsburgs,' wrote a Silesian, 'this province took a century to recover from the Thirty Years War; it has recovered from the Seven Years War with surprising speed.'

As in war, so now the body of Prussia beat to the rhythm of

Frederick's heart. He gave the orders, it was he who threatened, he who controlled. Once a year his ministers were summoned, not to discuss, but to listen while the King told them the sums he intended to grant each department of State. He mistrusted his 'bigwigs', as he called them. 'Men only look after what is theirs; the State is not the property of the ministers, therefore they have not its real welfare at heart.' If the ministers lacked public spirit, the junior officials lacked intelligence. 'Donkeys', was Frederick's favourite word for them. On a widow's request for a Civil Service pension he noted in the margin: 'I tied the donkey to the crib, why did he not eat?' A clerk who applied for promotion after thirty years' service got the answer: 'I have a heap of old mules in the stable who have done long service without being made masters of the horse.' Frederick hated the 'windbag brood' of officials and mocked their petty, title-hunting minds. When a tobacco storeman applied for the rank of *Kommissionsrat*, he appointed him instead *'Tabaksrat'* – Tobacco Master. A veterinary surgeon seeking the title of *Hofrat* (Counsellor) was made *'Viehrat'* – Cattle Adviser. As always in peacetime, Frederick spent several months in each year on tours of inspection, checking the work of State functionaries. He travelled in a thirty-year-old coach. When repairs were needed, they had to be done at night without his knowledge, for he professed to believe all such expenditure unnecessary – as a pretext, probably for striking such items from his officials' accounts. Wherever he stopped he inspected garrison troops and went into every detail of the local economy.

In July 1779, when Frederick was sixty-seven, he visited some marshlands north-west of Berlin that had been drained at his expense and were now settled with 300 families. The Royal Bailiff and Head Manager of the area was a conscientious and hard-working man named Fromme. His most outstanding gift was an extraordinary memory, of the kind that can learn timetables by heart. For a whole day he acted as the King's guide and informant. That night he recorded their conversation:

'*Frederick:* Who are you? *Fromme:* Your Majesty, I am the *Beamte* here of Fehrbellin. – What's your name ? – Fromme. – Haha! You are a son of the *Landrat* Fromme? – Your Majesty's pardon, my father was *Amtsrat* at Lehnin – *Amtsrat* ? That isn't true. Your father was *Landrat*. I knew him very well. But tell me, has the draining of the Luch been of much use to you here? – *O ja*, Your Majesty! – Do you keep more cattle than your predecessor? – Yes, Your Majesty. On this farm I have forty more cows, and altogether seventy more. – That's good. The murrain is not here in this area, is it? – No, Your Majesty. – Have you had the murrain here? – Yes. – You must use rock salt, plenty of it, then you won't get the murrain again. – Yes, Your Majesty, I do use it! But kitchen salt does nearly as well. – Don't you believe it! You mustn't pound the rock salt small, but hang it up so that the cattle can lick it. – It shall be done. – And how is your farm? – Two years ago I had the cattle disease. They all died. But I got no compensation. I can't get on my feet again. – My son, today I have some difficulty with my left ear; I cannot hear well. . . .'

As the King's carriage moved slowly forward Fromme was told to walk beside it so that he could answer more questions. After a time they came to a manor house belonging to General Ziethen. Fromme's record continues:

'Now His Majesty got out and was extremely delighted to see Herr General von Ziethen; talked with him of many things: whether the draining of the Luch had done him good; whether the murrain had been afflicting his cattle and whether he had tried using rock salt. Suddenly His Majesty stept aside, turned to me and called: "*Amtmann!*" (then close to my ear) "Who is the fat man over there with the white coat?" – I (also close to his ear): Your Majesty, that is *Landrat* Quast, of the Ruppin District. – Right.

'Now His Majesty went back to General von Ziethen and talked of various things. All at once His Majesty turned and said: "*Serviteur, Herr Landrat!*" As the gentleman was stepping forward, His Majesty said: "You can stay there, I know you. You are *Landrat* von Quast!" They had now yoked the horses. His Majesty took a very tender leave of old General von Ziethen, waved an adieu to those about, and drove on. Once we were out of the village, His Majesty took a luncheon from the carriage-pocket and for the rest of the drive ate apricots, nothing but apricots. . . .

'*Frederick:* Your tenants are in good case, I suppose? *Fromme:* Yes, Your Majesty. I can show from the Register of Mortgages that they have about 50,000 talers capital among them. – Good! May you keep them like that! – Yes, Your Majesty. It is very good for the subject to have money, but it also makes him insolent, like the subjects here, who have complained seven times about me to Your Majesty, in order to be free of socage! – I presume they will have had a reason. – Your gracious pardon; there was an inquiry and it was found that I had not oppressed the tenants, but had always been in the right and merely held them to their

212

duty. But there the matter remained: the tenants were not punished. Your Majesty always puts the tenants in the right and the poor official has to be wrong. . . . – Well, do what you will with the tenants, only don't oppress them! – Your Majesty, that would never enter my head.

'Now his Majesty came upon a number of peasants who were mowing rye. They had formed themselves into two lines and were wiping their scythes. *Frederick:* The Devil! These people will be wanting money from me, I suppose? *Fromme:* Oh, no, Your Majesty! They are full of joy that you have been graciously pleased to visit the district, *Frederick:* But I'll not give them anything! . . .

'We now came upon the territory of the *Amt* Neustadt. I brought up Herr *Amtsrat* Klausius to the carriage. . . .'

Frederick: What is your name?

Klausius: Klausius.

Frederick: Klau-si-us. *Na,* have you many cattle here?

Klausius: 1,887 cows, Your Majesty.

Frederick: And is the population also increasing well? Are there jolly children?

Klausius: O ja, Your Majesty.

Frederick: Who is that, to the right, over there?

Fromme: Bauinspektor Menzelius, who is in charge of the buildings here.

Frederick: Am I in Rome! These are all Latin names. What's the settlement called?

Fromme: Klausiushof.

Klausius: Your Majesty, it can also be called Klaushof.

Frederick: The name is Klau-si-ushof. And the other settlement?

Fromme: Brenkenhof.

Frederick: That's not its name.

Fromme: It is, Your Majesty. There is no other name for it.

Frederick: It is called Brenken-ho-fius-hof! . . .'

The King returned from each of his tours with wads of notes on the state of towns, villages, forests and fields:

On the estates of Graf Wallis they sell their flax to Bohemia; why is it not spun and treated in the County of Glatz? – The town of Striegau complain that they have no manufactures and no source of wealth; I do not see what can be done to help them unless some new manufacture can be started there – the preparation of vitriol or something similar. – The towns of Schweidnitz and Neisse lack roofing tiles; shall have to think about this. – N.B., for the tax-register of Glatz a

213

distinction must be made between the good, worthy nobility and foreigners. – When a farmer emigrates from Glatz his estate is confiscated. – Complaints from Schmiedeberg of oppression by merchants; investigate and send me a report. – More sheep could be kept in Glatz area if they were grazed in woods on the mountains; but question whether their wool would be good or not; at least it would help the poor country people who could live on goats' milk.

Silesia in particular was an object of Frederick's unremitting attention. Under the Austrians 2,000 troops had been stationed in the province, now there were 40,000. Then taxes had been low, now they were high. The nobles had been immune and lived a life of pleasure in Vienna; now they had to pay taxes, sit on their estates and cultivate the soil – and the King, if ill luck so willed, might come and examine the result at any time. State officials had been a rarity and those there were had been easy going, fond of good living and tolerant. Now, a tax collector crouched in a miserable office-cum-bedroom in every District town, usually a retired N.C.O. who collected the land taxes which village magistrates had to pay punctually on the appointed day. Despite a salary which barely kept him from starvation, he laboured on until his hands were too weak to tie the money-bags, his loyalty braced by a nod the King had once given him on his way through the town. A keener air was now blowing through this province; agriculture and the textile industry were beginning to flourish. Despite higher taxation the people were better off than before, though many looked back with regret to the milder climate of the Habsburgs. To be a Prussian was perhaps an honour but it was certainly no pleasure.

Frederick's economic policy aimed at making the State powerful and independent. For this purpose imports had to be reduced and exports increased, industry developed, immigrants attracted into the country and a reserve of ready money created. Frederick shared these basic ideas of mercantilism with all his contemporaries, but he applied them with greater energy. The intrusion of the State into every sphere of life was nothing new, but in countries with a weaker government there still remained scope for private enterprise. Not so in Prussia. The export of raw wool incurred the death penalty. If a sheep-farmer failed to make good he paid a fine of 1,000 ducats. If a well-to-do citizen wanted to marry, he had to buy porcelain from the royal manufactory before he could obtain a licence. But on the whole Frederick's innovations were salutary; he attracted thousands of immigrants to Prussia, founded 900 new villages, reclaimed 100,000 acres of marshland and made a start on 'ground clearance', i.e. the consolidation of farmlands; he planted 10,000 acres of woodland; forced the peasants to grow potatoes; and fought a ceaseless battle for feeding-stuffs: lucerne, lupins, clover and cattle turnip. He sent one of his tenants' sons to study agriculture in England, ensuring that he worked by requiring reports from him in diary form. The sight of waste land made him fume with rage. A barren area that his notes told him should be covered with ten-year-old trees made the forester concerned liable to immediate dismissal. He laid down the number of cows that should be given to new settlers, started instruction courses in dairy farming and specified the types of 'containers and machines to be used for butter making and how the same shall be kept clean.' Grain prices were regulated by his storage system: if the price of rye rose above twenty-four groschen, he sold from store at twenty groschen; if it fell to eighteen, he bought up and replenished. Thanks to this system he was able to absorb 40,000 people from Saxony and Bohemia when the rest of Europe had to go hungry. Grain prices in Prussia were often a third of those in southern Germany. He even planned to build mosques and make Tartars into good Prussian citizens. Fortunately, perhaps, the Tartars declined.

To get new industries started the King had often to give the entrepreneur a temporary monopoly or support him from State funds. He realised the disadvantages of this more clearly than other rulers: 'I have never favoured a monopoly, for it always has a bad result: the monopolist develops no real diligence or enterprise because there is no one to compete with him, hence he neglects his work and produces poor goods.' When the owner of a new leather factory demanded that the Silesians should sell him skins at fixed prices Frederick decreed: 'That won't do! They can sell him as many as they like, but there must be no compulsion.' The *Oberpräsident* of East Prussia applied for a subsidy for a sailcloth factory; he got a rude answer: 'You're not businesslike; there's nothing in it. People must do these things with their own money – they take the profit. When it's their own money they work harder and take more trouble.' The King certainly spared no pains to foster enterprise. One of his factories made small pictures of saints. Before production started, he had inquiries made as to which saints were the most popular. One day the garrison commander of Breslau received the order: 'I require to know the price that Breslau retailers pay for smoking tobacco, and also how much the soldier has to pay for the tobacco he smokes. I await your report at the earliest.' When Frederick discovered that large

215

quantities of rags were used in households for lighting fires he organised a rag collection, adding: 'It must also be arranged that the collectors carry a quantity of tinder with them to hand out to people and show them how it can be used equally well for lighting fires so that they do not have to burn so many rags.'

Frederick's tax policy was less successful, though in contrast to other European countries the State finances were strictly controlled and there was little or no extravagance. The expenses of the Court were kept to the minimum. Frederick exercised a rigid economy and the smallest increase in expenditure provoked as much wrath as though one of his generals had sold a fortress to the Queen-Empress. The head of the royal kitchens who had considerably exceeded the annual budget of 1,000 talers and incurred debts to the value of 488 talers was given two years' fortress detention, and the sentence was later increased to imprisonment. Frederick's only extravagance was the granting of 2,000,000 talers in 1763 for the construction of the New Palace, a huge, ungainly building erected between 1763 and 1769 in a corner of the park of Sanssouci. Apart from impressing Europe with the solvency of Prussian finances, the building's only use was to give work to a number of masons and artisans. Frederick himself never lived in it. Meanwhile, his foreign envoys had to use the same shabby coaches as their predecessors, and go on using them until the axles broke. Prussian officials were miserably paid, schoolmasters, for instance, getting between fifty and 100 talers a year. Travelling expenses were strictly controlled. Precise details had to be given, receipts attached and before undertaking a journey officials were told by their head of department how many days it should take.

Frederick had only two big expense items: reconstruction and development of the economy, to which he gave about 2,000,000 talers a year, and the army, which swallowed 13,000,000. He never allowed the State to run into debt, on the contrary, the budget had to show a surplus of 2,000,000 a year, which was then put to reserve. At his death this amounted to 51,000,000 talers. And with all his cheeseparing he tried to spare the poor. When the administrator of Taubenheim suggested cutting the salaries of lower officials Frederick answered: 'I thank the *Geheimer Rat* of Taubenheim for his good intentions and suggestions for economy, but I do not find them realistic. With food and everything so dear, the people of that class live miserably enough as it is, and they ought to have an increase rather than a reduction of salary. Nevertheless, I accept the principle of his plan

216

and will apply his suggestion to himself, deducting 1,000 talers from his annual salary on the understanding that he reports again at the end of the year to inform me whether this has proved beneficial or otherwise to his domestic convenience.' Claims for compensation (mostly for damage suffered during the war) were sifted rigorously. A Berlin wine merchant, for instance, alleged that the Russians had stolen eighty-two casks of wine from him. Frederick wrote in the margin of the claim: 'Why no mention of the damage he suffered in the Flood, when his cellars were under water?'

Anticipating the British system of graded income tax by a hundred years, Frederick wrote in his *Political Testament*: 'In financial administration, fairness and humaneness must both have a voice, but humaneness must come first and determine the type of impost; fairness demands that no one should pay taxes to the State beyond his capacity and that the payments should be proportionate: a man with only 100 talers to spend should not lose more than two of them, while anyone with an income of 1,000 talers could easily pay 100. Taxation should not affect the worker, the soldier or the poor man, but only the well-to-do and the rich citizen.'

Frederick attempted to offset the immense sums required for the army by improving methods of tax collection. In those days the most efficient officials came from France, where the system of tax farming required them to pay a fixed annual sum to the State, but anything above that sum went into their own pockets. Frederick abhorred tax farming because it led to exploitation, but he decided to separate the excise system from the existing machinery of State and hand it over to a newly formed department called the 'Regie,' which was run by French directors and employed 200 French and 1,800 German officials. No doubt Frederick hoped that the foreigners would be more ruthless in their methods. The head of the department, de la Haye, and his three co-directors each received a salary of 15,000 talers a year (Frederick's ministers got 4,000) and, between them, 5 per cent of whatever surplus they succeeded in collecting. This varied between 50,000 and 100,000 talers a year.

Frederick required the 'Regie' to abolish the excise duty on bread, but allowed it to be increased from two to six pfennig a litre on beer and to one pfennig a pound on meat, with the exception of pork, which, as the poor man's food, remained duty free. The duties on wines, liqueurs and spices were to be heavily increased. These taxes seem trifling by modern standards, but in those days they were felt to be oppressive. The coffee monopoly was even more disliked. The King chose to call coffee a luxury beverage because he wanted to stop 700,000 talers leaving the country every year in payment for coffee imports. 'In his youth His Majesty himself was brought up on beer soup; people today can just as well be brought up on beer soup, it is much more healthy than coffee.' So the King sold a pound of roasted coffee which fetched five groschen in Hamburg for twenty-four groschen. If a man bought twenty pounds in a single order, he was allowed a pound of raw coffee at nine groschen and a roasting permit. To stop smuggling, which was mostly in raw coffee, the King made it an offence punishable with three years' fortress detention to roast coffee without a permit. Four thousand disabled soldiers were appointed 'Coffee-sniffers' with the right to enter any house at any time of the day or night and nose round for the scent of roasting coffee. Often they brought coffee with them and then pretended they had found it. As a result there was a big drop in coffee consumption until de la Haye discovered that a lower price brought in a higher tax yield.

The 'Regie' became so hated its officials had to go about armed and the British Ambassador joked that the French were taking their revenge for Rossbach. But a tenth of the revenue raised by the 'Regie' went in salaries and expenses and the net yield of one to two million talers was due more to increasing prosperity than to the merits of the system. Whenever they could, the tax officials stole or took bribes – a 'nest of rascals' the King called them, and gradually sent most of the Frenchmen home. His older officials disapproved of Frederick's economic policy, but whatever their age, wisdom or experience, they were not employed to express their opinions, but to carry out his orders. Those few that dared to criticise became the targets of vulgar abuse. Ministers who suggested that foreign countries might take economic reprisals if wine imports were stopped were told they were obviously drunkards. In the economic crisis which swept Europe in 1766, the King called for a memorandum on the situation. The ministers had the courage to mention some of his own measures as contributing to the crisis. Their report was dismissed as 'obviously venal' and beneath it the King wrote in his own hand: 'I am amazed at the impertinent tale you send me. I excuse the ministers on grounds of ignorance, but the malice and corruption of the writer [of the report] must be punished in exemplary fashion, otherwise I shall never bring the rabble to heel.' The author of the report, *Geheimrat* Ursinus, was sent to a jail for a year, on the pretext of irregularities in his official conduct.

It is not easy to pass final judgment on Frederick's economic policy. There is much to show that, in the prevailing context, his measures were on balance sound. We have, of course, no accurate means of comparing the standard of living in Prussia at that time with her neighbours'. One thing is certain: the growth of Prussian power placed no great economic burden on the people. The weight of taxation per head was 1.6 talers on Frederick's accession and 1.8 talers at his death. We also know that the population of Prussia increased at a greater rate during this period than that of Hanover or Saxony. At his death the country had 5,750,000 inhabitants, of whom 3,500,000 lived in the original provinces, whereas the total population in 1740 had been only 2,200,000.

. . . . . .

Frederick hated injustice and cruelty. In his youth he had suffered from both. Allowing for the fact that, like all despotic rulers, he became increasingly arbitrary with age, at least with him arbitrariness never became a form of self-indulgence. Though blind to the possibility of any other form of government than absolute monarchy, he never looked on himself as anything more than a fallible human being called to rule over his fellow men. He believed in the principles of the Enlightenment and tried to give them effect, and though his cynicism was often offensive in private, in public affairs it was a valuable corrective to the bigotry and fanaticism of those who, unlike himself, did not think it possible they might be mistaken. Thus he abolished the death penalty for abortion and forbade the practice of forcing unmarried mothers to do penance in church. Beneath a sentence of death passed on a cavalry trooper for sodomy he wrote: 'The swine is to be transferred to the infantry.' No doubt it gave him pleasure to confound the over-zealous with mild irony and sweetly reasonable comments. On a heavy sentence passed on a blasphemer he noted: 'That the prisoner has blasphemed against God shows that he does not know Him; his defamation of myself I forgive him; but insulting a noble Counsellor deserves exemplary punishment – he shall be imprisoned for half an hour.'

But Frederick's concern for the underdog led him to commit a most curious blunder, though its ultimate effects were excellent. A man named Arnold had rented a water-mill from a Graf Schmettau at Züllichau. When called upon to pay large arrears of rent he claimed that he could not because a Herr Gersdorff had dammed the stream above his mill to make a carp pool, and

219

ever since he, Arnold, had been starved of water-power. The Küstrin Land Office gave Arnold notice to quit, whereupon he petitioned the King. Frederick ordered two officials to investigate the case. The facts showed that Arnold was in the wrong, but thinking to please the King one official reported in his favour. Now the Land Office was ordered to investigate. Their report stated that a second mill between Arnold's and the carp pool received plenty of water to drive the wheel and was in full operation; therefore the termination of his lease was justified. At this point, Frederick decided that honest Arnold was in the right and everyone else, particularly the landed gentry, was in league against him. He ordered his Supreme Court of Justice to go into the papers and report. The Grand Chancellor and Minister of Justice von Fürst was not enthusiastic. This was a test of strength. Had not Frederick himself decreed that the courts were not to pay 'the least attention to my instructions if there is anything in them subversive of established law'? Very well . . . The Supreme Court stood by the verdict of the Land Office and – intentionally or otherwise – did not even state its reasons for doing so. Now Frederick was doubly certain: a clique of nobles had shamefully conspired to pervert the course of justice. Miller Arnold's stream had turned to a trickle so that a country gentleman could have water for his carp. Plagued by gout and already not in the best of tempers, Frederick summoned the Grand Chancellor and the three judges who had prepared the report to attend on him at 2 p.m. punctually on Tuesday, 7th December, 1779, at the Palace. Frederick had been seeking a chance to get rid of his Minister of Justice; he had his eye on a young lawyer from Breslau, von Carmer by name, who had suggested to him a number of drastic law reforms. At 2 p.m. the four judges assembled before the royal presence. Frederick was reclining in an easy chair, one hand in a muff, each foot on a low stool. His hair was undressed and he was wearing a dressing-gown. 'Come closer!' he ordered. The men advanced till they were about six feet away. 'Now . . .' – and completely ignoring the Grand Chancellor, the King spoke to the three judges in a slow, deliberate voice, describing how poor Arnold had suffered and ending with the question: 'Is that justice?' 'No!' they chorused, while the Grand Chancellor remained silent. 'No!' the King echoed. 'Yet what does the Berlin Tribunal do?' Here the Chancellor, wounded to the quick, spoke for the first time: '*Kammergericht*, Sire, the Supreme Court of Justice, not a tribunal.' The recording clerk looked up. 'Put down "Tribunal of the Supreme Court",' said Frederick over his shoulder, then, balefully, to the Grand Chancellor: 'Your successor is already appointed. About your business, sir, on this instant! March!' And without a word the Chancellor marched. The other judges dared not open their mouths. Frederick fumed and scolded. As usual, the court's judgment had begun with the words: 'In the name of the King.' This particularly annoyed Frederick. '*Meinen Namen cruel missbraucht!*' he kept on exclaiming, striking the paper several times with his gouty hand. How much had the carp-fancier paid them, he asked the judges. They were too terrified to deny or even explain coherently why they had entered judgment against Arnold. The King had them taken to prison, quashed the judgment, reinstalled the miller, had the carp pond filled in and dismissed the Administrative President of Küstrin. The King's minister von Zedlitz was then instructed to take proceedings against the three judges, being advised that the lightest sentence required would be dismissal from office and a year's fortress detention. Zedlitz manfully refused, so Frederick sentenced them himself. His decision was made known to every court in the land so that 'they may thereby take warning and commit no such gross injustices, for they must know that the humblest peasant, yes, and even the beggar, is, no less than His Majesty, a human being and must be able to obtain full justice, all persons being equal before the Law.'

The case of the miller Arnold became known throughout Europe. Catherine the Great praised Frederick's humane action. In France, prints were published showing him holding the scales of Justice. D'Alembert spoke of 'judicial cannibals.' In *Die Aufgeregten* the youthful Goethe put the words into Frederick's mouth: 'I well know that the rich had many advocates, but the poor have only one – myself.' Abroad, the King's action was generally approved. At home, the Berlin populace was delighted, at Fürst's downfall and a joyful mob surrounded the Palace. Millers of less reputable character than Arnold were delighted, too, and soon the royal secretaries were deluged with petitions voicing every grievance from which a miller could suffer. Berlin Society, including the Royal Princes, hastened, on the other hand, to express sympathy with the fallen Chancellor and to deplore the distress caused to persons of quality by the King's well-meant but misguided action. And there seems no doubt that it was misguided. With hundreds of cases to choose from where the course of justice had been diverted to suit the nobility, Frederick had to pick on one which the courts had dealt with correctly and impartially. But once having made the mistake, he could not afford to undo it. He had made innocent judges suffer, but it had been in a good cause. Four months of their sentence were remitted, one was later restored to office and all four were rehabilitated after the King's death. The case had one excellent result: von Carmer was made Minister of Justice. His fresh, human approach came to be felt throughout the whole legal system, and it was he who introduced the *Allgemeine Preussische Landrecht*, one of the first progressive legal codes which conferred its blessings on Prussia for three generations.

The fact remains that the King's actions in the Arnold affair were, on balance, grossly unjust. Four judges, headed by the Grand Chancellor, were dismissed, disgraced and three of them imprisoned without any charge whatever being brought against them. Whether or not they were guilty of any offence – and as it happens they were not – they were treated by Frederick with total disregard for the rights he so eloquently claimed for beggars and peasants. The publicity he deliberately gave the case and the urgency, the time he spent on it, his threats and the violence of his language seem ludicrously excessive in relation to the case itself – the carp pool, the water-wheel and the miller's rent. If he was so concerned to have justice for this man, why did he not send for him and decide himself on the merits of his grievance? He did so in any case in the end, after setting the whole legal machinery of the State in motion and then discarding it as worthless. All the same, it was the only machinery in existence and to hold it up to popular derision was not calculated to enable beggars, peasants or anyone else to obtain impartial justice in the courts. If Frederick's aim in this affair was solely to protect the underdog then his actions appear nothing short of lunatic. But that was not his main purpose. Arnold and his water-mill gave him an excuse to remind ministers, judges, lawyers, the nobility and the gentry – in short, all who by reason of birth or office were in positions of authority – that they were expected to use their power for the general good and not for their own sectional interests. Frederick was the first monarch in Europe to transform the privileged nobility into a class of hard-working administrative officials. In France, Sweden, Poland and many of the German States the aristocracy still exercised enormous irresponsible power. In Prussia only the King possessed power by right; all authority derived from him. But if he called himself the first servant of the State, than all were its servants. The Prussian nobility was poor and had to live frugally. Wealth was no longer the key to power.

'The door to all offices of State must be closed to wealth as possessing no merit in itself and opened only to superior talents and outstanding services.' Seldom in any country have differences in living standards been so small as in Frederick's Prussia, and seldom has an upper class been called upon to work so hard in peace and give so freely of its blood in war for so little material reward. Arnold and his water-mill were transformed by Frederick into a symbol reminding all those who worked under him in an official capacity that their only inalienable privilege was the privilege to serve. Thus in this case the wrongs suffered by individuals were offset by the furtherance of social justice. Only those who have never held the reins of powers in their hands will believe that good can be achieved in this world except at the price of error and discomfort. It is only the idle who never make mistakes.

CHAPTER TWENTY-TWO

*

The Partition of Poland

As FREDERICK RODE HOME from the Seven Years War his future foreign policy was clear in his mind. He needed peace, and to ensure it he needed an ally. France was hostile. He had been deserted by Britain, and he thought that, secure in their island, the British would always be unpredictable friends. Maria Theresa he dared not trust, even if she was prepared to come to terms. There remained Russia.

But would a Russian alliance ensure peace? Catherine was a hard-headed, bellicose woman, one who sent her lovers for preliminary examination to the Court physician and for trial to her ladies, who drowned insurrections in blood while corresponding with Voltaire and Diderot on philosophy, a woman who filled Frederick with misgiving. And how long would she stay on the throne? Her subjects were by no means reconciled to this German princess who had climbed it with such indecent haste after the murder of the Czar, her husband. She was planning to win their love by conquest in Turkey and, worse from Frederick's point of view, by annexing Poland. Poland, she thought, was a plum ready to fall into her lap. But Frederick, too, wanted his bite, that strip of Poland that ran northwards to the shores of the Baltic and separated his territories of East Prussia and Pomerania. He wanted to round off his estates and he wanted Catherine's friendship – a difficult task to achieve, but not, he thought, impossible.

Six times as large and six times as populous as the Prussia Frederick had inherited, the gigantic Kingdom of Poland stretched from the Vistula to the Dnieper. But on this fertile country there rested a curse – the Polish nobility. One-tenth almost of the

14,000,000 inhabitants owned titles of nobility. All public offices were reserved to them, they were exempt from all taxes and dues, only they were entitled to vote in elections for a new king or to send representatives to the Imperial Diet. They held a monopoly in justice and administration and could not be put under arrest. Trade and business were barred to them on pain of losing their status. Military service was not highly esteemed, hence the only occupation they could pursue was farming. Estates were not passed on by primogeniture, but all male children inherited, with the result that the land was split up into ever smaller parcels, until it was said that a dog lying at the front door had his tail on the neighbour's soil. Thus apart from thirty wealthy families and 20,000 prosperous landowners, there were over 1,000,000 lesser nobles, called the *Schlachta*, living in dire poverty. These people were the laughing-stock of Europe. Unable to read and housed in louse-infested huts, they still proudly displayed the spurs which were the symbol of their nobility and even when begging wore them on their bare, dirt-encrusted feet. Many worked for wealthy magnates as coachmen or cooks, for they were allowed to enter the service of their fellow nobles and could even be thrashed by them – provided the chastisement took place on a carpet.

Under the dead weight of this all-powerful nobility, the lot of the serfs was truly desperate. The Venetian Ambassador in St Petersburg reported that no people in any part of the world were in greater distress. By decree of the Imperial Diet they were forbidden to teach their children to read or to send them to school. 'I see before my mind's eye,' wrote their fellow countryman Staszic, 'five-sixths of the Polish people. I see millions of wretched creatures, half naked, skins and rough cloth their only covering, disfigured by filth and smoke, breathing in gasps, with deep-sunk eyes, surly, degenerate and brutalised. They can hardly feel or think. They look more like animals than men. One barely realises one is in the presence of *Homo sapiens*. Exhausted by his day's work, the father sleeps with his naked children on rotting straw, on the same patch where his cow stands with her calf and the sow lies with her young.' Bread was a luxury to the serfs. They lived off rye pudding, cabbage, herrings and brandy. None of their mud huts had chimneys. Trade in the countryside was confined to stolen tree-bark and wooden spoons. There was no postal service. no apothecaries. Every winter wolves took toll of the people.

And what of the middle class? There was none! The town dwellers had originally been Germans, and German law had prevailed in the towns as recently as the Reformation. But when the Polish aristocracy had seized power, the Germans had emigrated westwards and now there were only six towns in the whole country with houses built of brick.

Existing miserably on their small acres, the *Schlachta* discovered a new means of making money. They succeeded in passing a law whereby not only every single resolution, but every measure proposed throughout one session of the Polish Diet had to be unanimously approved before it could be put into effect. Thus one dissident voice could paralyse the work of legislation. This meant that, in future, the vote of every member had to be purchased in advance. The result was that for nearly a century nine out of every ten sessions of the Diet achieved nothing. The Primate of Poland, Archbishop Lubienski, wrote despairingly: 'Such disorder is unexampled in history and one is forced to conclude that a kingdom based on so foolish a system must either fall a prey to its enemies or become a desert.' As for religious beliefs, Roman Catholicism was the only recognised creed and nearly half the population who were members of the Greek Orthodox or Protestant Churches possessed no rights whatever. Here again the lesser nobility found a way to enrich themselves by roving the country in armed bands, seeking out 'heretics' to despoil and murder. When they were able to afford boots, they wore one black and one red to signify fire and slaughter.

As the Polish Diet was not able to carry a single resolution for years on end, some other method of reaching decisions had to be devised. Once more a profitable solution was found. When political conflicts became acute, the armed bands of the *Schlachta* decided the issue by force of arms. Thus a kind of constitutional anarchy prevailed. The crowning calamity in this tortured country were the weak and dissipated Kings of Poland, who were drawn from the House of Saxony. Under their rule the nobility confined themselves to 'eating, drinking and loosening the belt.' No one thought of reform. The depths to which Polish prestige had sunk in the eyes of Europe are revealed by the Diet's resolution that no King of Poland might in any circumstances abdicate.

In the seventeenth century King Johann Kasimir of Poland had prophesied that thanks to her constitution Poland would one day be partitioned between Brandenburg, Russia and Austria and since then it had become the accepted practice for Polish kings to sell portions of their territory to the highest bidder. Thus Augustus the Strong had offered 'Polish Prussia' (the same strip of territory that Frederick now coveted) to the Hohenzollerns in

1700 in order to enlist their help against his enemies, and the 'national King' Stanislaus had repeated the offer in 1740. But Russia, the most powerful State in the East, had opposed these concessions, being anxious to obtain the whole of Poland herself. During the Seven Years War the realisation of this dream had come nearer owing to the fact that Poland, in gross breach of her neutrality, had given Russian troops free passage through the country.

When the King of Poland and Saxony died on 5th October, 1763, Catherine decided to go a step farther by arranging that one of her former lovers and also a one-time Polish Ambassador in St Petersburg, Stanislaus Poniatovski, should succeed him. Stanislaus was a handsome and noble nonentity, just the man to occupy a throne as Catherine's puppet. Through him she planned to endear herself to her Russian subjects by obtaining religious and political freedom for her Greek Orthodox co-religionists in Poland. It was useless to approach the strictly Catholic Maria Theresa, so Catherine suggested to the King of Prussia that they should co-operate in managing the election of the new King of Poland. Frederick was agreeable, but in return wanted an alliance with Russia that would avert an Austrian war of revenge and also guarantee him Silesia, and he replied in this sense to Catherine. Her answer was courteous but cunning. She was pleased, she said, that the King agreed to help her secure the election of Stanislaus as King of Poland and looked to him to fulfil his promise. As for 'more intimate' ties, they, surely, already existed and required no formal recognition. At the moment, unfortunately, she was so busy that she did not wish to burden the King with a longer letter. Frederick replied coolly: 'I shall await the moment when the weighty matters that occupy you allow you time to answer more precisely the letter which I have had the honour to write to you.'

Catherine was incensed. She had three good reasons for disliking Frederick: he was a formidable military commander with the best army in Europe, he despised women and he had procured her marriage and so, indirectly, her throne. In her first manifesto to her people she had called him the mortal enemy of Russia. And for personal reasons she did not want to alienate Austria, as Kaunitz was holding out hopes of making the murderer of her husband and also her present lover, Gregor Orloff, a Prince of the Reich, so enabling her in due course to marry him. Orloff was a handsome thirty-year-old Guards officer with the proven ability of reducing the strong-minded Catherine to the

227

status of an obedient slave. So she merely sent Frederick a few crates of water melons — 'I should have preferred a treaty of alliance,' he remarked — and spun out the negotiations. As Frederick expressed it, her intention was obviously to keep him amused with the prospect of an alliance until her candidate was elected King of Poland, and that being so, he said no more on the matter, but arranged instead for Turkey to send an ambassador to Berlin. 'I want to see if these Russians will show more eagerness to clinch matters if I, for my part, show none.'

Meanwhile, not daring to place the crown on her Stanislaus's head without the backing of one of the three Great Powers, Catherine was putting out feelers in Vienna and Paris. But there was no desire in either capital to obtain a Polish king from Catherine's bed and she was obliged to return to Frederick. On 11th April, 1764, the treaty of alliance was signed. It was to last for eight years. Each party guaranteed the other's territory, which meant that Catherine guaranteed Frederick's possession of Silesia, the same province that Russia had spent 120,000 lives and 60,000,000 roubles in an attempt to restore to Austria. The treaty also provided that Prussia should receive recompense if she were obliged to take joint action with Russia in Poland. Frederick himself looked on the alliance as a means of intimidating Austria. 'The best thing is that there are grounds for assuming the alliance will never be invoked; otherwise I should have been very foolish to let myself in for all this.' He was deeply gratified to be on good terms with Russia, for he had been one of the first men in Europe to appreciate her importance. Five years later, he wrote to Prince Henry: 'At the moment, my dear brother, I am in the closest accord with the Russians. May heaven keep them in this good mood which saves us from war. Russia is immensely powerful and in fifty years' time she will be making the whole of Europe tremble. Descended from the Huns who destroyed the Eastern Roman Empire, they will soon be reaching westwards and giving concern to the Austrians whose short-sighted policy first brought these barbarians to Germany and taught them the art of war.'

The Diet of Convocation to elect the new King of Poland foregathered at the end of August 1764. There being no Saxon candidate, Stanislaus Poniatovski was without a rival. Protests were raised, with French and Austrian approval, against his election on the grounds that Catherine would marry him immediately he had become King, so uniting Poland and Russia. Catherine tried to dispose of them by ordering her former lover to marry someone else forthwith. Instead, Stanislaus solemnly promised the Diet that he would marry only a Roman Catholic. As Catherine was officially of the Greek Orthodox Church this disposed of the French and Austrian objection; there remained the Poles. Whatever Stanislaus or anyone might say, they knew they were destined to become a province of Russia and in their despair they offered the Polish crown to Frederick's brother Prince Henry. But Frederick, with his mind now bent on peace and consolidation, was determined to have no hand in Polish affairs and refused even to consider his brother's candidature.

The election now went forward without a hitch. Opponents of Stanislaus were only able to summon 10,000 men under Prince Radziwill to give effect to their wishes and they were dispersed by Russian troops. At this election only ten men, an unusually low number, were actually massacred. The rouble did its work – to be exact, 3,000,000 roubles; the opposition, as Plutarch said of Demosthenes, suddenly developed a hoarseness caused by swallowing gold and silver, and, on 7th September, Stanislaus was unanimously elected King. 'Nothing seems to me so admirable,' wrote the fifty-two-year-old Frederick to the Czarina Catherine with that mild sarcasm characteristic of his later years, 'than the way in which you have carried out so many great things as it were effortlessly, and without the use of compulsion or force. . . .'

Stanislaus had promised Catherine to grant the Polish 'Dissidents', i.e. the Protestant and Greek Orthodox minorities, equal status with the Roman Catholics, and his first step was to propose a law granting freedom of worship to members of the Orthodox church. But when the King's spokesman tried to introduce the measure in the Diet, pandemonium broke out and he was lucky to escape with his life. Catherine now intervened with Russian gold. Eighty thousand of the nobility were bribed to do her bidding. The Bishops of Cracow and Kiev were arrested and sent to Siberia and a new Diet convened under the muzzles of Russian guns granted equal status to the Dissidents and, in February 1768, approved a treaty of eternal friendship between Poland and Russia which placed the Polish Constitution under Russian guarantee. It would have approved the Koran, said a bishop, if Catherine had so desired. Poland was now virtually a province of Russia.

Frederick was thoroughly alarmed. He had no desire to see Russia pocket her neighbour, and still less to send Prussian troops to defend Russia against an Austrian or Turkish attack provoked by Catherine's thinly disguised act of aggression. He urged moderation. Maria Theresa spoke of the criminal suppression of Polish liberties, of which she could not be a passive spectator, to which she could not be indifferent, which she was bound to view with concern, and almost, but not quite, spoke of unsheathing the sword – all of which had no effect on Catherine whatever. Now France decided to stir up the Sultan of Turkey to strike a blow for Poland, and in October 1768, after receiving large sums of money from the French the Sultan took the opportunity of a Russian trespass over his frontier to declare war and cast the Russian Ambassador into the dungeon of the Seven Towers. Six months later the Turkish armies were ready for the field, and soon after, the first battle was fought. 'Immense numbers of the Heathen were cast into Eternal Fire,' read the Sultan's communiqué, 'and some few of the Faithful assuaged their thirst at the springs of Paradise' – nevertheless, the Turks were decisively beaten in a victory, as Frederick said, of the one-eyed over the blind. But his own peril was thereby increased. 'Good heavens,' he lamented, 'why was not the affair confined to the election of a Polish king? Everything was going splendidly, and now this Dissident business has ruined everything.' For as Turkey had declared war on Russia, he was now obliged by treaty to support Catherine with 22,000 men or 300,000 roubles a year. He decided to pay, though he had always hated parting with money.

But Frederick was still left with the urgent problem: how to avoid being involved in the Austro-Russian war which now threatened, so helping Russia to retain Poland and obtaining nothing himself, probably, 'but a fine compliment and a sable coat.' One thing was clear. Catherine would never agree to end her victorious war against the Turks without some territorial gain; in other words, without risking a war with Austria. The solution was to find her compensation elsewhere, preferably in Poland, which was already under her influence. Instead of controlling the whole of Poland indirectly, she could be offered direct control of a part. From Frederick's point of view the plan had three advantages: it would prevent Russia and Austria going to war over Turkey, it might succeed in reducing Catherine's sphere of influence, and thirdly, as Catherine had promised that his help would not go unrewarded, it might procure Frederick the coveted link between Pomerania and East Prussia. Frederick ordered his ambassador in St Petersburg to approach Catherine on these lines. But, not surprisingly, Catherine found the suggestion unattractive. It would mean that she would not gain but actually lose by defeating the Turks. If Austria was determined to exploit the situation to her advantage, it would be better for Austria, Russia and Prussia to drive the Turks from Europe and a part of Asia so that Austria and Russia could then divide the spoils and Frederick have his corridor in Poland. But Frederick understood the hazards of war better than Catherine and he was horrified by her plan. Her appetite seemed to be growing alarmingly. The time had come to make it clear that if she went too far she might bring a Prussian-Austrian-Turkish alliance into being, and the way to achieve this was obviously to bring about an improvement in Prusso-Austrian relations.

Frederick might not have succeeded if he had been dealing with Maria Theresa alone, but since the death of her husband, the Reich Emperor Francis, in 1765 her son Joseph had been co-Regent of Austria. He had also been elected to succeed his father as Emperor. Joseph, now aged twenty-nine, was ambitious, well meaning and a firm believer in the principles of the Enlightenment. On becoming Regent he had given his private fortune of 22,000,000 ducats to the State. A tireless worker and indefatigable reformer, he believed that by the application of reason alone he could make the Austrian people happy. But if his Kantian mind had been able to grasp the fact, he would have realised that an unbridgeable gulf separated him from his deeply religious and music-loving subjects. He himself had no feeling for either music or religion. The light of his life was intellect. Instinct he mistrusted. His heart was cold. Unlike his mother he had no cause to loathe Frederick and in fact he admired and envied him. But he lacked wisdom, as his mother saw. 'It is high time,' she wrote at the end of one of her long letters to her son, 'to give up those puns and witticisms whose only object is to humiliate others and make them look ridiculous. One alienates all decent people by indulging in them and retains only the knaves and flatterers. After this sermon, which you will forgive, my heart loving you, as it does, and my country all too dearly, I should like to characterise your talents by drawing a comparison: you are as coquettish with your intellect as your sister Elizabeth is with her charms; so long as she pleases someone, whether it is a soldier on guard duty or a prince, she is content.'

When touring the battlefields of the Seven Years War in 1766, the young Joseph had tried to arrange a meeting with the King of Prussia, but for obvious reasons Maria Theresa had at that time forbidden it. At any rate, Frederick knew that Joseph was burning to see him face to face, and now, in 1769, he gave a hint to the Austrian Ambassador in Berlin that the project might be revived: 'We are Germans, what does it matter to us if the Russians and the Turks get in each other's hair? So long as we two, The House of Austria and I, understand one another well, Germany has little cause to fear war. The Queen-Empress and I have waged long, destructive and costly wars against one another, and what have we finally got out of them?' The Ambassador at once suggested a meeting between the monarchs. 'You are right,' replied the King. 'We will give each other our knightly word, like Francis I and Charles VI; that will be more binding than any treaty.'

The interview between Frederick and Joseph took place at Neisse in Silesia at the end of August 1769, and a second meeting almost exactly a year later at Mährisch-Neustadt in Moravia. On both occasions Frederick brought all his charm into play. He assured the Emperor that he was a changed man. 'In my youth I was ambitious; I am no longer. You think me full of bad faith; I know, and I have deserved it a little, circumstances required it, but that has changed.' He invited Loudon to sit next to him at table with the graceful compliment that he would rather have him as neighbour than opponent. He fasted with his guests because it was a Friday, and then, admittedly, nearly ruined the gesture by saying that during the whole of one Lent he had eaten no meat to find out whether the way to salvation was through the stomach. At the second meeting, where Joseph was host, Frederick put on the white Austrian uniform, spilt snuff over it and said: 'I am not cleanly enough to wear your colour.' Then, having brought only the one uniform, he watched an Austrian military review in it – until a cloudburst interrupted the spectacle. ('This man always brings us bad luck,' said Joseph.) Frederick got soaked to the skin and had to sit for some hours by a kitchen stove covered only by his cloak until his uniform was dry again. He listened, giving an impeccable performance as an attentive schoolboy, to a one-hour lecture by Kaunitz on the 'ten rules of politics,' then got up and embraced the Chancellor and asked for a copy of his notes. Afterwards, Kaunitz praised the docility with which the King allowed him to correct his 'confused and childish ideas'. Joseph, also, was full of enthusiasm:

When the King of Prussia speaks on problems connected with the art of war, which he has studied intensively and on which he has read every conceivable book, then everything is taut, solid and uncommonly instructive. There are no circumlocutions, he gives factual and historical proof of the assertions he makes, for he is well versed in history.

232

Joseph concluded his letter to Maria Theresa with the words: 'A genius and a man who talks admirably. But everything he says betrays the knave.' Maria Theresa already thought Frederick was a knave, but she must have been interested to learn he knew something about war. Frederick's opinion of Joseph was more detached: 'The Emperor is a man of lively intelligence and winning, attractive personality. He suggested a mutual reduction of the army, which I declined as politely as I could. He is consumed with ambition. At the moment I cannot yet say whether he aims at Venice, Bavaria or Lorraine, but one thing is certain: the moment he becomes sole ruler, Europe will be in flames.'

The Prusso-Austrian *rapprochement* which nevertheless resulted from these meetings filled Catherine with alarm, as Frederick had hoped it would. In October 1770 she invited his brother, Prince Henry, to St Petersburg. He stayed until February in the following year, was treated with the quintessence of courtesy by the Czarina, and, despite or because of his extreme ugliness seems to have possessed a strange attraction for her. All this, from Frederick's point of view, was to the good, for he was determined not to lose Catherine's friendship and the Russian alliance on which his whole policy depended – provided, that is, she did not drag him into a continental war. Then Catherine surprised all Europe by announcing the conditions on which she would make peace with Turkey: she demanded large areas on the Black Sea, in the Balkans and an island in the Mediterranean. Frederick was indignant. Such terms could not possibly be acceptable to Turkey or to Austria. Austria made it clear that she would fight, if necessary, with the Turks and Kaunitz concluded a secret alliance with the Sultan, promising armed assistance if the Russians advanced over the Danube. In return apart from 20,000 purses of gold (value, 11,000,000 guilders), Austria was to receive the Bukovina, at that time part of the Ottoman Empire.

Catherine was determined to acquire territory from Turkey which would place her armies on the north, east and south boundaries of the Austrian Empire, and Austria was equally determined to prevent this by going to Turkey's aid and, in doing so, extend her territory eastward towards Russia. It was a situation fraught with peril, particularly for Frederick, who, if war came, would inevitably find himself involved with nothing whatever to gain, and indeed, this time, everything to lose. Then an act of folly on the part of the Austrians suddenly presented him with a chance to break the deadlock. Austrian troops marched into some small areas of Poland of which a part had formerly belonged to Hungary, but which Hungary had solemnly renounced 200 years previously. These were not merely occupied by Austria, but formally annexed. What would Catherine do? The issue of war or peace depended on her. On 8th January, 1771, she mentioned the Austrian action to Prince Henry and said casually: 'Why should not everyone now take something?' And one of her generals added: 'Why shouldn't Prussia take the Bishopric of Varmia? After all, everyone must have something.' Henry reported these remarks to his brother, and Frederick now decided to suggest a partition of Poland to Austria and Russia. Catherine agreed. Kaunitz hesitated, fearing an increase of Russian power. 'I'm sorry,' said Frederick to the Austrian Ambassador, 'that my project has not met with her Imperial Majesty's approval. It had occurred to me as a means of reaching a general understanding; I must see if I can find twenty more ideas to put forward. Perhaps there will be one you can adopt. You see, I'm old. My brain is worn out. So I only get hollow ideas. But you should look at them on their merits and see what you think. Of course, in politics I'm a mere novice compared with Prince Kaunitz.'

But Maria Theresa apparently had scruples about annexing any sizeable part of Poland, though she could seize the more trifling areas without suffering moral indigestion. At any rate, she and Kaunitz now brought out their master plan: let the Polish cake be cut into three large slices; let Prussia take two and Russia one, and let Austria, as a reward for abstention, receive part of Silesia. 'What!' cried Frederick. Such suggestions should be held over until he had gout in the brain; at the moment, it was only in his legs. Joseph and Kaunitz had promised never to mention Silesia again. He declined to discuss the plan.

Kaunitz now realised that Austria could either claim her share or watch Russia and Prussia partition Poland without her. In the latter event, he would not only have lost a chance to acquire territory but have isolated Austria diplomatically. So Austria put forward her claim to Galicia and considerable areas south of Warsaw. 'You have a healthy appetite, I see,' remarked Frederick to the Austrian Ambassador. Austria then reduced her demand to Galicia; even then her share was greater than the Prussian and Russian shares combined: 600,000 Poles became Prussian; 1,800,000 Russian, and 3,000,000 joined the Habsburg Empire. In area, however, Galicia (less the city of Cracow) in the south-east was about equal to White Russia in the north-east, which Catherine obtained, and larger than West Prussia with its 20,000 square miles which Frederick received as the

234

coveted link which made East Prussia a strategic part of his other territories. The treaty of partition between Russia, Prussia and Austria was signed in August 1772. It robbed Poland of a quarter of her territory and over a quarter of her population.

When Maria Theresa received her signed copy of the treaty from the Austrian Field-Marshal Lacy in St Petersburg, she thanked him 'for this great gain, if it really is one.' But she complained that 'this great advantage for the State has been obtained without examining the question whether it was just or not.' A few weeks later she wrote to her youngest son Ferdinand: 'This noxious partition of Poland, which is costing me ten years of my life. . . . I can find no end to it, it oppresses and harries me so, it is poisoning my days. . . .' And before the treaty had been signed she had written to Kaunitz in agony of soul: 'When all my territories were being attacked and I hardly knew where I could be brought to bed in quiet, I found strength in God's help and the justice of my cause. But in this business, where justice clearly cries to heaven against us, I must admit that I have never felt so anxious in my life and so ashamed to show my face.' Finally to her son and co-Regent Joseph she wrote in tones suggesting that her letter was, perhaps, prompted by bitter arguments that had taken place between them:

All this has arisen because the principle was established that we should take advantage of the war between Russia and the Porte to extend our frontiers and obtain advantages which did not occur to us before the war. It was proposed to act after the Prussian manner, at the same time retaining the appearance of legality. . . . Throughout the misfortunes which have filled my reign we have at least tried to act with truth, justice and moderation in all things and with respect for our obligations. That gained us the confidence, I may even say the admiration, of Europe, and the respect even of our enemies. In the last year all this has been lost, and unfortunately I must confess to you that we have deserved it. Now I wish to remedy this by rejecting as false and noxious any attempt to draw profit from the present confusion and by considering how to get out of this sorry situation as quickly and as quietly as possible, without thought of aggrandisement, but solely in order to restore our credit and reputation and, if we can, the balance of power.

When approving the terms of the treaty Maria Theresa is said to have written the prophetic comment: '*Placet*, as so many great and learned men will have it so, but long after I am dead the results of this injury to all that has hitherto been held sacred and just will become apparent.' This sentence occurs in many history books, but not, unfortunately, in the original documents.

Why, it may be asked, if Maria Theresa was so strongly

opposed to partition did she agree to it, and why attempt to recover part of Silesia in exchange for a share of Poland which she thought it morally wrong to accept? Despite Frederick's cynical comment, 'She was tearful, but she took,' there is no reason to believe her scruples were not sincere, but they were private scruples which as a ruler she could not afford to indulge. She could not prevent Russia from acquiring territory at the expense of Poland and Turkey without going to war, and her only alternative to doing nothing was to support Frederick's policy; in other words, to try and limit Russian conquests by sharing in the spoils. '*Il faut hurler avec les loups*' – in a world dominated by power politics this was well understood, and likewise the corollary that if wolves are sheep it was the sheep's fault for being so weak. Thus only among the British, shielded by the sea from these harsh realities, was there much indignation over the partition of Poland. Elsewhere, prime responsibility for Poland's fate was ascribed to the Polish nobility, who had turned their country into a power-vacuum, secondly to Catherine's predatory designs, and in the third place to Joseph II, who had been the first wolf to descend on the fold. Frederick, in the circumstances, cannot be accused of turpitude, for though partition was hastened by his diplomacy and he had no scruples about accepting West Prussia, he would never have gone to war to obtain it. On the contrary, he favoured partition as the only means of preventing, less than ten years after the previous war, another conflagration which in due course would have engulfed the whole of Europe. At the same time, he achieved his double object with great skill. All the Great Powers were originally against him obtaining West Prussia; his main competitor, Catherine, equalled him in unscrupulous daring and in armed strength was far his superior. He had no one to support him but his own enemies, Austria and France. The Poles themselves were so weakened by internal anarchy that they counted for nothing, either as allies or enemies – for a nation of 14,000,000 inhabitants a situation surely without precedent in history! But the Austrians, the French and the Turks were obliged to play Frederick's game, and when all was over Prussia, the most feared and most hated country in Europe, had obtained without firing a shot the one province she needed to become a Great Power and Catherine's hopes of turning the Baltic into a Russian lake had been destroyed. The greatest benefit that the partition conferred on Europe, however, was that three land-hungry Powers had achieved their ambitions in co-operation instead of as enemies and without disturbing the balance of power. To this result the Polish nobility had made their unwitting contribution by setting a modest price on their votes for partition. Some were content with few hundred-weights of salt. A prince cost thirty ducats. So this major operation on the body of Poland passed off, as the Austrian Minister in Warsaw said, as though it had been a free and voluntary adjustment of territory. All the formalities required under the Polish constitution had been observed and the whole affair had not cost more than the Poles would be able to squander at the gaming tables in one day. Those who loved the Polish people spoke a different language, the Saxon Minister, for instance, who wrote of the truth behind the newspaper stories of 'Polish inconsequence' and 'laughable frivolity'. The truth was that, once they had money in their pockets, the Poles did terrible things; their licentiousness, violence and corruption boded ill for the future of their country. After voting away one-quarter of their territory, the members of the Diet had been given a great beanfeast. Wine had flowed. There had been music and torchlight processions and they had gone singing and shouting through the streets, proving to the world that Poland deserved her fate.

Frederick's first action after receiving West Prussia was to inspect it personally. He found it, as he told Prince Henry, 'a very good and advantageous acquisition, both politically and financially.' But the province was as uncivilised as Canada. There was no administrative organisation. The towns were in a pathetic state. In Culm, for instance, only one in eight houses was standing. The inhabitants seemed to be either Jews or monks. 'This piece of land,' concluded Frederick, 'is going to give me a load of work.' He filled the chief administrative post, that of *Oberpräsident*, himself, and spent some time in the province every year. He abolished serfdom at once and reduced feudal service to sixty days in the year. The peasants were given the right to own and inherit land. The administrative board in Marienwerder received the order:

In the performance of its functions the Board must give close and serious attention to ensuring that officials do not deal with the inhabitants in the harsh Polish manner, because His Majesty has abolished all slavery and serfdom and desires to see his subjects looked on and treated as free people. . . . Finally, not the smallest distinction must be made between his Catholic and Evangelical subjects, but they must be heard and in every way treated by the Board without regard to their religion on the same absolutely impartial footing.

Officials were obliged to learn Polish. Some estates belonging to the Polish landed aristocracy were sequestrated, but against compensation. The practice of forcibly expelling proprietors belongs to later centuries. Church property was put under State administration, the owners receiving one-half of the previous yield. 'Our bishops,' wrote Frederick to Voltaire, 'retain 24,000 talers of their revenue, the abbots 7,000. The Apostles did not have as much. One can reach an understanding with them on the basis of relieving them of the cares of this world so that they may devote themselves without distraction to attaining the heavenly Jerusalem which is their true home.' The King also informed his officials that he intended to treat the Catholic priesthood better than the Catholic Austrian Government were able to do. German farmers were settled in the province, schools started and the Prussian legal system was introduced. A canal was built joining the Rivers Oder and Vistula. Gradually the forlorn and brutish inhabitants were instilled with new life by the example of orderliness, self-discipline and hard work. These qualities have been called Prussian; perhaps in the first place they were Frederick's.

*

CHAPTER TWENTY-THREE

Thief Catches Thief

A CLOSE STUDY of the rulers of Europe convinced the Emperor Joseph II that he was a cut above them all; an extremely clever, capable and high-minded prince. He mingled with his subjects and identified himself with their problems. He had played skittles with the citizens of Spielberg, sat for a moment in the dungeon of the local prison to seize intuitively a picture of the criminal mentality, and had laughingly held one handle of a plough while a capable farmhand had guided it with the other. Only recently, in October of this year 1777, he – or was it Kaunitz? – had prised the fair province of the Bukovina from the Sultan's senile grasp, a feat doubly praiseworthy in that he had done nothing to deserve the territory. And yet, with all this to his credit, he was not respected as highly as some other monarchs. His mother, for one. Catherine, that revoltingly immoral creature, for another. And Frederick of Prussia – why did people insist on calling him a hero? Presumably because when someone had dropped a province he had picked it up. Well, perhaps one day the chance would come to him, Joseph. One day quite soon. . . .

The chance for aggrandisement came to Joseph in December of that year – 'an opportunity,' he called it, 'such as occurs only once in centuries.' In that month the Elector of Bavaria died without issue and was succeeded by Charles Theodore, the Elector Palatine. Officially, Charles was also childless, but a large and extravagant troop of bastards enabled him to experience at least one of the joys of honest parenthood – perpetual indigence. Impelled by poverty and enticed by Kaunitz, he therefore decided to surrender Lower Bavaria and the reversionary title to the Upper Palatinate to the Habsburgs in return for immediate cash. In

January 1778 the bargain was signed and Austria occupied the valuable territories which increased the German-speaking population of the Empire, rounded off its frontiers and formed a link with Maria Theresa's detached Swabian possessions.

So far, so good. Joseph was optimistic to the point of euphoria. No trouble could arise from Charles Theodore's heir, his nephew, Duke Charles of Zweibrücken, for the simple reason that, granted the spirit to protest, he lacked the soldiers to enforce his objections. 'As the King of Prussia will not risk acting alone,' wrote Joseph, 'the whole affair – if I am not mistaken – will pass off very quietly.' And if it did come to war, said Joseph gaily, and he were defeated, there would be no shame in succumbing to 'the hero of the century,' and if he won, the victory would be doubly glorious. Kaunitz was more cautious. He thought it impossible to predict 'the wild, almost demented aberrations of a mind such as his [Frederick's], continually dominated as it is by passion and predatory ambition.' As for Maria Theresa, she was disgusted with the whole affair: 'If war comes, then do not count on me to do anything more. I shall retire to the Tyrol and end my days there in solitude, bemoaning the sad fate of my House and my people.'

'As the King of Prussia will not risk acting alone' – here lay Joseph's great mistake. Frederick had no intention, as he said, of acting Don Quixote for the feeble princes of the Empire and his intervention had nothing to do with idealism, but he saw clearly that it was necessary to intervene for three reasons. The first two he expressed in a letter to Prince Henry: '. . . To let Austria usurp despotic authority in Germany is to furnish her with arms against ourselves and make her far more formidable than she is today.' The second reason was an extension of the first: Austria might become so strong 'that one day we might be unable to resist her.' The third reason was explained in an autograph letter to the Emperor Joseph himself. Joseph was co-Regent of Austria and also Emperor of the German Reich. By agreeing to purchase the title to parts of Bavaria and the Upper Palatinate he had implied that the Emperor was at liberty to terminate at will the hereditary rule of the Reich Princes over their respective States. But this, wrote Frederick, was 'contrary to the laws and customs of the Reich. . . . As a member of the Reich I consider myself directly concerned to maintain those freedoms and privileges of the German Reich by which limits have been set to the power of its supreme Head. . . . I love and honour your person and I shall certainly regret having to fight against a prince endowed with such excellent qualities and whom I personally esteem. These are

240

the thoughts which I submit according to my humble lights to Your Majesty's higher discernment.'

This letter was dated 13th April, 1778, and was written in the King's own hand, without the assistance of secretaries, from his army headquarters in the field. For he had already guaranteed Duke Charles of Zweibrücken his Bavarian heritage and already assembled his forces. The humble tone of the letter – though strictly correct coming from a prince of the Reich to his Emperor – and the numerous spelling mistakes which it contained caused mother and son much ribald amusement. Joseph's reaction, when he had managed to stop laughing, was to claim that he had not been acting as the supreme Head of the Reich, but as 'the Archduke of Austria'. This, and the mannered conceit with which he ended his reply was altogether too juvenile to make any impression on the sixty-three-year-old Frederick. 'I shall await with composure,' concluded Joseph, 'whatever it pleases you to reply or to do. I have learnt so much of real value from Your Majesty that, were I not a citizen and disturbed by the imminent sufferings of some millions of human beings, I might also say that I would not be averse to Your Majesty going further and teaching me how to be a general.'

Frederick now made a practical suggestion. If Austria raised no objection to Prussia obtaining Saxon Lusatia in exchange for Ansbach and Bayreuth, which were due to revert to her by treaty, he was prepared to see Austria retain part of the territory she had occupied in Bavaria. Frederick was anxious to obtain Lusatia, as it formed an enclave between Silesia and Brandenburg. Maria Theresa favoured this suggestion, but the clever Joseph took it as a sign that Frederick was weakening: 'One must conclude that the King's desire for Lusatia is very great, but his warlike ardour very small. Hence if we maintain a reasonable but firm tone, the great Frederick with his Xerxes army will eventually moderate his Quixotic language on behalf of Germany and abandon the rest for the sake of peace for his old bones.' Flushed with the arrogance of youth, Joseph was in no mood to consider a compromise. In fact he was hoping to get the whole of Bavaria by giving Charles Theodore the Austrian Netherlands in exchange or by making him King of Galicia. But Maria Theresa opposed the first idea because it would mean a loss of revenue from taxation and the Elector had no desire to be King of anywhere. Meanwhile, Frederick was sent a non-committal reply, and Joseph happily set about planning his next move in the diplomatic game. But the sands had run out. On 3rd July, 1778, he received instead of the expected compliments and counter-suggestions a declaration of war and two days later the King of Prussia marched into Bohemia at the head of 100,000 men.

At once Joseph plummeted from airy optimism into the nether pit of despair. Within a fortnight, the 'old bones' had become 'this great soldier' and Joseph was writing: 'In this highly dangerous war the fate of the monarchy may hang on a few moments' bad luck. The enemy is indeed a great soldier and one who, as everyone knows, will stop at nothing. He is definitely superior to us in numbers and we are definitely without allies. The monarchy will have to rely entirely on its own resources. . . .' Joseph clamoured for 40,000 recruits and an immediate increase in taxation. His mother wanted peace at any price, and declared that if he was afraid to make it for fear of being thought weak she was ready to take the blame on her own 'grey head, which in any case is now good for nothing else.' Maria Theresa then wrote the first letter she had ever addressed to the hated King of Prussia, saying that her age, her desire for peace, and her alarm at having two sons in the army had prompted her to express, without the Emperor's knowledge, her 'desire to resume and conclude the negotiations hitherto directed by him.' At the same time she sent a plenipotentiary with a draft settlement. Frederick replied courteously, promising to postpone military operations while terms were being discussed. He found the draft too vague, added to it and sent it back. Maria Theresa, prompted perhaps by Kaunitz, then made the highly immoral offer to evacuate the whole of Bavaria if Frederick would renounce his claim to Ansbach and Bayreuth. Frederick replied that the Margraviates had nothing to do with the matter under discussion.

Meanwhile Joseph had been informed of his mother's action and was fuming with rage. He called it a 'capitulation', threatened to retire to Florence and wash his hands of the whole affair. Later, he changed his mind and wrote to Maria Theresa that he would sign anything so long as no one asked him for advice. Maria Theresa was deeply distressed. Beseeching God to soften her son's heart, she wrote to Joseph: 'We were a Great Power, we are no longer, we must bow our heads and at least save the wreckage and make the people that remain to us happier than they have been during my unfortunate reign. You and I must speak the same language.' But Joseph refused to express an opinion on her peace suggestions.

Meanwhile, Prince Henry had skilfully outmanoeuvred Loudon and was advancing deeper into Bohemia. Loudon took fright and offered to resign. Then Joseph started preparations for the evacuation of Prague. His appetite for war was proving better than his digestion. Maria Theresa, on the other hand, though peace-loving, was not a coward and she cancelled his orders. Frederick, who had marched with one Prussian army into Moravia, now ordered his brother in Bohemia to attack. But Henry, though an elegant tactician, preferred to do nothing. He found a pretext in the incapacity of his generals. 'No brains! In this respect we have sunk right down. That is the result of despotism and of the bad examples which ruin a whole nation.' Too many of the senior officers were, in fact, over age. But the main difficulties in coming to grips with the enemy were lack of forage and the fact that they had installed themselves in fortified positions and would not risk an encounter in the field. So, towards September, the war began to peter out without any major engagements having taken place. The troops' main activity was pillaging, hence it became known as The Potato War. The King is said to have had one narrow escape. When he was riding on reconnaissance a Croat suddenly aimed a musket at him from behind a bush. With unruffled calm, Frederick raised an admonishing finger and said 'Now, now!' whereupon the startled enemy lowered his gun and stood to attention while the King rode past.

In the middle of September lack of food forced both Prussian armies to withdraw, thousands of non-Prussian troops deserting on the way. The King spoke sarcastically of the 'heroic deeds of the seventy-year-olds,' and planned to do better in the following year. He himself was ready for peace at any time provided Austria disgorged most, if not all, of the territory she had seized in Bavaria, and his feelings were echoed by all in Vienna bar Joseph. Throughout the winter he brooded and pondered how best he could save his face; Frederick's agents reported he was usually drunk by mid-afternoon. Finally, by the Treaty of Teschen, which was not signed until May 1779, he agreed to evacuate all Bavaria except a small area between the Danube and the Inn and the Salzach with 60,000 inhabitants. Prussia obtained nothing, not even the cost of the previous year's campaign. But Frederick had won considerable political advantages. He had curbed the Emperor's ambition and by championing the cause of one of the German States he had made himself the potential leader of them all against Austrian encroachment. He was no longer looked on as the Emperor's rebellious vassal, but as his rival for German leadership.

The peace had been signed on Maria Theresa's birthday. Eighteen months later she died as bravely as she had lived. Typically Austrian in her open-mindedness, spontaneity and warmth of feeling, in her love of music and domestic comfort, in her lack of logic and not least in her inability to meet the harsh realities of life with an equally hard-headed realism, she has ever since been both the symbol and the pattern of the Austrian mentality. Her happiness sprang from the Austrian virtues and her sorrows from the same sources as those of her people, and it was because she was a ruler after their own heart that the conglomeration of territories she inherited was passed on to her heirs as a State.

The Viennese mob took advantage of her funeral to demonstrate against high taxation. Frederick, who had always respected Maria Theresa, wrote to d'Alembert: 'She has done honour to her throne and to her sex. I have made war against her and have never been her enemy' – and won with this facile tribute a round of applause from the French Academy. Joseph was now sole ruler of Austria. A new phase was beginning. Frederick had only to recall his own career to realise that youth, ambition and a powerful army formed an explosive mixture. He was full of concern. He said the Austrian Ambassador in Berlin probably had one task: to keep Joseph informed on the state of the King's health so that 'the hell-hound', as Frederick called him, could attack Prussia the moment he was dead. In that same year of 1780 Joseph visited Catherine in St Petersburg. A letter to his Berlin Ambassador confirmed Frederick's suspicions. 'The only jewels which could give me pleasure,' wrote Joseph, after he and Catherine had dispensed with the customary exchange of gifts, 'would be Schweidnitz, Glatz, Neisse and Kosel; but you will understand that it will take time for the jewellers to acquire them.' Kaunitz, on the other hand, favoured a more devious and subtle course than Joseph and advised the Berlin Ambassador to remove all concern which the heir to the throne might feel regarding 'any hostile intentions which might be carried out after the death of his uncle: such personal reassurance is the easiest way to encourage the Crown Prince's taste for luxury and extravagance and that is the most certain means of undermining the Prussian machine and inducing its gradual collapse.'

Frederick was in a difficult position. He knew well enough that as two young and ambitious sovereigns Catherine and Joseph would tend to draw together, as the plans of either would be baulked by the other's hostility. If they could sink their rivalry, the Ottoman Empire, which at that time included the whole of the Balkans, would be at their mercy. He, on the other hand, both politically and, as an ageing man, personally wanted only one thing: security, and that meant the *status quo*. But to obtain it he would need other and more reliable friends than Russia. In France a daughter of Maria Theresa was Queen and her husband, Louis XVI, was, in Frederick's opinion, 'unfit to govern.' There was still England, but since the separate peace of 1762 he mistrusted her. The only alternative was to try to cross Joseph's plans and cement the alliance with Russia. Frederick sent Prince Henry to St Petersburg, saying that in order to prevent evil it was necessary to pay court to the Devil. He suggested in vain a tri-partite alliance with Turkey and rejected Catherine's counter-proposal to partition what remained of Poland. Clearly, the woman was incorrigible, and more clearly still when, in 1781, she concluded a defensive alliance with Joseph and gave notice that she did not intend to renew the treaty with Prussia when it expired in 1784. Meanwhile, Joseph had paid her a second visit. They sailed down the Dnieper in a State barge, and exchanged saccharine flattery. 'Yes, madame, you have given me a taste of that sweet satisfaction which is beyond the power of chance or changes of fortune to impair, namely a deep inner contentment with oneself, and when I read your letter I could not help thinking, my years after all had not been quite wasted, for Catherine applauds me' – to which Catherine was ready with her answer: if Voltaire had known Joseph he would have quoted the Bible test, 'Blessed be the womb that bore thee.' She now told the Emperor of her plans. She had insisted on one of her grandsons being christened Constantine because she intended to make him head of a revived Greek Empire based on Constantinople. In return for his support Joseph now demanded the greater part of the western Balkans and portions of the Republic of Venice. Catherine recognised a fellow jackal and the friendship cooled somewhat.

Frederick was beginning to realise that his alliance with Russia was already as good as dead. He was seventy-two now. At the end of a long life was he to leave Prussia without a single ally? In desperation he turned to the only supporters he could muster: the German princes. After long negotiations he succeeded in uniting fourteen States* in the League of Princes, pledged to uphold their rights against the Emperor. The League came into being in July 1785. Its advent was hastened by the alarm felt among German princes at Joseph's latest offer of the Austrian Netherlands to the Elector of Bavaria in return for the whole of the Electorate. Instead of King of Galicia, he was now to be

* Anhalt, Ansbach, Baden, Brunswick Hanover, Hesse-Kassel, Gotha, Mainz, Mechlenberg, the Palatinate, Saxony, Trier, Weimar, Zweibrücken.

known as King of Burgundy. From the Austrian point of view, the idea was excellent, for as parts of Baden and Württemberg were already within Joseph's territories under the name of Hither-Austria, the addition of the whole of Bavaria might have led eventually to the whole of southern Germany coming under the Habsburgs, and possibly the future German Reich might then have been centred on Vienna instead of Berlin – or else been permanently divided.

Meanwhile the great majority of the German States, now combined in the League and headed by Frederick, were strongly opposed to Joseph's manoeuvre. As Prussia could not deter him alone, Frederick asked for French assistance. The French had at first welcomed the prospect of Austria evacuating the adjacent Netherlands, particularly as Joseph now offered them Namur and Luxembourg in return for their support. On the other hand, Austrian aggrandisement was always to be feared, and Frederick, backed by most of the princes of the Reich, was not to be lightly antagonised. Louis XVI, who was Joseph's brother-in-law, pondered, but could not make up his mind. Frederick was indignant, fearing 'that at this decisive moment France may lack energy and finally get a nose-bleed. Gods! What miserable people we have to deal with! Surrounded by this cowardly and venal rabble, how are we going to maintain the Reich Constitution on our own and oppose the boundless rapacity of this accursed tyrant in Vienna? I must admit, it drives me to distraction. More than half-way to the next world, I have to be doubly alert and active and retain all these odious projects in my mind which the accursed Joseph is hatching daily. So I am condemned to enjoy no peace until a little earth covers my bones.'

But when Frederick wrote this letter the danger was already past. Louis XVI had done what the timorous always do – asked each of six ministers for a 'memorandum'. They, in turn, had held a meeting and, as usual when two or three are gathered together, the cautious policy had won the day. So Louis was advised that it would be extremely dangerous to allow Austria such an increase of territory, and Louis agreed. Now England joined her voice in protest, and before long Joseph was reading an ironic note from France: she would approve his plan if he could obtain the consent of Prussia. Joseph quietly withdrew.

*

CHAPTER TWENTY-FOUR

Frederick's Army

WITH HER 5,000,000 INHABITANTS Prussia was not capable of supporting an army of 180,000 men, so only half was enlisted within the country. Town-dwellers were exempt from military service and the recruits came from the land. In peacetime they served for two months in every year. The rest of the army consisted of foreigners. Von Boyen, later to become Scharnhorst's assistant, gave it as his considered opinion that the foreign troops were largely useless. Their real calling was not soldiering, but collecting enlistment bounties. No sooner had they joined one army than they took the first opportunity to desert and join another. They supplemented this income with theft and confidence tricks. In war it was, in any case, the practice to compel prisoners to change sides. It is said that if they refused they were denied medical assistance. The King kept this international mercenary proletariat together by giving them good food – a pound of beef per week – and especially by savage punishments. It is hardly an exaggeration to say that one half of the army was kept busy guarding and thrashing the other half. A favourite trick was to pair good and bad soldiers together. If one deserted, the other was made to run the gauntlet. To make desertion more difficult it was a standing order in wartime that camps were not to be sited near forests and at night tents had to be continually inspected. At sunset, guards were doubled, cavalry patrolled the perimeter of the camp, and if there was standing corn sharpshooters were posted in it. Judging by the precautions taken when in the field, it might have been an army of slaves.

The main deterrent to desertion was fear of being made to run the gauntlet. Frederick had none of his father's sadistic love of cruelty, and if he retained this barbarous punishment it was quite simply because without it a good half of his army would have melted away. The offender was made to run naked down a lane of a hundred or more soldiers standing six feet apart, each of them armed with a hazel switch about two and a half feet long. The man's hands were tied together over his chest and an N.C.O. saw to it that he did not run down the lane too fast. Soldiers that did not strike at him with all their strength were themselves made to run the gauntlet. After running to and fro several times the wretched man was in a terrible state. Often he collapsed before completing the punishment. Then the remaining blows were given him lying down.

But all this merely kept the army together; something more was needed to make it a fighting machine. If troops were to advance into the muzzles of 300 enemy cannon, it was necessary, wrote Frederick in one of his testaments, that they should fear their own officers more than death. 'Experience has shown that the quality of the troops depends entirely on that of the officers: a good colonel, a good battalion.' Frederick's officers were a dedicated and fanatical body, saturated in the quasi-mystical ideals of courage and self-sacrifice, ruthlessly hard on themselves and on their troops and ready to accept death in battle as their natural end. Such men were to be found in the Prussian nobility; from it and from no other class in society Frederick's officers were drawn. He called the nobility the finest jewel in his crown. He demanded the utmost from his officers, but he would and could not offer them high pay – a lieutenant received fourteen talers a month – and indeed a purely material reward would in a sense have been inappropriate to their essentially spiritual achievement. Men who are prepared to give their utmost, including their lives, are insulted by an attempt to assess their value in cash. Instead, Frederick paid them in more appropriate coin by giving them, second only to himself, the most honoured position in the State. He could do so without infringing the rigid caste system of semi-feudal Prussian society because his officers were, in any case, members of a privileged social class. This, no doubt, was one reason why Frederick never accepted a member of the bourgeoisie, however capable, for a commission. But whereas the ostrich feather in the hat, powdered hair and other outward distinctions of the nobility had formerly been worn by right of birth, they were now the badges of service. A young nobleman who was not an officer was in Frederick's eyes a 'wretch.'

The King took good care that the self-respect acquired in war was maintained in peace. One of his regulations for officers

248

reads: 'As His Majesty desires a noble and respectable corps of officers in his army, the good conduct of all officers must be ensured. Lax practices unbefitting an officer, such as drunkenness, refusal to pay debts, patronage of low coffee houses and brothels must not be tolerated by commanders, nor must officers be allowed to consort with common people or townsmen, but must confine themselves to the society of their equals or those above them, so maintaining good conduct and ambition.' It followed that intermarriage with the bourgeoisie was also frowned on. On such alliances Frederick poured expressive if not very coherent abuse, calling them in his peculiar German: 'Stinkert Fet und Schmierige Butr.' Young officers were refused permission to marry, however eligible the bride: 'My dear Major General von Bronikovski, in reply to your submission of the 12th of this month concerning the marriage of your sister to the Cornet* von Zmiesky, I have to tell you that the Hussars are not expected to seek their fortune through the vagina, but by the sword. Ich bin Euer wohlaffektionierter König, Friedrich.'

In more recent times, for instance between the years 1900 and 1914, foreign visitors to Berlin can hardly have failed to notice the extreme arrogance of Prussian officers towards German civilians. This was no part of Frederick's system, but a latter-day perversion of it. He had said that all were equal before the law and possessed basic rights as Prussian citizens, and he meant it. 'No garrison commander or officer in charge of troops,' ran one of his orders, 'must in any circumstances take it upon himself to arrest a civilian. Any complaint must be made to the municipal council. Should any officer, whoever he may be, so far forget himself as to strike or use insulting language towards a citizen he shall be arrested immediately, court-martialled and punished. This is my express will.'

Frederick's officers were not only the moral but also the economic backbone of his army. Per month, company commanders were paid the sum of three talers and five groschen for each man in their unit. Out of seventy or so Prussian citizens in a company, between fifty and sixty would be on leave for ten months in the year, so that the commanding officer would save 2,000 talers in the same period. The foreign contingent, on the other hand, cost him 500 talers a year in recruiting expenses, for he was responsible for procuring replacements for deserters. He also had to pay for the clothing of his unit. Uniforms were supplied by the regi-

---

* Cornet (cavalry) and ensign (infantry) were the most junior of the commissioned officers and carried the colour.

ment at a fixed charge of one taler five groschen a year. Thus, like the Condottieri of the fifteenth century, Frederick's company commanders had also a commercial function. Their own pay was adjusted to allow for the profits derived from it, and even when they had reached the rank of General they still retained their companies. The system had the advantage of reducing the size of the army quartermaster branch and also of giving the company commander a financial interest in keeping down desertion. But, for the same reason, it led to a continual deterioration in the troops' uniforms and boots and after the Seven Years War the King abolished it in most regiments.

Such, in outline, was the instrument of Frederick's glory, the army with which for seven long years he withstood the onslaught of half Europe. Though it had been created by the Prince of Anhalt-Dessau and the foundations of its morale had been laid by his father, Frederick William, its supremacy as a fighting machine was due to Frederick alone. It is no recommendation for a commander to be loved by his troops and indeed love and hatred in the ordinary sense do not apply to the attitude of an army to its leader. If he leads them to victory, they will follow him. If he is hard on himself, they will accept the most merciless treatment, even to Frederick's 'Die quietly, can't you!' to a wounded soldier crying in agony. Finally, if they achieve glory together, their identities tend to merge; there is a bond between them and, like Frederick's Guardsmen, troops may call their commander by the familiar 'thou', or 'father'. All this applied to the Prussian army under Frederick. He may, as has recently been pointed out, have made many mistakes and lost many battles. His victories may have been due in part to the fact that he was opposed by superannuated generals and as a King answerable only to himself could take greater risks than they. But to ascribe his victories solely to the superior qualities of his troops is to deny him any effect on them, good or bad, and this is obviously nonsense. In 1806, when he stood as conqueror beside Frederick's grave in Potsdam, Napoleon said: 'If he was still alive, we would not be here.'

Napoleon must remain the most exacting, the most expert of Frederick's critics and the best qualified as being nearest to him in time. After pointing to a number of Frederick's errors, Napoleon came to the conclusion: 'He was principally great at the decisive moments, and that is the finest tribute to his character that could be paid.' Napoleon particularly praised Frederick's daring. Frederick himself preached initiative to his generals:

'There has never been a man who succeeded in all his plans. If you make only small plans you will never be more than an average individual, but even if only two out of ten large-scale undertakings which you have planned succeed, you will make your name immortal.' To his cavalry he extolled the spirit of attack: 'The King hereby forbids all cavalry officers on pain of being cashiered with ignominy to allow themselves to be attacked by the enemy in any action whatever throughout their career; it is the Prussians who must always attack.' And similarly to the infantry: 'Battles must be decisive. Have at the enemy! Give him a good salvo in the nose at twenty, at ten paces, and then immediately bayonet him in the ribs.' Frederick disliked artillery as unsporting and with comic indignation called the excessive use of it an unheard-of abuse.

Another of Frederick's military virtues which Napoleon praised was his ability to retain complete control of his troops in battle. One of his officers related: 'When marching against the enemy he was usually with the advance guard and the army followed him in a number of columns so that the whole mass could be rapidly deployed according to his orders. If he found the enemy, his practised eye took in with great speed the advantages and disadvantages of the whole neighbourhood, the strong and weak points of the enemy's position, the approaches to it, the key points on the seizure of which the success of the operation would depend, and if it then appeared possible to attack the enemy with advantage the plan was made at once. The advance guard was given its positions, the adjutants flew back with orders for the columns which determined their line of advance and the formation they should adopt. Within a few minutes the whole army was drawn up in the most exact battle order and often a vigorous attack had started before the enemy had time to realise his danger.'

During the Seven Years War, Frederick had been obliged to obtain some of his officers from the middle classes. After the Peace of Hubertusberg these men were only retained in the artillery and the engineer corps; their place was taken by foreign officers. A number of reforms were introduced, including the appointment of army inspectors, among them young officers. Generals were released from service until, on the King's death, only one remained. Administrative changes were made until no two regiments, hardly, were organised in the same way. The ageing Frederick's severity increased as his power declined. Circumstances were never taken as an excuse for failure: invariably the commanding officer was blamed, and often in the most

251

scathing language. Before the King held one of his inspections the dependants of senior officers joined together in prayer that the head of the family might be spared disgrace, for good conduct and efficiency were not enough – the royal praise or criticism was a matter of whim. Thus, two years before his death, Frederick wrote to the Silesian General Tauenziehen:

When I was with you, I mentioned that my army in Silesia had never been in so bad a state. I will now repeat that in writing. The regiments could not be worse if I made cobblers and tailors into generals. It is not my intention to lose battles through the inefficiency of my generals and next year, therefore – if I am still alive – I require you to assemble the army between Breslau and Ohlau and for four days before my arrival at the camp carry out exercises with the ignorant generals and teach them their duty. Whoever does not then fulfil his duty shall go to court martial, for I should think it blameworthy for any country to retain people in service who take so little interest in their profession. You are to inform your whole Inspection that this is my will.

But the military system which Frederick perfected was already out of date. The difficulty he was now finding in maintaining the efficiency of his army was the first sign of the decay, which, twenty years later, was to produce the disaster of Jena. The days of the small, highly trained army with aristocratic officers and peasant soldiers were over. It was to be supplanted by the levies of the French Revolution, by the field-marshal's baton in every trooper's knapsack and by national armies sprung from the spirit of nationhood which Napoleon's oppression provoked. In strategy, the parade-ground attack in which troops marched shoulder to shoulder towards the enemy with officers on the flanks and N.C.O.s in rear was also passing. In future, light, quick-firing artillery would loosen up the order of battle, make units more independent and allow that speed and freedom of movement which Napoleon used with masterly effect. Above all, the eighteenth-century conception of limited war had gone for ever. When East Friesland had been overrun by the French in the Seven Years War and the inhabitants had been visited with savage reprisals for attempting revolt, Frederick had shown no sympathy with them. Civilians, he declared, had no business to meddle with war. If they opposed their rulers, whether these were Frenchmen, East Frisians, or Prussians, they were rebels and deserved their fate. But soon the countries of Europe would be fighting for survival against an enemy who threatened annihilation. Soon there would be no longer officers, other ranks and civilians, but only – manpower.

*

CHAPTER TWENTY-FIVE

Frederick and the World of Ideas

No RULER IN WORLD HISTORY has written as much as Frederick. As he himself confessed: 'As soon as I have a spare moment, the itch to write seizes me; I cannot resist this frivolous pleasure; it amuses me, distracts me and puts me in a better frame of mind for the work which I have to do afterwards.' He composed thousands of verses, one or two comedies, several epic poems, half a dozen major historical works, two long political testaments, memoranda, treatises and essays on political questions, numerous literary dialogues, satires and parodies, military treatises and a rhyming dictionary. His private correspondence fills sixty volumes; his official political letters have been published in forty-four volumes, but there are more to come. From the first word to the last all this vast output was written in French.

Frederick was also an insatiable reader. 'I have read more than all the Benedictine friars put together. . . . Without my books I would have gone mad.' Frederick liked to call himself a thinker rather than a man of action. When his deeds made him famous, he felt like a philosopher 'who has marvellously strayed from his sphere.' During the siege of Schweidnitz he read Cardinal Fleury's thirty-six-volume history of the Church, extracted long passages and had them printed separately for his personal use. Five sets of his basic library consisting of two or three dozen books uniformly bound in bright red morocco were distributed between Sanssouci, Potsdam, Berlin and Breslau, with the fifth set reserved for use in the field. The library included French translations of the masterpieces of Greek and Latin literature, the works of Corneille, Racine, Boileau, Voltaire, Montesquieu, Bossuet, Pascal, Locke and other philosophers and also a number of historical works. Frederick was steeped in classical French literature; in a letter home, d'Alembert wrote that he could quote no major passage with which the King was not conversant. But the library contained no German books; the King could understand the spoken but not the written language.

Frederick was a child of the Enlightenment. He believed in the supremacy of rational thought, he detested everything that reason could not penetrate. We are inclined nowadays to deride the logic-chopping rationalistic outlook, but we should not forget that the dawning of independent thought held much of the effulgence that belongs to youth in every sphere. Rejoicing in its new-won freedom from the fetters of superstition and prejudice, the intellect felt entitled in those days to claim sovereign powers over life. No one doubted that the task of literature was to set up firm principles for action and cure humanity's ills and that the task could be fulfilled. Enjoying life, confident of penetrating its secrets and believing in progress, men chose to ignore what Reason failed to explain. Gaiety was their key-note, for they were sure of themselves, sure of their ability to create the best of all possible worlds. So at night, when the flute trilled in the blue, silk-lined rooms of Rheinsberg or Sanssouci and the company danced, chatted, or watched theatricals, the very statues and temples in the moonlit park seemed infused with a cool and airy optimism. Certainly, it filled the heart of the brilliant, handsome young man who was heir to a throne and felt he had already inherited paradise. Longing to embrace the whole of creation, he rhymed:

> If my soul like Thebes had a hundred doors
> I would bid joy enter in tens and scores

– and if tiresome learned allusion was one of these joys, that did not make him the less sincere.

But if Frederick was a child of the Enlightenment, this only applied to his cast of mind and limitations of intellect. His personality was too complex to be labelled, as Dilthey had suggested in an excellent essay, *Friedrich und die deutsche Aufklärung*. Those, he writes, who were able to study Frederick at close quarters were at once attracted and repelled, fascinated and baffled by his fluid, contradictory character. Sometimes the discordant elements seemed to fuse, at others to predominate singly in rapid succession: 'the disposition to enjoy life in cheerful company, conversation, music, reading or in literary creation – and the awareness that the ruler must sacrifice himself to the State;

the ambitious military commander in pursuit of fame – and the philosopher-king anxious to contribute to the welfare of his people and the progress of mankind; the king who cultivated friendship and treated men of letters as his equals – and the authoritarian despot: self-surrender, abandonment, almost, to the impresssions of the moment – and a heroism in confronting fate unequalled since the days of ancient Rome.'

Frederick faced public and private tribulation without the comforts of religious faith. But he rejected atheism, perhaps from a sense of monarchic solidarity. 'As we have to penetrate the labyrinth, I will be guided only by the thread of reason. Reason compels me to assume that an Intelligence rules over this world and keeps the machine working as a whole. I imagine this Intelligence as the orginal source of life and movement.' But he repeatedly stressed that the supreme Intelligence was not concerned with the fates of individual men, though at the end of his *Histoire de Mon Temps* he did recommend Prussia to the care of Providence, 'if human misery is not beneath her attention.' On the other hand he was too much the master of his own fate to accept the popular argument that suffering was incompatible with the existence of a benevolent deity.

As regards free will, Frederick held different opinions in youth and maturity. As Crown Prince he had written to Voltaire: 'You act according to a principle, according to sublime reason, and therefore according to necessity.' But as King he was obliged to believe in some measure of free will, as he explained in a letter to d'Alembert: 'Whence have all human beings a feeling of freedom, how do they come to love it? Would this be possible if freedom did not exist? I dare to surmise that there is a contradiction somewhere in the system of fatalism; for if one accepts it, one must also consider laws, education, punishments and rewards as superfluous and pointless. If all is necessary, then nothing can be changed. But my experience proves to me that education can do a great deal for men, that they can be improved and given an incentive.'

His answer to the question of immortality was much less ambiguous. The capacity for thought, considered Frederick, derived from our physical organisation and both would perish together. The mind was like a flame. Both needed nourishment. When the wood had burnt to ashes the flame was extinguished. In his testament Frederick wrote with lofty detachment: 'Without regret I return the breath of life which has inspired me to beneficent Nature which lent it to me, and my body to the elements of which it is composed.' In this testament he also expresses the essence of his philosophy: 'Our life is a hurried transition from birth to death; in this short interval the task of man is to work for the welfare of the society of whose body he is a member.' But Frederick had always been wary of metaphysical problems because he considered the human intellect incapable of solving them. Ethics seemed to him more important because of their practical application. He was concerned, not to know why he was alive or what happened to him after he was dead, but being alive to discover how he should act. He did not believe in the innate goodness of human nature. To a correspondent who had extolled it he replied: 'You do not know the accursed race to which we belong.' But he did believe that men could be changed for the better by the use of reason: 'I could wish that the motive force of egoism could be directed by proving to men that it is to their own advantage to be good citizens, good fathers and good friends, in short, to practise all the moral virtues. And as it is indeed so, it ought not to be difficult to convince them.' So, in old age, he reached a gentle and realistic humanitarianism: 'Those who consider all men to be devils and rage cruelly against them are seeing them through the eyes of a fanatical misanthrope. Whoever thinks they are angels and leaves them to their own devices is dreaming like a feeble-minded Capuchin. But he who believes that men are neither all good nor all evil, who rewards good actions above their deserts and punishes bad ones more lightly than is due, who shows consideration to the weak and humanity to every man, that person is acting as a reasonable man should.' But one should beware of imagining that these admirable though somewhat trite principles of Frederick the philosopher were consistently applied by Frederick the King. In 1776 the British Ambassador, Sir James Harris, wrote: 'Although as an individual he often appears and really is humane, benevolent and friendly, yet the instant he acts in his royal capacity these attributes forsake him and he carries with him desolation, misery and persecution wherever he goes.' The contrast is over-drawn, nevertheless it reflects the existence in Frederick of two almost separate beings: the affectionate, sensitive, contemplative idealist who was always ready to believe that his opinions might be mistaken, and the ruthless, cynically realistic man of action, the despot who never doubted that he held a monopoly of wisdom and who shaped Prussia to his will, ferociously indifferent to the hardships and sufferings he caused. Yet in some curious way these two beings were not psychologically antagonistic. Each refreshed the other. A friendly, almost tender literary conversation on the eve of a great battle – and next morning the commander would awake with courage renewed, mind cleared and heart rearmoured against adversity. Frederick to Voltaire: 'You came into the world that I might know happiness.' The King: 'If I wanted to punish a province, I would have it ruled by men of letters.'

In old age, Frederick's interests narrowed and his prejudices deepened. Mathematics and the natural sciences were dismissed as mere playthings, astronomy and geometry as valueless to navigation. In agriculture, the practice was everything, theory was irrelevant. Electricity? A pastime for the curious. Sublime Reason's earthly interpreters, the Encyclopaedists, he mostly disliked – Diderot for his arrogance, Rousseau for his politics, Holbach for his aggressive atheism. D'Alembert, on the other hand, seemed 'a very nice fellow' and Frederick corresponded with him for twenty years. But here again, though no trace of personal rancour or petulance marked their letters, the King did not always see eye to eye with the philosopher – on Church questions, for instance. Frederick declined to offend the pious after Voltaire's death by installing his bust in a place of worship. Voltaire, he told d'Alembert courteously, would certainly feel bored there. He also refused to build a Temple of Reason in Potsdam. Apart from the fact that experience had undermined his confidence in the ultimate triumph of reason, he had no intention of being accused of blasphemy by his subjects.

Frederick's personal attitude to Christianity was of the 'nothing but' kind. Voltaire's mockeries had laid bare the distinction between religious faith and historical fact, and the contrast between his father's pious words and his mad and fumbling cruelties had filled Frederick with revulsion for organised religious worship. To him personally, the Church was based on superstition and it bred hypocrisy. His reaction was to interpret Christianity by the light of primitive reason: 'Like all forces in the world, Christianity had modest beginnings. The hero of this sect is a Jew from the scum of the people, of dubious origin who weaves some good moral doctrines into the insipidities of the ancient Hebrew prophesies. Miracles are ascribed to him and at the end he is condemned to a shameful death. Twelve enthusiasts spread his teaching from the East as far as Italy, win adherents by the pure and saintly morality which they preach and – apart from some miracles which excite people of fervid imagination – teach nothing by Deism. . . .'

But in his public capacity Frederick saw the danger of mocking established and venerated institutions and he held too low an opinion of average human intelligence to believe with d'Alembert and others that once superstition had been derided out of existence cold reason could take its place. When Voltaire told him of a young Frenchman who had been condemned to death for damaging a religious statue and failing to take his hat off to his village priest when the latter was carrying the Host, the King's attitude reflected the experience of the ruler: 'Remember what Fontenelle said: "If I had a fistful of truths I would think twice before opening it." The mass of people do not deserve to be enlightened. If you ask me whether I would have passed so severe a sentence, my answer is: No. I would have suited the punishment to the crime. I would have said: You broke the statue, so you must repair it. You failed to remove your hat to the priest when he was carrying the well-known object, so for fourteen days you must appear in church without a hat. You have read the works of Voltaire, so you must study the *Summa* of St Thomas under the parson's supervision. The dizzy fellow would have been much more severely punished in this way than he was by his judges, for boredom lasts a century, but death only a moment. Toleration must allow every citizen the freedom to believe what he will. But it should not extend to condoning the insolent rowdyism of young hot-heads who grossly insult objects venerated by the people. That is my view. It is consistent with the measures necessary to ensure freedom of thought and the public peace – and that is the prime object of all legislation.' And elsewhere: 'Believe me, if philosophers founded a system of government, within fifty years the people would have created some new superstition, have set up other idols – would be praying at the grave of the founders or calling on the sun. Some aberration or other would thrust out the pure and simple cult of the Supreme Being.'

Frederick even recommended that Voltaire should not give his history of Louis XIV to the general public, stating roundly: 'Nothing is more absurd than the desire to root out superstition. Prejudices are the people's reason. And does this stupid people deserve to be enlightened?' King Frederick's tolerance was largely one of contempt and political expediency.

· · · · · ·

Though Frederick once told the poet Gottsched that he had never read a book in German and that he spoke the language '*comme un cocher*,' he freely expressed views on German literature and devoted a thorough discussion to it in his treatise *De la Littér-*

ature Allemande, which was published in 1780, but for the most part had been written twenty years before. Seldom can a writer have been so profoundly ignorant of his subject. With one exception, Goethe's drama *Götz von Berlichingen*, which he thought 'detestable', Frederick had read nothing of Lessing, Klopstock, Wieland, Herder, Kant, Winckelmann or of Goethe himself. But it was enough that they were Germans, ignorant of the French language and the wonders it could perform, for Frederick to know that they were men hopelessly adrift on the turbid waters of the barbaric German tongue without even a star, a standard of excellence, to guide them to the harbour of literary merit. And if proof were needed, the fact that they imitated the bad, base and boring plays of the Englishman Shakespeare showed that they were heading for the rocks or rather, the rocky mountains of Canada, whose savages, said Frederick, might find Shakespeare's 'abominable pieces' to their taste. Yet the literary future was not without hope. German culture had been retarded by the Thirty Years War. German literature might yet astonish Europe if a concerted effort were made to preform the language and improve prose style. At present, 'it is physically impossible even for the most brilliant writer to master this harsh language.' Frederick found it cumbersome, particularly the syntax which placed the verb on which the whole meaning of a sentence depended at the very end. It was also ugly; the verbs *to give*, *to take* and *to say*, for instance: *geben*, *nehmen* and *sagen*. The last syllable was mute in each case. 'Let an *a* be added to these endings, so that they become *gebena*, *nehmena*, *sagena* – this sound is pleasant to the ear.' Frederick, in other words, missed the even stress given to syllables in French. Finally, a German ruler was wanted with a real interest in literature who would patronise the best writers and bring them to the fore. This ruler could not be Frederick. The great days of German literature were yet to come – but come they would: 'Like Moses I discern the Promised Land from afar.' The King believed that with this treatise he had made a solid contribution to the furtherance of German culture. 'You may laugh,' he wrote to d'Alembert, 'at the trouble I have taken to convey some small idea of good taste and Attic spice to a people who hitherto have known only how to eat, drink, fight and make love. But it is human to want to make oneself useful, and often a word falls on good soil and brings forth unexpected fruit. . . .' Attic spice, or an understanding of the Greek spirit, was indeed needed to wean German literature away from imitations of French classicism and so enable it to achieve independence, but the teacher was

Lessing, not Frederick, though the fruits were ultimately to be that same calm humanitarianism that glowed in the ageing King when the fires of Rationalism were spent.

. . . . .

And what of Frederick's own creative talent, both literary and musical? His verses are diligently rhymed prose. His comedies and epic poems are paltry. His prose style, on the other hand, is splendidly clear and fluid. But his verse lacks feeling and sincerity. Both qualities are found in his musical compositions. Frederick was a passionate flute-player. Until his teeth began to fall out in old age, he practised assiduously, often for several hours a day. He composed over a hundred sonatas and concertos, all of them consisting of intricate elaborations on some simple main theme which he embroidered with elegant and cheerful figurations, runs, trills and cadenzas. Here, too, of course, he was a rationalist: 'It always pleases me when I find that music provides scope for intelligence. I enjoy a learned-sounding piece of music as much as clever conversation at table.' In his music he succeeded sometimes in giving expression to deep feelings. At a competition held in 1869 one of his marches was chosen as the Spanish national anthem. It was retained until 1922. His musical taste did not develop beyond the preferences of his youth. Anticipating a fashionable word, he rejected Haydn and Mozart as 'degenerate.' In music his overburdened spirit found relaxation and a refuge and his innate sensibility an outlet.

CHAPTER TWENTY-SIX

*

Growing Old

HE WAS SEVENTY-TWO NOW, walked with a bent back and a stick, perpetually tormented with gout. But he still got up at 4 a.m., read the official correspondence, dictated replies and marginal comments, attended parade sitting for hours in the saddle, received foreign visitors, and then, punctually at noon, as ever, sat down with his guests to dinner. Getting settled in his chair was something of an ordeal, but once he was seated the pain eased.

He was wearing the uniform of the Life Guards. It was so old and dusty the blue coat looked like a winter's sky. The gold epaulettes were lustreless, the once black, now yellowed jackboots were held together at the tops with tape, the sash looked to his visitors as though it dated from his accession. The blue streaks on the faded red cuffs were obviously ink. From a pocket the old man produced a couple of jewelled boxes oddly at variance with his shabby clothing. From each he took a pinch of Spanish snuff, and, judging by the smudges on his coat and reddish-brown face, not for the first time that day. No one spoke. All eyes were on the King. Now, with furtive glances round the table, he was fishing a hunk of meat out of the plate in front of him and laying it, still dripping with gravy, on the table-cloth to cool for his greyhound. Did someone wince? The old man gave another glance, piercing this time, towards the offender, then very slowly and deliberately took some scissors from his pocket and began to cut his nails. That done, he poured some coffee into a glass of champagne, took a gulp and began to speak – and at once the quirks, the oddity, the self-neglect of the old man sitting crouched like a vulture in his chair were forgotten.

He spoke quickly and lightly in a soft, low voice, and he spoke with style. He might have been reading from a thrice-chiselled manuscript, his sentences were so firm and pregnant. But reading suggests monotony; this monologue was charmingly spontaneous – all fire and wit, or mockery, and nothing loose or trivial. The talk came from a swift and penetrating mind. Perhaps some of his guests had been expecting to find a soured and misanthropic autocrat; but here was a charmer. He spoke of art, war, medicine, literature, religion, philosophy, ethics, history and legislation, of the fine eras of Augustus and Louis XIV, of the Greeks and of the good company they must have been, of the frankness and valour of Henri IV, of the rebirth of letters, the chivalry of Francis I, of the domineering Maupertuis, of Voltaire and his indiscretions, of d'Argens the over-anxious, and of Jordan the beloved, Jordan the good friend – he would never have a better – Jordan, whom he missed, even now, after nearly forty years. . . .

After talking for nearly five hours with an occasional pause, only, to ask a guest to supply a fact, the King rose from table to give his instructions to a young diplomat who was to be his ambassador in Turkey. First, he told him of the purpose of his mission, of the interests of Prussia and of the other European Powers, and of the Turks and how to deal with them. Then he sent for a clerk and began to dictate the new ambassador's instructions, pausing at the end of each paragraph to explain its purport. Half-way through he stopped the dictation and, playing with the greyhound that had meanwhile jumped on to his knees, encouraged the young diplomat to talk so as to see whether he had fully understood his wishes. Then the dictation was resumed. There was no: 'Now let's see, how far did we get?' The King remembered, and took up the thread at once. The clerk then disappeared with the lengthy document and Eichel, the private secretary, came in for signatures. He told the King that Podewils wanted advice on how to reply to a Note from Britain – to reply at all seemed to involve embarrassment for Prussia. Such problems held no difficulties for Frederick. 'I want nothing to do with it,' he wrote to Podewils. 'You produce an answer, in Austrian style: courteous, but vague, meaning neither "yes" nor "no", but quite simply incomprehensible.'

The day's work was done. It was about half past eight. The old man went straight to his bedroom – he never took food in the evening – undressed without help and, covering himself with an old sable rug, was asleep before the clock on the garrison church struck nine.

. . . . .

262

The years had their routine no less than the days. Six, nine months ahead it was possible to predict what the King would be doing on a certain day. Sometimes it seemed indisposition would prevent him keeping an engagement, but when the time came, the old man would suddenly recover, as though he were able to will himself better. From Christmas till 22nd January he held his big receptions in Berlin, and this, if ever, was the time when the Queen saw him. On 23rd January, the eve of his birthday, he would go with a sigh of relief to Potsdam to avoid the ovations. Once, to mark the occasion, he had a dromedary precede him carrying his three hundred snuff boxes. In April he transferred to Sanssouci for the military reviews. In May he toured Pomerania and West Prussia. He never visited East Prussia because the nobility had paid homage to the Czarina during the Seven Years War. In June he went to Magdeburg, when the annual budget was settled. In August he visited Silesia. In September he attended manoeuvres, and he returned to Potsdam in November.

In the closing years of his life – in 1784, 1785, 1786 – Frederick, as Carlyle rightly said, showed himself to be a sound-hearted, brave old man. 'Life, my dear Darget,' he had written to his former reader in 1778, 'is a mean affair when one gets old. One must resign oneself to dying suddenly or to fading out slowly, bit by bit. But there is a way of being happy and that is to rejuvenate oneself in imagination, disregard the body and to the end of the play preserve an inner cheerfulness, so strewing the last few steps of the path with flowers.' Frederick worked and did his duty to the end, and though almost all his old intellectual friends had gone and on most days he was surrounded at the dinner table by his trusted but not very brilliant generals, he managed, as we have seen, to snatch a little gaiety from drab infirmities and colourless routine. Foreign visitors were always calling; some, like the Prince de Ligne, were witty and intelligent and could put the King in the old malicious, mocking, scintillating humour. Though his temper varied and he could still be brutally harsh, he never withdrew into morose despondency. He had a right to please himself. Many visitors, upon reaching the Presence at last, were curtly dismissed, but some, to their own amazement, saw those extraordinary eyes – which never grew old – rest on them with interest and enjoyed long conversations in which the King put them completely at ease. At table some ridiculous remark could still make him burst out laughing, and as always he enjoyed embarrassing his guests; Baron Pöllnitz, for instance, who was suddenly called upon to answer: 'Tell me, what was the man's name you sold the fake silver to at The Hague?'

The King seldom saw his wife. On his return from the Seven Years War, his greeting had consisted of one sentence: 'Madam has grown more corpulent.' 'This is my old cow, whom you already know' had been his manner of introducing her to his sister Ulrike. He had failed to remember their golden wedding day. He was on equally cordial terms with other adult members of his family. The futile and dissolute heir to the throne, Frederick William, son of his brother, Augustus William, filled him with contempt. In thirty years' time, said Frederick, there would no longer be a Prussia. Prince Henry he mistrusted and disliked, while he himself was at times an object of hatred, for instance when he ordered the Prince's bedfellow, a certain Herr von Kaphengst, out of Berlin.

But the King was not lonely, because he was not introspective. He was not a self-pitying individual, but remarkably detached. His loud lamentations during the war and his attitudinising to de Catt had sprung not from weakness but from strength, the ability to stand back from himself, to sit with the audience and be moved by the tragic predicament of King Frederick on the stage. 'His high spirits,' said Catherine, the cleverest of his contemporaries, 'sprang from his superiority over his fellow men.' Superiority implies detachment. But Frederick was also not lonely because he still had his friends – friends of the heart. These were his nephews and nieces. 'They are good children and I am very fond of them,' he reported – and to a niece: 'Many thanks, dear child, for the nice things you say to your old uncle. He does not deserve them. He is a decrepit old chatterbox who must be sent by the shortest road to the Beyond, where he can continue his twaddle. But you don't think of him like that. With your tender heart you take an interest in the old skeleton, because he is a relative and because in your natural goodness you wish well to every man. As long as I live I shall love you and feel tenderly towards you.' But Frederick's favourite was his nephew Henry, whom he loved as his own son. When the boy died at the age of eighteen, the King composed a funeral oration which was read before the Academy. On reciting it to his *Lecteur* Thiebault he was overcome with emotion and had to break off, silently handing over the manuscript.

So the old King with the face of granite could still weep and smile. There was no doubt he was capable of deep emotion – had a softer heart, some would say, than he cared to show. Yet sensibility alternated with the most callous indifference to hu-

264

manity and with a cruel delight in affronting delicacy of feeling in others. This combination of cynicism and sentimentality is certainly distasteful, but it hardly deserves the shocked indignation of historians, for what is surprising is not Frederick's instability of temperament, but the survival in him of natural feeling in any form. In his early years he had been deprived of all that a child must have if it is to grow into a balanced individual: love, protection and a consistent attitude towards him on the part of his parents. His father was cruel and unpredictable, determined to mortify him, to stifle his natural self and substitute the tangled mass of contradictions, doubts, lusts, fears and ungovernable emotions which comprised his own personality. His mother was affectionate, but she was also a frivolous and frightened woman whose feeling for her son was neither strong nor consistent enough to shield him from his father's persecution. So the young Fritz was left without prop or support to fight for very survival against a father's attempts to kill him in spirit and, if that failed, quite possibly in the flesh. And the murderer was also a king. There was no one, literally no one, to gainsay him. He could lock the boy up for life and no protest would be raised by any one of his 4,000,000 subjects. He was answerable only to God, and God, he said, had given him proof of his benevolence. If the child ran away, no one in Prussia would give him shelter, perhaps no one in the world. He had to stay – and be dragged by the hair, thrashed, humiliated and goaded continually by the reminder that he was destined to rule the same country as his father, yet was utterly unworthy even to breathe the same air. But this was not the worst. If his father had been consistently hostile, that would at least have been one unalterable fact in the child's chaotic world. But like all sadists, Frederick William sentimentalised over his victim. After the blows would come blubbering embraces. Fond glances – mostly in public – would throw the child into confusion and bring hope and the suppressed desire to love and be loved welling up in a heart already hardening against adversity. Then Fritz would be defenceless; relief and joy would overwhelm him – until a cuff or a snarl would suddenly freeze up every nerve, every spring of emotion in his body and once again he would be face to face with the tyrant. Frederick William mocked his weak digestion; it is a wonder that he could eat at all.

It was not by taking conscious thought, of course, that the child, the boy and the youth survived these torments with reason intact. Long before he was capable of analysing his predicament, Fritz must have reacted to it instinctively. In the child's experience, his father's will was paramount. His orders were obeyed, not only in the home, but in Berlin and, indeed, to the limits of Fritz's world. His mother, on the other hand, could only weep and clasp him in impotent distress. The conclusion was obvious: love was weak and hatred was strong. Fritz also knew that it was dangerous to give way to feelings of tenderness, for his father would never accept him as he was and the moment the boy sought his affection he interpreted it as a sign of weakness and dangled a bargain before his eyes: if you throw away your true self and become the child I want you to be, I will love you and look after you. Thus Fritz was faced with an agonising and tragic choice: he could either accept the bargain and kill a part of himself or defy his father and take the consequences. In fact, his strongly assertive nature fought with the instinct of self-preservation and he compromised, concealing but not abandoning his real interests which his father scorned and feigning enthusiasm for the plodding, conscientious performance of administrative duties which Frederick William found so attractive. Thus Fritz survived and, amazingly, emerged from the ordeal not only with his life, but with a shining intellect, high spirits, the capacity to feel and the ability now and then to experience affection and to inspire it. But all this was bought at a heavy price in bitterness and a sense of futility. Fritz had gained a crown, but lost part of himself. His eternal suspicion of his fellow men, his callousness, his erotic cynicism were his scars. A deeper scar remained, the memory of that terrible day when his jailers had dragged him to a window and forced him to watch the execution of the only human being with whom he had enjoyed friendship on equal terms. Frederick William had expected his heart to be 'softened by grief', but from then on it was closed to all but the ex-valet, Fredersdorf, children and dogs.

*

CHAPTER TWENTY-SEVEN

Frederick the Great?

THE OPINIONS EXPRESSED by German historians on Frederick II as a man, as a king, as a patriot and as a citizen of Europe are innumerable and widely divergent. Their value depends, of course, in each case on the writer's degree of erudition, but also on the standpoint from which he views his subject and the political and moral criteria he applies to it. The Pan-German or *Grossdeutsch* historian will have something entirely different to say from the *Kleindeutsch*, the Prussian patriot from a cosmopolitan intellectual like Thomas Mann. Even the historian's own personal ambition plays a part. Those who seek to pass definite judgments are less likely to be sound than those who realise that, whatever opinions they may express, they can be no more than a contribution to a perennial debate.

Here, we will discuss three questions: did Frederick achieve the goals which he set himself? This is a political question. What moral judgment should be passed on his actions? And finally, what effect did he have on the course of German history? This last, as we shall see, is a question which permits a variety of answers.

Frederick's main object was clear: he wanted to make Prussia a Great Power. And he achieved that object. In 1786, when he died, the country was larger and more powerful than on his accession, and in prestige particularly ranked among the great nations of Europe. All this would not have been so, of course, if Frederick had succumbed in the Seven Years War. That he successfully defied an overwhelming coalition and emerged the moral victor, without loss of territory, is perhaps his chief claim to greatness. But was this due entirely to his own efforts? Some historians say no. If the Empress Elizabeth of Russia had not died in January 1762 they believe he would have been defeated, Prussia would have been reduced to the status of a Margraviate and Frederick would have gone down to history as another Charles XII of Sweden, a bold and death-defying warrior who brought ruin on his country. Only chance, say his critics, saved him from this fate. This may be true, but the contrary is equally plausible. When Elizabeth died, Austria was already tiring of war and had been forced to reduce the size of her army owing to financial difficulties. And even if she had lived, Frederick's negotiations with Turkey might have drawn troops from the Russian army facing him. In any case, Elizabeth's death would have made no difference if her successor, the Czar Peter, had not been a fervent admirer of Frederick's, and far from being a mere matter of luck that admiration was directly due to the King's fame, which, as we have seen, played so large a part towards the end of the war in paralysing the military and diplomatic efforts of his enemies.

In winning Silesia during the War of the Austrian Succession, however, Frederick achieved an undeniable success and perhaps a greater one in frustrating Austrian attempts to recover the province. During this war he also succeeded in preventing French aggrandisement at the expense of Austria. His Polish policy was also successful; without going to war he prevented Catherine from annexing the whole country and obtained West Prussia. Finally, he won an almost bloodless victory by stifling Joseph's Bavarian plans.

As against this, Frederick made big mistakes. The Treaty of Westminster achieved precisely the opposite of what he had intended, though the English alliance did not affect the issue of peace or war, as Austria and Russia were determined to fight in any case and Frederick's prospects would hardly have been better with France as his ally and England his enemy. It has also been said that he was gravely at fault in allowing Russian friendship to cool during the last years of his reign. But how could he prevent it? Only by hobbling in the wake of the young and hot-headed Catherine and sharing in her Turkish adventures. A glance at a map will show that no part of the Ottoman Empire was contiguous with Prussian territory, that, short of flying, no Prussian army could have reached European Turkey and that no Austrian ruler, let alone the ambitious Joseph, could have afforded to allow Prussian troops on both the north and the south sides of the Austrian Empire.

Frederick's greatest achievement in the military sphere was

undoubtedly his survival of the Seven Years War. Here he gave literally all he had got – his last ounce of courage, resource, endurance, resilience – and not only in the field, but in foreign affairs, the recruiting of his soldiers, finance, administration, agriculture; he was the hub that set all in motion; his the spirit that swept the field at Rossbach, that dared to look disaster in the face after Kunersdorf, that hypnotised his enemies and that turned him, its possessor, into a figure of legend. 'The heroism of the defence,' says Professor Trevelyan, 'makes us forget the shoddiness of the original robbery.'

And what of internal affairs? Did Frederick realise his youthful dream of making his people happy? He preserved the absolute monarchy and the social stratification of Prussia as they had been in his father's days. In economics he was, like most contemporary rulers, a mercantilist. His financial wisdom did not extend beyond a treasury bursting with cash. Twenty years after his death, all these principles had been superseded, but they were the ideas of his time and within their framework his achievement compares favourably with that of other European States. His State Bank, the royal porcelain factory, reclamation and settlement of marshland, his encouragement of the silk industry, above all, the example of hard work and service to the State which he set his subjects at least enabled them to bear the heavy burdens of war without falling below the level of prosperity prevailing in the rest of Germany. They were lucky, for it was not so much their comfort that concerned Frederick as their ability to support his expansionist foreign policy. That came first. 'We ape the Great Powers,' he had once said, 'without being one.' His measures to foster industry and agriculture and his maintenance of the existing social structure were intended to equip the country to stand the strain involved. His efforts to create an impartial judiciary no doubt sprang in part from the injustices he had suffered as a youth, partly also from his philosophical ideals, but not least from his determination to ensure that the nobility were not immune from punishment if they fell below the exacting standards of duty and service he imposed on them.

To his contemporaries, the main driving force in Frederick's character appeared as restless ambition. More accurately, it was a determination to make good, a compulsive drive to make the world admire and fear him and so eradicate the injustice of his father's scorn. And he had to triumph in the capacity for which his father thought him totally unequipped – as a soldier. On his accession, the Powers at whose expense he would necessarily have to acquire territory, if he gained it at all, were Russia, Austria and France. Their rulers were not a whit more scrupulous than Frederick, and in foreign affairs territorial expansion was the accepted policy of them all. But they could afford to wait. Their power was already great and their prestige, unlike his, did not depend upon performance, but was inherent in their very title. They were the 'Haves'; he was a 'Have not'. From the first, they eyed him with suspicion. Twelve weeks after his succession, the Herstal affair confirmed their worst fears: the jaunty young King was a highway robber. Then he stole Silesia, and to keep it changed his diplomatic front five times in five years. Indignation mounted. The vocabulary of three languages was ransacked for epithets bad enough to apply to the Demon King. Thus, to this day, Frederick the Great has remained interchangeable with Frederick the Knave, for the adequate reason that his knavery was successful. But this alone does not account for the intensity of feeling, ranging from semi-adoration to the deepest repugnance, which this King has always aroused. His contemporaries saw him as different from other men; some detected a strange virulence of spirit which at times made him seem almost superhuman, others believed he was erotically abnormal. The sequestration of his wife, the exclusion of all women from his daily entourage, his contempt for the feminine virtues, his attachment to handsome pages, and what remains of his correspondence with Fredersdorf – all this tends to confirm the belief. Voltaire, one of the few who had the independence and audacity to speak openly, supplied details.

It remains to consider Frederick's effect on the course of German history. Certain facts are unquestionable: he established Prussia as a Great Power and set her on the path which was to culminate in the leadership of Germany. He dealt the death-blow to the old conception of German unity as a loose agglom-eration of States owing allegiance to the Emperor; in place of this outworn political structure he kindled the fires of spiritual unity by arousing the admiration of all Germans for his deeds and for the heroic qualities of mind and spirit which he had demonstrated in their achievement. For the very reason, how-ever, that there was so much to admire in him as a human being and that his lifelong aims had been achieved, the question of whether they were laudable aims and whether his qualities had been put to the right use was entirely overlooked and Frederick became the lodestar which future generations of German patriots uncritically accepted as their guide – not the Frederick who wrote,

270

'A ruler should consider it his calling to relieve human misery,' but the Frederick of this passage in his *Memorabilia:*

I must admit that it is very difficult for a man drawn into the cross-currents of European politics to preserve an upright and honest character. Constantly in danger of betrayal by his allies, abandonment by his friends and of being crushed under the weight of envy and jealousy, he is finally confronted with the terrible alternatives of either sacrificing his people or breaking his word. In the smallest as in the largest States the urge to expand can be considered the basic rule of government. The passions of princes are restrained only by exhaustion. These are the established laws of European politics which every statesman must accept. If a prince were less concerned for his advantage than his neighbours, they would always be the stronger and he, though the more virtuous, would be the weaker. This, I agree, seems in many ways the opposite of private morality. But it is the morality of princes who, by tacit agreement and on the basis of numerous historical precedents, have granted one another the privilege of seeking only their own advantage. To achieve it, they employ negotiation, subterfuge and intrigue or else fire and the sword. They are the first to mock at the conscientious observance of treaties which, in truth, amount to no more than false oaths. One must hope that a more enlightened age will hold honestly in greater esteem. I do not wish to defend statecraft, I am simply explaining the reasons which, in my opinion, oblige every prince to act deceitfully and misuse his power.

*

CHAPTER TWENTY-EIGHT

Death

ON 23RD MAY, 1785, an eight-year-old boy was standing by the Halle Gate in Berlin waiting to catch a glimpse of the King as he rode home after reviewing his troops. All round him in the square and beyond, in the Wilhelmstrasse, were dense crowds of people. Looking up he could see every window crammed with expectant figures. All were bare-headed; all were silent. Soon there came a clatter of hooves. The boy craned forward. Years later, he recorded what he saw:

The King came riding on a big white horse. He was wearing a plain blue uniform and red cuffs, red collar and gold shoulder-bands, a yellow waistcoat and black velvet breeches. The hat was properly looped up with the peak set in front, in correct military style. Behind him rode a number of generals, then his adjutants and finally, the grooms. The King rode quite alone in front, answering the bows of the onlookers by continually taking off his hat. All faces showed an expression of reverence and confidence. The only sounds were the clopping of the horses' hooves and the shouts of the Berlin street-boys who capered before him, flinging their caps in the air and darting up occasionally to wipe the dust from his boots.

The King turned into the forecourt of the Palace, the double doors opened and the aged Princess Amalia, who was lame, came swaying down the shallow steps, leaning on two ladies, to meet him. As soon as he saw her, he put his horse to the gallop, then halted, quickly dismounted, took off his hat, embraced her, gave her his arm and led her up the steps again. The double doors closed and all had vanished. But still the crowd stood, bare-headed and in silence, all eyes gazing at the spot where last he had been seen, and it was some while before each man collected himself and quietly went his way.

And yet nothing had happened, no pomp, no fireworks, no dis-

272

charge of cannon, no drums and fifes, no music, no culmination of some great event! No, only an old man of seventy-three, ill-dressed and covered with dust, was returning from his laborious day's work. But everyone knew that this old man was working for him, had devoted his whole life to the task and had never yet missed a single day. Round about, near and far could be seen the fruits of his labour, and so the sight of him inspired reverence, admiration, pride, confidence – in short, all the nobler feelings of man.

But the King referred to his subjects as '*canaille*', riff-raff, and took a different view of their admiration. 'But,' objected one of his guests, 'when Your Majesty entered the city yesterday and the people flocked to see their great King, they were not riff-raff.' 'Put an old monkey on a horse and send it through the streets, they would do just the same,' came the swift retort. 'Tired of ruling over slaves,' wrote the King a few months before he died. But he did nothing to free them.

And now he was seventy-four. Year by year his health had been getting steadily worse. He was suffering from gout, dysentery, colic, abscesses on the ear and knees, cough and dropsy. But he would not give in; he flogged himself on like 'an old jade.' At a military review in August of the previous year, 1785, he had sat in the saddle for six hours in torrential rain without bothering, even, to put on his cloak. Four weeks later, he had a sudden attack of angina pectoris. His first words when the pain had ceased were: 'Not a word of this to anyone!' He continued to work, but was very short of breath, slept badly, and throughout the winter of 1785–6 lived immured in his Palace of Potsdam, summoning his secretaries at 4 a.m. instead of at six. 'My condition obliges me to impose this burden on you, but you will not have to bear it for long. My life is drawing to a close. What time I have left I must put to good use, for it is not mine, but the State's.'

When spring came, the King moved to Sanssouci. He had always thought it a disgrace, unworthy of a soldier, to be seen driving in a carriage, but this time he was too weak to ride. So he set off very early in the morning, reaching the Palace by a circuitous route, so that no one would see him. He had erysipelas now, and asthma. The only way he could breathe was to sit day and night in an easy chair. But the work went on, from 4 a.m. to 11 a.m. each day, the King seeing his ministers and regulating every detail of his military, civil and political affairs with a clarity of intellect, reported one of them, greater even than when he had been in his prime.

Rumours that the King of Prussia was dying had long since reached the Courts of Europe. Members of the Prussian Court had already ordered mourning when Frederick sent for the famous Doctor Zimmermann of Hamburg. The doctor prescribed an infusion of dandelion, in German, 'Lion's tooth.' Jokingly, the King wanted to know which lion, but took the medicine and felt so much better that his appetite revived. Zimmermann, very rightly, had put him on a strict diet. To his horror, he found his patient drinking large quantities of soup. 'This soup consisted of a bouillon extracted from the very hottest and strongest substances. With each plateful, the King took a large dessertspoonful of ground nutmeg and ginger. Then he ate a generous helping of beef prepared in the Russian manner, that is, stewed in a pint of brandy. After that, came a large quantity of an Italian dish consisting of equal quantities of Indian corn and Parmesan cheese mixed with garlic juice and baked in butter until a hard crust had formed round it about the thickness of a finger. A broth made of the hottest spices was then poured over the whole. Finally, after praising the splendid appetite which the dandelion had given him, the King ended the scene with a whole plateful of eel *paté*, again so hot and spicy that it might have been baked in Hell.'

The King had a relapse. Four days later, despite Zimmermann's warnings, he was on horseback, riding Condé, the big white horse that the small boy had seen in Berlin in the previous year. He rode for three-quarters of an hour, some of the time at the gallop. Then he collapsed. Rallying again, he advised Doctor Zimmermann to return to his patients in Hamburg. He felt sure they had need of him. 'Then,' records the doctor, 'the King removed his hat with indescribable charm and dignity and said: "Fare well, my good, my dear Herr Zimmermann. Do not forget the good old man you have seen here." '

Frederick awaited the end with stoic calm. His minister Hertzberg, who was with him daily during the last weeks of his life, reported that, although clearly in great pain and unable even to shift his position in the chair where he sat night and day, the King never allowed the smallest sign of discomfort to appear in his features, but remained unvaryingly cheerful, calm and, to all appearances, contented. He never spoke of his ailments or of dying, but conversed in the most pleasant and intimate manner on recent events, literature, ancient and modern history, and particularly well on horticulture in connection with the gardens which were still being made on his orders at Sanssouci.

274

On 14th August, 1786, Frederick was still dictating to his secretaries. 'To the Head of Excise: Your Account of receipts and expenditure was received yesterday, 13th August. But it lacks detail. I require full particulars.' On Tuesday, the 15th, he woke much later than usual, seemed confused at first, but then regained his usual clarity of mind, dictated military orders, went through the Cabinet work and gave his secretary four quarto pages of instructions for an ambassador leaving to take up his post. On Wednesday morning, the 16th, the secretaries arriving at the usual hour were told to wait: the King was sleeping. But Frederick had lost the power of speech. He was nearing the end. All day and on into the night, he slumbered, stirred occasionally, then relapsed into coma. At 11 p.m. he heard the clock above his head strike the hour, and asked: 'What o'clock?' 'At four,' he was heard to murmur, 'I will get up.' At midnight he opened his eyes and saw that one of his dogs was shivering. From a slight movement of his hand an attendant judged that he wanted a quilt put over it. From midnight, the King's faithful valet, Strützki, knelt with one knee on the ground and held his master in his arms to ease his breathing, as he kept slumping in his chair. For over two hours he knelt motionless while the King's breathing grew weaker. At twenty minutes past two, it ceased.

The mood in Berlin on the day of Frederick's death was described by Count Mirabeau: 'No face which did not show relief and hope, not one regret, not one sigh, no single word of praise. This, then, was what became of so many battles won, so much fame, a reign of almost half a century so full of so many great deeds. All were longing for it to end; all congratulated themselves that it was over.'

Frederick's successor at once abolished his most unpopular measures: tax-farming, the tobacco monopoly and the duty on coffee. All Frederick William II's decrees bore the unmistakable stamp of good will and of the desire to mitigate the harsher aspects of his uncle's system of government. In the army, too, many desirable and useful reforms were made. Disabled officers and soldiers were more regularly provided for, clothing was improved, tactics and training were brought up to date in the light of experience which Frederick in his old age had left unexploited.

Yet none of these benefits could make good the loss of that masterful will and relentless driving force. Frederick had demanded only two things of his subjects: obedience and hard work. He had looked after the rest. He was the mainspring of the whole machine. The State that he bequeathed was an inverted pyramid. The whole weight of government had rested on him. Only a genius and a man of steel could support it. But his nephew was a mediocrity, and from the early hours of Thursday, 17th August, 1786, the whole structure of Prussian efficiency, vigour and power began to crumble until, on 12th October, twenty years later, the humiliation of total defeat at Jena kindled the spirit of national pride which was to bring about the unification of Germany.

Index

Frederick William I, King in Prussia, birth of, 15; marriage, 16; characteristics as ruler, 19–20; his Code of Regulations for State Officials, 20–1; his choleric temperament, 21; encourages immigration, 21; the 'Plus-Maker,' 21; creates Prussian military machine, 22–3; his passion for tall soldiers, 22; fails to acquire Jülich and Berg, 24–5; his loyalty to the German Emperor, 24; his weakness as a diplomat, 25; his contempt for his son Frederick, 26–7; regulates Frederick's schooling, 26–8; relations with his wife, 29; assaults Frederick, 30; his letters to Frederick, 32, 59, 64–5; and the Double Marriage Project, 33–9; his attempts to discipline Frederick, 35; his hatred of George II, 36; and Frederick's attempted 'desertion', 42–54; restores Frederick to favour, 57–8; plans Frederick's marriage, 62–8; death of, 80–1; and the Prussian army, 250

Frederick II (the Great), King of Prussia, contemporary respect for, 7–8; youthful characteristics of, 8; favourable judgments on, 8–10; Thomas Mann on, 9; Leopold von Ranke on, 9; unfavourable judgments on, 10–11; as military commander, Napoleon on, 10, 177, 230; his vanity, Bismarck on, 10; his enigmatic character, 11; his genealogy, 12–16; birth of, 17; his schooling, 26–8; his father's contempt for, 27; learns French as mother tongue, 28; assaulted by his father, 30; his lack of religion, 30; visits the Court of Dresden, 31; attempts to ingratiate his father, 33; accompanies father to Saxony, 37, 40; publicly chastised, 40; plans flight from Prussia, 40; refused asylum in England, 41; his debts paid by George II, 41; accompanies father to Ansbach, 41; his attempted flight, 42; placed under arrest, 43; imprisoned, 43; before court of inquiry as 'deserter', 45–6; submits to 'will and mercy' of the King, 46; offers to renounce succession, 48, 63; court-martialled, 49–50; forced to watch execution of his best friend, 51–2; renounces Calvinist beliefs, 53, 58; signs act of submission, 53; released from prison, 54; studies provincial administration, 55–8; his versifying, 57, 60, 74, 76, 84, 89, 118, 132, 134, 171, 172–3, 183–4, 193–4, 205, 253, 254, 260; attends Wilhelmina's wedding, 59–60; his first and last flirtation, 60; his betrothal, 66–7; marriage, 68; soldiering as Crown Prince, 71–2; intellectual pursuits at Reinsberg, 73; his first letters to Voltaire, 74–6; becomes a Freemason, 77; relations with his father, 77–8; his *Antimachiavel*, 78–9; accession of, 82; invades Prince-Bishopric of Liège, 84–5; plans seizure of Silesia, 90–1; his motives, 90; invades Silesia, 92; legal claim to Silesia, 93; occupies Silesia, 93; his flight from field of Mollwitz, 95–6; concludes alliance with France, 98; concludes Convention of Kleinschellendorf with Austria, 101; makes peace with Austria, 105; concludes alliance with France and Bavaria, 107; relations with Russia, 108; captures Prague,

Fromme (royal bailiff), recounts a day with Frederick, 211–4

Fürst, von (Prussian Grand Chancellor), 220–1

Galicia, transferred from Poland to Austria, 234

Gaxotte, Pierre (French historian), on origins of Seven Years War, 140

George William, Duke of Celle, 13

George II, King of England, 15, 33, 38, 41, 62; seeks enlargement of Hanover, 98; supports Frederick over Silesia, 112; animosity towards Frederick, 143, 194; death of 204

George III, King of England, accession of, 204; policy of, 204

Ginkel (Dutch Ambassador in Berlin), 47

Glatz, 244

Goethe, Johann Wolfgang von, 8; on victory of Rossbach, 174

Gooch, Professor, on origins of Seven Years War, 140

Görlitz, 170, 186

Gotter, Count, 92

Grumbkov (Prussian War Minister), 30; and Double Marriage Project, 33–4, 38; and Frederick's 'desertion' as Crown Prince, 45, 48, 54, 58, 59, 60; and Frederick's marriage, 63–8

Hacke, Colonel (Prussian Adjutant-General), 81

Hanover, 43, 98

Hanover, Treaty of, 112

Harrach, Count, 116

Hasse (German composer), 160

Hastenbeck, Battle of, 168

Henry, Prince of Prussia (brother of Frederick), 165–6, 185; appointed Prussian Generalissimo, 192; defeats Austrians at Freiberg, 208; visits Empress Catherine, 233; Frederick's mistrust and dislike of, 264; mentioned, 193, 240, 242

Henry, Prince of Prussia (nephew of Frederick), 264

Herstal, ownership contested by Frederick, 34; war over, 85

Hesse-Darmstadt, 42

Hesse-Kassel, 161

Hildburghausen, Prince, 170

Hildesheim, 98

Hille, *Kammerdirektor*, 54, 56, 58, 63

Hochkirch, 185

Hohenfriedberg, Battle of, 112–3

Holstein (Prussian) General, 199–200

Holy Roman Empire (German Reich), 23; army of, 170; defeated at Rossbach, 173; Diet of, outlaws Frederick, 169; undermined by Joseph II, 240–1; and the League of German Princes, 245–6

Hotham, Sir Charles, 36–9

Hubertusberg, Treaty of, 208

Hülsen (Prussian) General, 199–201

Hyndford, Lord, 101

James (VI of Scotland, I of England), 12

Jena, Battle of, 10, 276

Jenkins's Ear, war of, 88

Jordan (friend of Frederick), 91, 94, 113, 262

Joseph II, German Emperor, his personality, 231; his two meetings with Frederick, 231–2; his opinion of Frederick, 232–3; obtains the Bukovina from Turkey, 239; attempts to acquire Bavaria, 239–46; quarrels with Maria Theresa,

282

242; visits Catherine of Russia, 244–5

Karl Albert, Elector of Bavaria, 100; crowned German Emperor, 103; concludes treaty with Prussia, 107–8; death of, 110
Kassel, Battle of, 208
Katte, Johann Hermann von, plans flight from Prussia with the young Frederick, 40–1; arrest of, 45; court-martial of, 48–50; sentenced to death, 50; executed, 51–2
Katte, Lieutenant-General von, 51
Kaunitz, Prince (Austrian Chancellor), favours friendship with France, 144–5; determined to crush Prussia, 148; builds alliance against Prussia, 150; rejects alliance with Britain, 206; makes secret alliance with Turkey, 233; mentioned, 180
Kay, Battle of, 190
Kayserling (friend of the young Frederick), 113
Keith, the brothers, pages at the Prussian Court, 36–43, 48–9
Kesselsdorf, Battle of, 114–16
Khevenhüller (Austrian) Field-Marshal, occupies Munich, 104
Kinsky (Austrian Minister), 103
Kleinschellendorf, Convention of, 101–2
Kloster-Zeven, Convention of, 168–9
Knobelsdorf (architect); 88; designs Sanssouci, 123
Knyphausen, Count, 150
Kolin, Battle of, 8, 164–5
Königsberg, 169
Königsmark, Count, 14
Kosel, 187, 244
Koser, Reinhold (German historian), on Convention of Kleinschellendorf, 102

Kunersdorf, Battle of, 190–1
Küstrin, 43, 45, 51, 54, 58

La Mettrie, 137
Landshut, Battle of, 196
League of German Princes, the, 245, 246
Leczynski, Stanislaus, 68
Lehmann, Max (German historian), on origins of Seven Years War, 141
Lehwald (Prussian) Field-Marshal, 162; defeated in East Prussia, 169
Leignitz, Battle of, 197
Leuthen, Battle, of 175–8
Liège, Prince-Bishop of, 84–5
Loudon (Austrian) Field-Marshal, 182, 185, 196–8; plans to kidnap Frederick, 203; out-manoeuvred in Bohemia, 242
Louis XIV, King of France, 87
Louis XV, King of France, 108, 147–8, 201
Louis XVI, King of France, 245, 246
Louis, Prince, of Brunswick, 113
Lubienski, Archbishop (Primate of Poland), 226
Lusatia, Saxon, 241
Lynar (Danish) Count, 168–9

Maaseyk, 85
Macaulay, Thomas Babington, 11; on Maria Theresa, 149; on battle of Rossbach, 174
Mährisch-Neustadt, 232
Mann, Thomas, 7, 140, 267
Mannheim, 41
Mannstein (Prussian) General, 163
Maria Josefa, Queen of Saxony, 159
Maria Theresa, Queen of Hungary and Bohemia, Archduchess of Austria, 47, 63; character of, 89; marriage of, 88; appeals to

BISMARCK
A. J. P. Taylor

Otto von Bismarck, 'The Iron Chancellor', was the
driving force behind the unification of Germany in
1871, but his influence was still felt in the twentieth
century. This biographical study of Germany's
outstanding soldier and statesman is both witty and
scholarly and gives historical perspective to a highly
readable personal account. 60p. 221 pages.

MENTOR PAPERBACKS
from New English Library

Please supply:

T21688 ....copies **BISMARCK** (60p)

Please include package and postage costs of 10p per copy.
I enclose cheque/P.O. for £.............. payable to New English Library Ltd.

Name ....

Address ....

....

New English Library, P.O. BOX 11, FALMOUTH, CORNWALL

THE THIRTY YEARS WAR

J. V. Polisensky

This detailed analysis of one of Europe's most
turbulent periods spans a century in its consideration
of the underlying contributory factors of the war
and contains a Marxist assessment of the grass-root
contemporary conditions in Bohemia and Moravia.
95p. 320 pages.